SCIENCE SERVING FAITH
by Henry Nelson Wieman

ÆR

American Academy of Religion
Studies in Religion

Editors
Charley Hardwick
James O. Duke

Number 46
SCIENCE SERVING FAITH
by Henry Nelson Wieman
Edited by
Creighton Peden and Charles Willig

SCIENCE SERVING FAITH
by Henry Nelson Wieman

Edited by
Creighton Peden and Charles Willig

Scholars Press
Atlanta, Georgia

SCIENCE SERVING FAITH
by Henry Nelson Wieman

Edited by
Creighton Peden and Charles Willig

© 1987
The American Academy of Religion

Library of Congress Cataloging in Publication Data

Wieman, Henry Nelson, 1884-1975.
Science serving faith.

(American Academy of Religion. Studies in religion ; no. 46)
 1. Religion and science—1946–   . 2. Jesus
Christ—Person and offices. I. Peden, Creighton,
1935–   . II. Willig, Charles. III. Title.
IV. Series: Studies in religion (American Academy of
Religion) ; no. 46.
BL240.2.W519   1987   261.5'5   87-9441
ISBN 1-55540-131-7 (alk. paper)
ISBN 1-55540-132-5 (pbk. : alk. paper)

Printed in the United States of America
on acid-free paper

CONTENTS

A SCIENTIFIC BASED CHRISTIANITY

Henry Nelson Wieman is one of America's most noted Twentieth Century thinkers who spoke to the need for developing a philosophy and theology founded upon a scientific approach. In the Nineteenth Century, geological and evolutionary discoveries led to an intellectual revolution focusing on whether reality is to be understood in terms of pre-scientific philosophies and religions or whether the scientific method is to be the guide. Wieman spoke directly and forcefully to this continuing issue and attempted to demonstrate the contributions of the scientific approach that would enable Christianity to adapt to the modern world. To a reader encountering Wieman for the first time or after a period of some years, an introductory review of the man and his thought may be helpful. This can best be accomplished by a brief biographical sketch, followed by a synopsis of his method, metaphysical view, doctrine of God, and Christology.

Biographical Data: Wieman was born in 1884 into the family of a Presbyterian minister. He died in Grinnell, Iowa, on June 19, 1975. During his childhood he developed a strong passion for religion. Park College provided his undergraduate education, and it was there he developed a passion for philosophy, with Josiah Royce becoming his prophet. After completing studies at San Francisco Theology Seminary, Wieman studied in Germany at Jena and Heildelberg Universities, coming under the influence of Eucken, Windelband and Troeltsch. After several years in the parish ministry, he began his Ph.D. studies at Harvard University, with the influence of Bergson fresh in his mind. At Harvard he studied under William Earnst Hocking and Ralph Barton Perry, but more decisively he came under the influence of John Dewey and William James.

In effect Wieman had joined the revolution in theological, philosophical and scientific thought dating from the evolutionary controversy of the 1860s, which was making a concerted attack upon Idealism. F.E. Abbot, writing at the time Wieman was born, indicated that the clash between evolution and Idealism was the dominant intellectual issue:

> The theory of Phenomenism *versus* the theory of Noumenism; the theory of Idealistic Evolution *versus* the theory of Realistic Evolution; and the Mechanical theory of Realistic Evolution *versus* the Organic theory of Realistic Evolution,—these are the vital philosophical prob-

lems of our century, and their solution must determine and decide that
of the vital religious problem of Theism, Atheism, and Pantheism.[1]

Wieman participates strongly in the intellectual movement rejecting Idealism, but his developing theology retained a striking element of his idealistic past. This idealistic influence is seen in his doctrine of God as the
Supreme, Sovereign or Absolute Good who gives meaning to the relative
goods of human existence. It is wise to bear in mind this idealistic influence
in Wieman's thought, even though it becomes colored and reshaped by his
increasing empirical emphasis.

After completing the Ph.D., Wieman taught at Occidental College until
1927 when he became Professor of Theology in the Philosophy of Religion
Chair in the graduate school of The University of Chicago. Prior to Chicago,
Wieman had encountered the writings of A.N. Whitehead and was influ-
enced by Whitehead's analysis of sense awareness as an awareness of "the
whole occurrence of nature." From this encounter Wieman wrote his first
book, *Religious Experience and the Scientific Method*, in which he concentrated upon the need and possibility of developing a more objective sense of
the reality beyond immediate subjective experience. On the basis of this
book, Wieman was invited to lecture at the Divinity School at the University
of Chicago. Those attending report that Wieman's reputation was already so
great that the room was full, with a crowd standing on the lawn outside the
windows. Shortly following this lecture, Wieman moved to Chicago to begin
the most productive phase of his career. Upon retiring from Chicago in 1948,
he taught several years at the University of Southern Illinois at Carbondale.[2]

Method: Since the Darwinian controversy, liberal religious thought has
been moving towards an accommodation of traditional Christianity to the
scientific approach. In the 1870s John Fiske's "Cosmic Philosophy" enabled
evolution to be viewed as God's way of doing things. By the early part of the
20th Century, the encounter between science and religion focused on the
issue of whether God existed. Wieman established his place in American
religious thought by redefining this issue so that the question is not "Does
God exist?" but "What is the character of God?" By definition he asserts that
God exists. Wieman's line of reasoning is as follows: We have experiences
which we call religious. They are religious because we experience a saving
quality in our lives, i.e., there is Something within our experiences which
saves us. That Something in human experience which saves is by definition
God. Since humans neither cause nor can forsee that these religious experiences will occur, they are not the creator of these experiences. This Some-

---

[1] F.E. Abbot, *Scientific Theism* (London: Macmillan, 1885), p. viii.

[2] For those interested in a more detailed intellectual biography, cf. H.N. Wieman, "Intellec-
tual Autobiography," *The Empirical Theology of Henry Wieman*, ed. Robert W. Bretall (New
York: Macmillan Co., 1963), pp. 1–18, and Creighton Peden, *Wieman's Empirical Process
Philosophy* (Washington, D.C.: University Press of America, 1977), pp. 17–25.

thing which produces the religious experience is God. God produces the religious experience by giving a direction of value to a particular becoming process. God works through the development of culture as it centers on a particular situation, in order to transform the situation into being a saving situation.

The experience of God is not knowledge of God, and knowledge of God is what Wieman initially is seeking. The foundation of possible knowledge is the God-given experience, which is the basis of what Wieman calls knowledge by acquaintance. God produces the experience and one's task is twofold in relation to the experience: (1) to find if the experience is an experience of God, and (2) if it is, to determine the characteristics of God in the experience, in order that one can live in more adequate relationship with God. It should be noted that Wieman is saying that knowledge of God is *not* an end in itself, but that living in relation to God on the basis of knowledge is the desired end.

A certain method must be followed before one can gain knowledge of God, or any knowledge at all. Wieman calls this method the scientific method, the empirical method, the common sense method, and the method of reason. "The scientific method" appears to be his favorite term, but he asserts that "If one does not want to give the name of science to these inquiries, the matter need not be argued."[3]

Wieman employs the concept "problem solving," which may better eludicate the true character of his scientific method. As he explains, "The word 'God' should indicate a problem above all others imperative for human existence, a problem of such sort as to bring into action all the resources of the individual and of society to find a working solution. . . ."[4] One has a problem. One has an experience in which one is interested, thinking it a religious experience. Wieman asserts that it is part of one's nature to have a sub-rational urge towards those things which are super-rational. By super-rational he means those things which happen which one cannot understand fully. When one has an experience, this sub-rational faculty responds to the God-given super-rational possibilities of the experience; thus, the possibilities become a "lure." This lure of interest is given in the possibilities of the experience. Humans do not create the lure; God is responsible. Wieman calls this lure the grace of God. He also calls this God-given lure the revelation of God by the Holy Spirit. We are transformed in the experience in such a way that we can learn of God. We must carry out the intellectual inquiry, but it is God in the form of the Holy Spirit Who makes possible our efforts:

---

[3] H.N. Wieman, "Bernhardt's Analysis of Religion: Its Implications and Development," *Iliff Review*, 1954, p. 53. For an attack on Wieman's use of the term "scientific method," cf., Edwin Aubrey, *Present Theological Tendencies* (New York: Harper, 1936), p. 32ff.

[4] H.N. Wieman, "Reply to Dr. Williams," *The Empirical Theology of Henry Wieman*, p. 113.

Now this transformation by "the holy spirit" is what (rightfully) can be called revelation. It is not the giving of knowledge, but it is the giving of an attitude or disposition of the personality which enables one to acquire knowledge of God's way. It redirects the interests and desires and attentive awareness so that one can learn of God by the ordinary methods of intelligent inquiry.[5]

Wieman's scientific or problem solving method presupposes an initial revelation by God in the particular religious experience. God reveals the super-rational possibilities of the experience. By designating this revelation by traditional phrases such as "the grace of God" and "the transformation of the holy spirit," Wieman relates the foundation of his scientific method to the Christian tradition. He contends that it is our responsibility to use the scientific method to discover the implications of God's revelation and to act upon this information.

The scientific method not only enables us to get knowledge; it also transforms the character of experiences because it transforms the habit of response. One develops a scientific attitude toward God, this means that an attitude is developed which enables a person to be more responsive to particular localized data. This development of a scientific attitude implies that one cannot assume a completely detached role in the process of religious inquiry. Proper use of the scientific method, in the religious inquiry, will enable one to be more attuned to the scientific experiences in which God's revelation occurs. Using the scientific method in a completely detached manner would cause one to consider all experiences on an equal basis. Wieman rejects this postivistic approach and calls for a scientific attitude which enables one to be more attuned to the specific revelation of God.

For Wieman, the scientific method is used incompletely unless there is a faith-commitment. Gaining knowledge of the God-human relationship is important, but this knowledge is of limited value until we act upon it, by making an absolute faith-commitment to God. Since Wieman places the faith-commitment as the goal of the scientific method, it is possible to question whether his method is truly scientific. From Wieman's perspective; however, the true scientist does not gain knowledge for the sake of gaining knowledge. The scientist seeks knowledge in order to act upon it. The scientific method is used in gaining knowledge of the God-human relationship for the purpose of acting upon this knowledge, an act which is an absolute faith-commitment to God. The knowledge gained is important because it enables people to commit themselves to the true God and not to some figment of their distorted needs.

Metaphysical Position: Before considering Wieman's doctrine of God, it will be helpful to look at his metaphysical position and the way he views metaphysics. Wieman had a distrust of metaphysics from the beginning of his

---

[5] H. N. Wieman, *The Growth of Religion* (Chicago: Willett, Clark & Co., 1938), pp. 442–3.

writing because of its speculative tradition. In his earliest book he states that "metaphysics in the sense of that reasoning which abjures experience and the conclusions of scientific thought, is futile."[6] Metaphysics must be metaphysics of the universe, nor that which transcends the universe. Metaphysical knowledge must be within the bounds of human knowledge, or it is not knowledge at all. Wieman rejects any form of speculation as providing metaphysical knowledge. Since we can not know a beginning or final end of the universe, such questions are not within the proper scope of metaphysical consideration. Revelation in the traditional, supernatural form is rejected as a source of metaphysical knowledge. As Wieman explains, "Final outcomes, as well as all original beginnings, are entirely beyond the scope of our knowing. Anyone who claims to know by revelation or otherwise the ultimate beginning and end is deceiving himself and others."[7] In essence what Wieman is doing is limiting metaphysics to the universe and metaphysical knowledge to what can be known on the basis of human experience and the knowledge scientifically gained from such experience.

Wieman's metaphysical view begins with the universe as the given. The universe is the primary event or the basic nexus of events, which contains an infinity of events. As the primary event, the character of the universe is neutral, in the sense that the universe does not shape the ultimate character or direction of the becoming events. By ascertaining that the universe is neutral, Wieman makes clear that he does not view the universe as God. As the basic nexus of events, the universe remains constant while all the events which make-up the universe are a process of change. If the structure changed, the universe would cease to be. Thus, it is self-evident that changeless structures are necessary in order for there to be change.

As events come together and form a nexus of events, a "conjunction" occurs. A conjunction is a new or more complex event made-up of strands of events. No event or conjunction can ever be repeated. Qualities, or values, are the things of which events are made. The qualities include the possibilities of an event. When a conjunction occurs in such a way that the qualities of the events included in the conjunction fulfill to a greater degree their possibilities, while at the same time they are enriched through an association with other events, there is increase of quality or value in the universe. When this increase occurs on the human level, there is an increase of meaning, or qualitative meaning. A conjunction that brings about such an increase of value is good. When a conjunction results in the limitation of the qualities and of the possibilities of the events concerned, there is a decrease of quality in the universe. When this happens on the human level, there is a decrease in meaning. Such a decrease is evil.

[6] H.N. Wieman, *Religious Experience and Scientific Method* (New York: Macmillan Co., 1926). p. 12.

[7] H.N. Wieman, *The Source of Human Good* (Carbondale, Illinois: Southern Illinois University Press, 1964), p. 92.

The universe, being neutral, does not determine whether there shall be an increase or a decrease of value. The events themselves cannot forsee the developments to occur within a conjunction; therefore, the events can not be responsible for the developments. Since everything that happens occurs because of processes within the universe, there must be some process or processes which are responsible for this development. Within the universe there are processes towards decreasing value and a process towards increased value, or in other words a process for good and processes for evil. Since decreased value is a disintegration of value, the processes which caused these decreases are plural by definition, because their structures are oriented to disunity. The increase of value is an integrating process, in the sense that it works for its unity of value. Being a process for a unity value, the process of integrating value must be one process. The process which works for increased value can be metaphysically designated as "God." God is not the value itself, but is the source of value. Wieman speaks of God as the process of progressive integration of value within the universe or as the highest value. While God is part of the cosmic whole, God is not the universe. As the integrating process of highest value, God must work with the events that are given. All possibilities are limited to the possibilities inherent in the events; God is so limited.

God and humans are both participants in the events of the universe. God's revelation occurs in these events in such a way that, if people use their capacities, they can understand what conditions are required in order that God should bring about the increase of value. God reveals what the conditions are, and people have the responsibility to dedicate themselves to God by living in such a way as to create the conditions in which God can save them. God can not transform the world or people in any other way than that which conforms to the nature of the events involved in the situation. One's responsibility is to discover under what conditions there is an increase in value through conjunctions, and then to structure the conditions of the conjunctions in order that there will be an increase of value in the universe. In more theological terms, the task is to understand what are the conditions under which God can transform lives and then to dedicate those lives to God, in order that God can save them. In essence, according to Wieman's metaphysics, God is that process or function within the universe which is a source of highest value or, from a human perspective, the source of our salvation. Metaphysically, it is God who increases values or saves the world.

Doctrine of God: Wieman begins by saying that God is that process in the universe which is Supreme Value. By the term "Supreme Value," he means that God is that something upon which we are most dependent for our security, welfare and increasing abundance. God may be much more than this, but God is this by definition. Starting from the premise that "God" refers to that which saves us as we can not save ourselves, Wieman uses a variety of terms to establish the distinguishing characteristics of God. In the

Method of Private Religious Living, he develops a view of God as the "integrating process" at work in the universe. This integrating process works in the universe whether we know of it or not; but when we do know this process, we know of it on the basis of our human experiences. The term "mutuality" becomes the key for understanding the distinctive nature of God. The process carries in its existence and in its possibilities the patterns which make possible the most rich and complete mutuality there can ever be. It is the nature of God to function in the universe in such a way as to bring about the greatest degrees of mutuality possible. Our responsibility is to open to God's functioning in order that this mutuality can occur. Mutuality occurs when we are being integrated with ourselves, our fellow humans, with God and the total universe to the greatest degree possible. This is salvation; it is the good; it is the highest value; it is God—God working.

In *Normative Psychology of Religion* he develops his thoughts on "the principle of value." This principle is a further attempt to explain the integrating process as it functions on the level of human existence. As Wieman explains, "The principle of value which we propose is this: Value is that connection between enjoyable activities by which they support one another, enhance one another and, at a higher level, mean one another."[8] The term "connection" becomes the key concept in the principle value. Value does not lie in the events themselves, but in the connection of these events. Therefore, increase of value does not occur by an increase of events; rather it occurs by increase of the functional connection between these events. The principle of value also requires "meaning," which Wieman defines as "the added factor of human appreciation and use of this mutual support."[9] When one gains meaning from the connections, value occurs in such a way that there is "growth of value." This growth of value should not be confused with universal programs; it only means that, within the scope of the conditions under consideration, there is an increase of value. Since growth of value includes the connections and the meaning, growth means much more than that which is or might be; growth itself is a process which increases what is, in order that it may approximate what might be. This process of growth is the supreme value; it is the sovereign God.

In the *Growth of Religion,* Wieman continues to develop the concept of Growth. He posits or formulates two types of growth, the competitive and the connective. Competitive growth relates to the individual and leads to limited growth. The connective type transcends the individual and joins the individual constructively to others in order that unlimited growth can occur. The second type of growth is "creative synthesis," in the sense that is the union of diverse elements in such a way that a new relation transforms them

---

[8] H.M. Wieman and R.W. Wieman, *Normative Psychology of Religion* (New York: Thomas Y. Crowell Co., 1935), p. 46.
[9] Ibid., p. 48.

into a whole which is very different from the sum of the original factors. This growth is the work of love, where love means "the formulation of bonds between diverse individuals whereby each works to conserve the system as a whole, and the whole works to reserve the parts in relation to one another which constitutes the system."[10] Since God is the unlimited connecting growth of meaning which is the work of love, God is love.

In his most important work, *The Source of Human Good*, Wieman speaks of God as the "source of human good," "the creative good," "creativity," and "the creative event." Wieman asserts that human good can be increased only by progressive accumulation of good through a sequence of generations, but this good can not accumulate so long as we seek the creative goods of life. It is necessary that we seek, understand, and commit ourselves to some general principle of goodness in order that the unique goodness of each situation can occur. We must seek and promote that kind of transformation which is the source of qualitative meaning, not seek the qualitative meaning as an end. What we must seek and commit ourselves to is the source of good, the creative event.

Wieman makes a distinction between the structure of an event and the process or function of the event in reality. He makes this same distinction in discussing God as the creative event. "Creativity" and "creative event" can not be separated, but the two terms carry an important distinction in understanding the fullness of his doctrine of God. The sovereign God is creativity, in the sense that God is the character, structure, or form which enables the events of human life to be creative. If God were not this structure of creativity, the reality of the creative event could never occur, and we could not be saved. Creativity is changeless, and because it has this structure, the creative event can change and meet the relative conditions of human life in order constantly to save us.

Wieman is trying to assert that God is both transcendent (creativity) and imminent (the creative event). Creativity is an abstraction which we infer because of the knowledge we have concerning the imminence of God. The creative event is not an abstraction; it is the concrete reality in human experience which saves us. As creativity God gives a changeless structure to our inter-personal events in order that the possibility of creativity can be realized. As the creative event God is the actualized reality of this possibility as it occurs in the event, transforming human understanding and appreciation, and thus, saving us. Humans do, however, have an important role in the creative event. It is the responsibility of humans to open themselves up by dedication to the source of good, in order that they can be saved. Practically speaking, humans carry out this dedication by creating the attitude or conditions which are necessary for life to be transformed continually, making it possible for the creative event to occur in each changing situation.

---

[10] H.N. Wieman, *The Growth of Religion*, p. 327.

In his latter writings, Wieman speaks of God's "creative transformation." God is creative transformation because God saves by transforming lives in such a way that the greatest value can occur in each situation. God creates the potential value in each situation, and God creates the human mind in such a way that it is able to appreciate these values in order that they may become actualized in concrete situations. Because everyone has been transformed, humankind now has a standard whereby to judge good and evil. One does not establish these standards; it is God who makes possible this standard and creates human minds in such a way that the standard is applied. One continues to have the responsibility of creating conditions by which God can save, but the conditions for creating are now very relevant. One must make the faith-commitment, but, in effect; it is God who creates the situation in which one can respond in faith, and it is God who transforms those minds and total selves in order that the faith-commitment can be made. It is true that the will of God can be blocked by creating false ideals about God, and for this reason it is necessary to follow the method previously stated in order to check propositions and actions and be sure that devotion is to nothing but the sovereign God. Evil is very real and does occur every time humans create the conditions which limit the highest value, which is potential through God in each situation. Although evil is a real factor, God is the sovereign source of salvation. It is God who creates the world with its infinite possibilities of highest value; it is God who transforms people in order that these possibilities can occur. While Wieman's doctrine of God gives emphasis to God's being imminent in human experiences, it is necessary also to keep in mind that he also stresses the transcendence of the sovereign God. This transcendent emphasis can be seen in Wieman's use of the term "super human" in relation to God, a term which means beyond or more than human in capacity or normal human power. Super human does not mean supernatural. As Wieman explains, "God is that force functioning in nature within the context of human experience that saves man when he is saved. It is super human because it operates in ways over and above the plans and purposes of men, bringing forth values men cannot foresee, and often developing connections of mutual support and mutual meaning in spite of, or contrary to, the effort of men."[11] In essence, God is super human in the sense of doing what one can not do when one's doing is defined as producing what one intends and images before it occurs. Humans can and must work with this super human function by creating the conditions in which they can be open to being transformed. Creating the conditions is what Wieman calls being intelligently and devotedly religious, which means to carry out the scientific method with the understanding that it is God who saves. Yet humans can never understand how the super human God brings about salvation. Through God's imminent functioning, one knows that God saves; but be-

[11] H. N. Wieman and R. W. Wieman, *Normative Psychology of Religion*, p. 52.

cause one does not know how God does it, one knows that God transcends
limited human experiences and understanding.

Christology: In his earliest writings Wieman provides some clues to his
Christology. In the *Wrestle Of Religion With Truth* (1927), Jesus is compared
with Buddha and Mohammed as a vehicle through which glimpses of the
beauty of the universe are possible:

> In Jesus, so we Christians believe, there shines more of the unex-
> plored and mysterious goodness of this universe, and in him there is
> more promise of that unimaginable blessedness that may sometime flood
> the world, than in any other. Through him we make better contact with
> that which lifts the value of human life to the highest level. . . . but it
> would be a very narrow-minded Christian indeed who would say that the
> life of Jesus is the only quarter in which the most precious object in this
> universe is to be found. [12]

In the passage just quoted, Wieman seems to imply that it is in Jesus' life or
personality that we make better contact with that which directs our lives to
the highest level. By 1930, in an article entitled "Appreciating Jesus Christ,"
Wieman contends that he made a mistake in supporting the orientation
which sought to emphasize the personality of Jesus. As he explains, "All we
can take over from Jesus Christ into our own lives must be the method, the
course of procedure, the principles—if there are any such—by which he
achieved the marvelous qualitative richness of his own unique personality.
But people can not make the personality of Jesus their own, simply because
no one personality can ever be another."[13] The problem is to find the
principles by which Jesus lived. Wieman argues that these principles can be
established by following the scientific method, which will provide the conditions to be met and the specifications to be fulfilled in order to promote these
highest goods. The discovery of these principles is possible because they
belong to all humankind; they did "not belong to Jesus in any special way."[14]

In an article entitled "Was God In Jesus?," Wieman attempts in 1934 to
explain the unique principles established by Jesus from the perspective of a
philosophy of organism. He asserts that, if humans are justified in turning to
Jesus for knowledge of God and for the compelling reality of God, there must
be something in Jesus which can be identified as the mark of superhuman
deity. This "something" is the way Jesus lived or functioned so as to demonstrate that humans are bound together in an organic unity. Wieman argues
that "this fact about the life of Jesus is plain, namely, for him all the riches

[12] H.N. Wieman, *The Wrestle Of Religion With Truth* (New York: Macmillan Co., 1927), p.
127.

[13] H.N. Wieman, "Appreciating Jesus Christ," *The Christian Century*, October 1, 1930, p.
1181.

[14] Ibid., p. 1184.

and all the fulfillment of life were to be found in this organic unity where in the good of each is the good of all and the good of all the good of each. Also evil of each is the evil of all and the evil of all the evil of each."[15] In demonstrating this basic functional interdependence and unity for humanity, Wieman contends that the deity came to focus in Jesus. By stressing Jesus' functional nature, humans are able, based on observation and reason, to gain an understanding that the identifying mark of God is organic unity.

In 1939, Wieman wrote an article for *The Christian Century* entitled "Some Blind Spots Removed." In this article he indicates the desire to relate his religious inquiry more closely to traditional Christian thought and to demonstrate scientifically how the essential religious insights of the Christian tradition relate to contemporary understanding. As previously indicated, essential to Wieman's theology is a transforming good within each concrete situation for which humans are not in any way responsible nor which they can predict or anticipate. Wieman now calls this transforming good by the more traditional term "the Grace of God." He contends that history tells us that there has been a growth of this transforming good, especially in inter-personal relationships. At this point, he provides insight into his Christology, as he asserts that this growth and its potential is the living Christ:

> This growth of connections of mutual support and enrichment, this growth of the bonds of potential meaning which fills each concrete situation with infinite fullness of value to be appreciated, is a living Christ because it issues from that historic situation in which Jesus Christ, regardless of our theological interpretation of his personality and teachings, was used by a process of history to initiate and promote such a growth.[16]

A further insight into his emerging Christology is found in Wieman's growing appreciation for the Church as a historical institution. He now asserts that this growth of good, this Living Christ in our midst, is a way of life which must be fostered by a historical community which is committed to this way of life. What makes this committed community different from every other community is that its way of life, with its hopes, ideals, and moral principles, is crucified with Christ, and must, therefore, keep a distinctive relationship with the original, historical community which formed around Christ Jesus.

With the publication of *The Source of Human Good* in 1946 Wieman's Christology emerges in full form. In this book Jesus is presented as a catalytic agent who "started a chain reaction of creative transformation . . . simply by being the kind of person he was, combined with the social, psychological, and historical situation of the time and the heritage of Hebrew

[15] H.N. Wieman, "Was God In Jesus?," *The Christian Century*, April 25, 1934, p. 589.
[16] H.N. Wieman, "Some Blind Spots Removed," *The Christian Century*, 1939. p. 117.

prophecy."[17] Wieman contends that there were direct consequences in the individual and collective lives of the disciples of Jesus. First, there rose in the group a unique degree of mutual awareness and responsiveness so that each person was deeply and freely receptive and responsive to the others. Next the meanings derived from each other, due to this enhanced condition of mutual awareness and responsiveness, were integrated with the meanings previously acquired. As Wieman explains, "each was transformed, lifted to a higher level of human fulfilment. Each became more of a mind and person, with more capacity to understand, to appreciate, to act with power and insights; for this is the way human personality is generated and magnified and life rendered more nobly human."[18] A third consequence follows the first two. Since the disciples were more sensitive to and appreciative of the world as seen from the perspective of others, their personal and collective reality was richer in terms of meaning and quality. Due to their enlarged capacity to gain the perspectives of those they encountered, there developed an expanded depth and breadth of community among themselves and all people. Thus, the result of Jesus' functioning as a "catalytic agent" was that the Disciples found themselves living in a community miraculously deeper and wider than had previously existed. Wieman is careful to point out that this power leading to creative transformation was not in the man Jesus. Rather, Jesus was in or a part of this power—a power that can be understood in part as emerging in a cultural context. This creative power occured in the interaction between these individuals in such a way that their minds, personalities, appreciable world and community were transformed:

> What happened in the group about Jesus was the lifting of this creative event to dominate their lives. What happened after the death of Jesus was a release of this creative power from constraints and limitations previously confining it; also the formation of a fellowship with an organization, ritual, symbols, and documents by which this dominance of the creative event over human concern might be perpetuated through history. Of course, there was little if any intellectual understanding of it; but intellectual understanding was not required to live under its control in the culture then and there prevailing, for men did not have our technology.[19]

Wieman also addresses the issue of whether the teachings of Jesus should be considered of pre-eminent importance. If the teachings are considered in isolation, Jesus becomes only another wise person. Thus, the

[17] H.N. Wieman, *The Source of Human Good*, p. 40.
[18] Ibid., p. 40.
[19] Ibid., p. 41. cf. H.N. Wieman, "What Is Most Important In Christianity?" in Cedric L. Hepler, ed., *Seeking a Faith for A New Age, Essays On The Inter-Dependence of Religion, Science and Philosophy* (Metuchen, N.J.: Scarecrow Press, 1975).

teachings must be considered part of revelation, with revelation being understood as the complex transforming event that occured between the Disciples. The power is derived from the events and not from the teachings: "The teachings may well be a necessary part of the total occurrence. But events rich in value and events transformative of human existence run deeper than ideas and doctrines and are mightier."[20]

Jesus as the Christ or as the transforming agent is not limited to the group of Disciples but provides world-transforming efficacy. What Christ has done can be simply stated: "the reversing of the order of domination in the life of man *from* domination of human concern by created goods *over to* domination by creative good."[21] This event provides salvation by continuing to be efficatious in a fellowship made continuous in history. God is incarnate in these creatively transforming events, revealing God's forgiveness of sin and assurance of saving the world. Wieman is attempting to explain his Christology in terms of the ancient Christian doctrine of God's revelation, forgiveness of sin and salvation expressed by way of Jesus Christ.

Science Serving Faith: Wieman continues his general theological position premised on the contention that God is divine creativity operative in human existence. This divine creativity functions so as to sustain, save and transform humankind towards the greater good. The problem is that "this divine creativity is latent and ignored, generally, until it is revealed by rising to a level of dominance over all that overlays and opposes it in human life."[22] This rise to dominance is described as a transformation called the saving event, creating an ever deeper appreciative understanding of the unique individuality of others. Whenever this transformation occurs, it is the revelation of God. What the *New Testament* essentially records is the experience the Disciples had with or because of Jesus. This was a transforming experience which revealed Jesus to be Christ. It is not the man Jesus, his teachings or his resurrection which is important.[23] Wieman rejects the controversy over whether the reanimated body of Jesus moved and spoke, contending that the only important point is that the saving power of the creative transformation continued with them after Jesus was gone. While the revelation of God in Christ is not the only example of this divine creativity at work, it is historically significant due to the chain of creative events which flowed from it:

This event initiated a sequence of events in history which changed the order of society in certain ways, redirected the course of history and,

---

[20] Ibid., p. 217.

[21] Ibid., p. 269.

[22] H.N. Wieman, "Science Serving Faith," unpublished manuscript (Archives: Southern Illinois University Library at Carbondale), Chapter One, p. 16.

[23] Cf. H.N. Wieman, "Reply to Horton," *The Empirical Theology of Henry Nelson Wieman*, pp. 190–3, and Ibid., "Reply to Weigel,"pp. 354–377.

when required conditions are present, continues to bring about a reorganization of the personality of individuals so that inner conflicts cease to
be disruptive interpersonal conflicts cease to be destructive, and social
conflicts can be resolved in ways beneficial to the parties concerned.[24]

In this book Wieman stresses the need for modern cultures, with their
fantastic powers, to be guided by divine creativity. This is only possible if
persons search out and provide the conditions most favorable for creative
interchange to occur. It has been possible previously to look to the Christian
tradition for the required conditions. Wieman explains what conditions
humankind can learn from the Christian religion:

> One of these conditions is that the individual come into vital associa-
> tion with the fellowship in which this transforming event takes place.
> Another condition is that the individual recognize the need to be trans-
> formed. This is called confession and repentence of sin. A further
> condition is that the individual accept as the ruling concern the life-
> giving interchange in Christ which delivers from fragmentary and self-
> destructive forms of existence.[25]

While these conditions are universally acknowledged in the Christian
religion, modern secular-scientific cultures require more accurate specifications of these conditions in order that intelligent action can be applied to
meet them. This specification requires the employment of the scientific
method. While Christ is the actual operative presence working to transform
humans from the corruption of evil and toward the greater good, it is science
which can provide the descriptive understanding about the required conditions. This does not mean that the Christ event can be reduced to a set of
scientifically described structures, but it does mean that science can provide
"descriptive accuracy sufficient to guide intelligent action by serving Christ
and in recognizing this event beneath the forms of diverse systems of
symbolism."[25] However, it is necessary to understand that the knowledge of
the conditions provided by science will not itself enable the power of Christ
to change human lives. One must be committed to creating the conditions,
but one is only able to make this commitment because of some experience of
the transforming power of divine creativity—of Christ. Wieman notes that
this conforms to Christian understanding "when it is asserted that commitment of the individual to Christ is a gift of God's grace."[27]

In all his writings, Wieman turns to the social sciences, especially
psychology, for the best information on understanding the conditions suppor-

---

[24] H.N. Wieman, "Science Serving Faith," Chapter One, p. 8.
[25] Ibid., Chapter Three, pp. 2–3.
[26] Ibid., Chapter Four, p. 18.
[27] Ibid., Chapter Three, p. 5.

tive of the creative event. A most interesting contribution in this volume is his discussion of how Eric Erikson illustrates the kind of knowledge that can be scientifically gained. Wieman contends that this emphasis on a commitment to what sustains and develops wholeness of being compares to Erikson's idea of successful identity formation. All persons go through a series of crises. While traditional Christianity speaks to the crises, in the complicated conditions of modern living, dominated by science and technology, which exercise enormous power over the conditions of human existence, the insights of the Christian religion will not ordinarily be helpful in dealing with these crises. It is at this point that the research-science of Erikson becomes significant.

The first crises presented by Erikson is "trust vs. mistrust." It is essential that the infant develop adequate trust, especially in relation to the mother. For this trust to develop in the infant, the mother must be sustained by a deep-laid organization of personality, reaching far beyond her conscious purpose and good intentions. The mother is able to generate this trust in the child because of her experiences which have generated this trust in her. Wieman asserts that "what sustains the trust in the infant is God in Christ when this expression refers to that kind of interchange continuing through history which creates mutual trust and profound concern between individuals when required conditions are present."[28] When we speak of this basic trust later in life, we refer to the religious concept of "faith."

The second crisis that Wieman attributes to Erikson is "autonomy vs. shame, doubt." All children have experienced this which leads them to a condition of shame and doubt about their self-worth, resulting in the pretense to be something other than their true selves or the attempt to hide and sink into oblivion. Wieman contends that the solution to this crisis is to be found in the resources God revealed in Christ: "This is so because the sense of autonomy, independence, self-confidence, and self-worth will develop to the measure that the interchange between the small child and one's parents is the kind creating recognition and appreciation for one another of the genuine individuality of each."[29]

The concept "initiative vs. guilt" designates the third crisis. According to Erikson the best way to deal with guilt is to promote identity formation. Wieman explains this version of Erikson's insight by saying that guilt needs to be focused so as to promote wholeness of being and the commitment of faith:

> This way of treating guilt requires two things. It requires first that one acknowledge one's self for what one truly is with whatsoever guilt and virtue are in one. Only when one does this can one meet the second requirement, that is, to commit oneself as one truly is, guilt and all, to

---

[28] Ibid., Chapter Seven, p. 29.
[29] Ibid., Chapter Seven, p. 30.

the divine creativity of interchange able to weave this guilty self into the fabric of life to create a goodness not otherwise possible. Thus does the self, guilt and all, become something precious.[30]

While Wieman discusses the other crises, these three serve to illustrate his belief that Erikson, although focusing on the problem of health, is essentially dealing with religious issues. However, there is a basic difference when the focus is conceived to be a health rather than a religious problem. For a health problem one only needs to commit to the regime and treatment required. But the development of a person into wholeness of being requires a commitment in faith to divine creativity.

Wieman contends that the Christian religion, employing scientific research, can speak to the crises of the modern world, as illustrated in the discussion of Erikson's work. He proposes seven ways that the Christian religion must function if it is to bring the salvation of Christ to modern persons, "when Christ means what carries people most successfully through the major crises of human life to the end of our salvation."[31] This sevenfold approach is designated as cognition, education, evangelical, institutional, cultural, historical, and philosophical-theological. In the cognitive emphasis, the Christian religion is responsible for developing the best possible intellectual understanding of what is called for in the commitment of faith. Education is required to enable the individual in society to be sustained through the crisis of formation. The evangelical conduct required of Christians in the modern world is to live so as "to respond with appreciative understanding to the unique individuality of the other person." The institutions supported by Christians must be re-shaped so as to help as people undergo the crisis of personal development. The Christian religion must also develop a cultural perspective which will include an understanding of the significance of science so humankind can integrate science into the comprehensive view of the way life should be lived. The historical and philosophical-theological responsibilities are a part of the effort to broaden perspectives in order to better understand human experiences and to develop an adequate ideology for guiding decisions in this scientific age.

In essence, Wieman is pointing out that the purpose of the Christian religion is to assist people, in a given social and historical context, to understand and to commit to that which creates, sustains, saves and transforms towards the best that human life can ever attain. Since its inception Christianity has made significant adjustments in its sevenfold manner of relating to the changing cultural context. The adjustments of Augustine to Neo-Platonic philosophy and Aquinas to Aristotelian philosophy are but two examples of major cultural adjustments in the Christian religion. But today

---

[30] Ibid., Chapter Seven, p. 31.
[31] Ibid., Chapter Seven, p. 38.

the social-historical condition has changed radically and swiftly due to the scientific revolution, with its new view of reality and the tremendous power available with this revolution. The old understanding of Christ, held over from previous times, is not fitted to guide the commitment of faith for many modern persons. What is required is a re-shaped Christology based on the intellectual understanding afforded by science. Only when science is put to the service of the Christian religion can the revelation of God in Christ be made intelligible so that people can understand this revelation and commit themselves in faith to divine creativity.

Creighton Peden
Augusta College
Augusta, Ga. 30910

PREFACE

Henry Wieman began *Science Serving Faith* in the early sixties, clearly intending the work as his major statement on Christology. When he put the manuscript aside, he had a relatively complete draft of chapters one through eight, and a much less complete draft of chapter nine. (This original manuscript is available in the Special Collections at Morris Library at Southern Illinois University.) In its rough manuscript form, the volume appeared much less finished than it actually was; as a result, no attempt to publish it was made by Wieman's family or friends after his death in 1975.

When we began work on the manuscript, our intent was to make available Wieman's thought at the end of a long and brilliant career as the pre-eminent spokesperson for empirical theology. The most difficult immediate task was to decipher Wieman's handwritten additions and corrections. Fortunately we had the able and invaluable assistance of Mrs. H.N. Wieman. Numerous other editorial decisions had to be made, for which we relied upon Wieman's *Source of Human Good* as our style "standard." In addition, we took the advice of several publishers and scholars on Wieman and made the somewhat controversial decision to remove gender distinctions—a decision, we realize, that some readers may regret. In all editorial matters, however, our purpose was to present Wieman's ideas clearly and accurately. In this we believe we have succeeded.

In addition to Mrs. Wieman, without whose courtesy and patience this volume would not exist, we would like to thank Frissy Peden for many hours of proofreading and Carolyn Kershner for typing the final manuscript.

Creighton Peden
Charles Willig
Augusta College
December 1, 1986

SCIENCE SERVING FAITH

Henry Nelson Wieman

CHAPTER 1
SCIENCE AND REVELATION

The life-giving center of the Christian faith can be called its heart. On it all else depends. It sends the quickening pulse to all parts and to it the life-blood returns to be renewed and sent again to the extremities. This heart of Christianity is not the man Jesus nor his teachings. It is not any institution nor set of doctrines. It is not any theology nor ritual nor symbol nor form of worship. All these might be called the veins and arteries, or bones and tissue of Christianity. Without them there would be no Christian religion. But they are not the life-giving center. In distinction from all these, the heart of the Christian faith is the revelation of God in Christ with that revelation's saving and transforming power.

In dealing with the question of the relation of science to the Christian religion, the understanding of divine revelation is crucial. The interpretation given to the revelation of God in Christ determines what relation science can have to the Christian faith. When revelation is understood in one way, there is continuous conflict between "revealed truth" and "scientific truth" or with "science so falsely called." When revelation is understood in another way, scientific knowledge is allocated to one area and revelation to another, and the two are so completely separate that they seem to have no bearing on one another. A third interpretation of divine revelation is possible, however, and when it is accepted the two sources of knowledge are mutually corrective and mutually helpful. In other words, we can have a view of revelation of such sort that scientific or empirical knowledge pertains to the field of revelation as much as to any other.

The "revelation of God in Christ" has been interpreted in diverse and contradictory ways throughout the history of Christianity. Today conflicting doctrines claim to set forth the truth involved in this confession of faith that God is in Christ. Many accept the words without any attempt to specify what is meant by them. Yet nothing intelligible can be said about the Christian faith which is not based upon an understanding of revelation. Such being the case, it is apparent that we cannot begin to discuss the relation of science to the Christian religion until we make plain what we understand to be the meaning of the words "God revealed in Christ". In order to do this we shall examine what four outstanding representatives, now dominating the field of religious thought, have to say about it. If there were one single, clearly formulated, widely accepted and undisputed, understanding of the referent indicated by the words "God in Christ," it would not be necessary to begin with this study of conflicting doctrines before undertaking a discussion of the relation of science to the Christian religion. But among theologians today there is no unanimity on this manner.

On one point first of all let us be clear. "The revelation of God in Christ" refers to an actual event along with a sequence of events occurring through subsequent history, this sequence issuing forth from the initiating event and continuing through a fellowship. No matter how false may be the interpretation given to the words "revelation of God in Christ," the error lies in giving a wrong interpretation to this event and the historic sequence following from it. On the other hand, no matter how much truth might be affirmed in any doctrines about the revelation of God in Christ, the revelation would not be in this true doctrine about the event. The revelation would be in the event itself, not in what theologians might correctly state about the event.

This distinction between (1) the event with its sequence in history and (2) what theologians say about the event, is a distinction of first importance. Certainly we need to have a correct understanding of the events. Without this understanding, confusion overtakes discussion of problems pertaining to the Christian faith. Nevertheless, important as it is, intellectual understanding of the event is not identical with the event itself. Correct understanding of what one should eat to gain good health is not identical with the actual event of eating health-giving food. So it is with the actual event of revelation. Doctrine about the event may be true or false, or mixed with partial truth and error to all degrees. The event still stands with its essential characteristics, regardless of the truth and regardless of the error in all the doctrines about it that have been set forth throughout the history of Christianity. Indeed, doctrines about the revelation of God in Christ can be true and can be false only when they do refer to a sequence of events having essential characteristics which remain, regardless of what is affirmed and denied in these diverse and conflicting doctrines. A true doctrine about the revelation is a statement correctly specifying the essential characteristics of the event. A false doctrine is one attributing to this event with its sequence of subsequent events certain features which do not characterize them.

The problem is exposed, not solved when we say that the revelation of God in Christ is an event combined with subsequent events reaching down through history in our own time and into the personal existence of each of us as individuals. This statement about revelation shows us how we should proceed and what we should try to discover. It directs us away from misleading lines of inquiry and directs us toward the area where true statements about revelation may be found.

The revelation of God in Christ involved words with their meanings. But the event in which these words of revelation were involved was a transformation in the organization of personality of those who received the revelation. This is the distinction we here wish to make and to emphasize. It is the distinction between doctrines about the revelation and the revelation itself. The revelation is a transformation occurring when required conditions are present. It is a transformation of the individual, of society and of the course of history. It is a transformation whereby the individual, society and the course of history are saved *from* the self destructive propensities of human existence and *saved* unto a divine creativity operating in human life to fulfill God-given potentialities resident at the level distinctly human.

This transformation of human existence, which cannot occur unless required conditions are met, does involve the use of words with meanings. Words used in this way and with this kind of meaning did occur in the interchange between Jesus and his disciples. According to the record, this kind of interchange transformed the lives of those involved and did it in such a way that the transforming interchange continued in the fellowship of the disciples after the death of Jesus.

This transformation of a person's way of life, reaching consciousness in the form of a statement vividly apprehended, may indeed be the voice of God. It may come when a person is alone, but mere solitude without prior interchange of the kind which occurred between Jesus and his disciples will not produce creative insight. It will not redirect the conduct of life in the way that saves from the self-destructive propensity of human existence. Jesus alone in the wilderness may reach his major decisions; but from all we know about the conditions of his life and about human life generally, these decisions would not have occurred as they did if Jesus had not spent his life in interchange with the books and persons transmitting the life and teachings of the Hebrew prophets.

So it has been with all the great creative transformations which have occurred to individuals in solitude, whether it be St. Paul or Augustine or Luther or any other. Always a kind of interchange was required, endowing words and symbols with the kind of meaning which transforms the lives of individuals from the drive toward self-destruction to the drive toward ever deeper appreciative understanding of people for one another. This appreciative understanding of one another, when deep enough and wide enough and free enough, is that mighty creative communion of each- with-other wherein a human being can find a resting place, the goal of one's existence, the condition which one's nature craves. It has been called the Kingdom of God.

In this discussion we seek to understand a certain kind of event called the revelation of God in Christ. This kind of event is distinguished from all others by one essential characteristic. It is a transformation of human existence from the drive toward self-destruction to another kind of drive, here called the divine creativity, which creates in human beings ever deeper appreciative understanding of the unique individuality of one another. This transformation is wrought by the kind of meaning which words and other symbols can convey. The technical name for this kind of meaning, derived from the Greek, is *kerygma*. So, in seeking to understand the event of God in Christ, we are led to seek an understanding of the meaning which produces this transformation. But then we find that any meaning conveyed by words and other symbols must be derived from interchange among and between persons. This interchange endows the word with meaning; otherwise it is merely a sound and not a word. Words and other symbols convey one or another kind of meaning, depending on the kind of interchange which gives them the meaning they have for the persons concerned.

This brings us to the question we must answer if we are to distinguish from other events the kind of event which is the revelation of God. The question is this: What kind of interchange endows words and other symbols with the kind of meaning which can transform lives after the manner called salvation?

Our inquiry now comes to a single point. We seek to identify the kind of interchange which occurred between Jesus and his disciples. This interchange continued by way of the crucifixion and resurrection in the fellowship of the disciples and has been transmitted with intermittent but recurrent transforming power down to our time. In seeking to understand what is meant by the words "revelation of God in Christ," we must be able to distinguish this creative and transforming kind of interchange from all the many other kinds which occur in human life.

Reference to the "resurrection" calls for some interpretation of this word. Again we must avoid entering into controversies which do not pertain to the problem presently under consideration. We are here concerned solely with one feature pertaining to the resurrection. This one feature is the resurrection of that kind of interchange whereby human existence is saved from its drive toward self-destruction and is endowed with a drive toward that kind of communion between each and all wherein the noblest possibilities of human existence are attained. This was accomplished by way of resurrection. Controversy over whether the reanimated body of Jesus moved and spoke in the fellowship of the disciples need not concern us. The important point is that the saving power of divine interchange continued with them after Jesus was with them no more. On the third day after the crucifixion, the disciples found themselves engaged in the same liberating, sustaining, and transforming interchange which they had experienced with Jesus. Perhaps they had no way to tell about this experience except to represent it as though the body of Jesus was still among them. After their story had been transmitted from mouth to mouth for several years without its being put down in written form, it may have come to be told in such a way that the bodily presence of Jesus was a part of the story. Or was the bodily presence actually there and necessary for the continuing of the saving power of God revealed in Christ?

So far as concerns the purpose of the present discussion, this question can be answered either way. The one fact that is essential to the revelation of

God in Christ is that the power of God unto salvation was continued as an operative presence to subsequent generations, transforming the lives of individuals when required conditions are present, and pointing out the way of life that people choose, socially and historically, if the imperative demands of human existence are ever to be satisfied. These imperative demands are unconscious, ignored and overlaid by other interests prior to that awakening which comes when the hidden potentialities are aroused by the kind of interchange the disciples had with Jesus. If the bodily presence of Jesus risen from the grave was necessary for this to be accomplished, then so it was. If the bodily presence of Jesus was not necessary, then let the facts be as they may. The point is that this transforming power was resurrected after the crucifixion and did continue as an operative presence in the fellowship of the disciples. Furthermore, it can rise again in our midst today with saving and transforming power, and ever again arise, when required conditions are met. Does it always involve, even with us today, the invisible but bodily presence of Jesus risen from the grave? Let all persons answer that question as they can; but when controversy over that question excludes from consideration the essential reality, we have missed the meaning of the revelation of God in Christ. The essential reality is the saving power of the kind of interchange which Jesus had with his disciples.

As mentioned earlier, we shall examine briefly in the next chapter what four outstanding theologians of our time are saying about the revelation in Christ. We shall find that they disagree radically with one another, not only about the resurrection but also about other matters of importance. When disagreements are as strong as these, all cannot be correct because the affirmations of one are often denied by the others. Indeed when such disagreements occur, there is great probability that not more than one can approximate the truth, and even he may be far from it. But this need not dismay us. An event did occur which transformed the lives of individuals. This event initiated a sequence of events in history which changed the order of society in certain ways, redirected the course of history and, when required conditions are present, continues to bring about a reorganization of the personality of individuals so that inner conflicts cease to be disruptive, interpersonal conflicts cease to be destructive, and social conflicts are resolved in ways beneficial to the parties concerned. The problem is to understand this kind of event and its required conditions.

We seek this understanding so that we can act intelligently and effectively in providing the conditions most favorable for the occurrence of this saving event which transforms the lives of people when required conditions are present. We need to do this at whatever time and place we may occupy and in our dealings with whatsoever difficulties may confront us. Obviously there is one first condition which must be met if we are to do anything at all of this sort. This first condition is our own commitment of faith. Without this no intelligent and effective action in service of Christ can be undertaken. But neither can such action be carried through if we are ignorant of the other conditions which a devoted disciple should seek to provide in order that the transforming power of Christ may spread and grow and deepen among people.

A further condition required for the saving event to occur is the state of mind called confession and repentance of sin, humility and ever-deepened commitment. But these words do not specify with clarity what is required until more accuracy of specification is given to them by proper inquiry and understanding.

In addition to the subjective conditions just mentioned, pertaining to the individual who undertakes action in commitment of faith, other conditions of a more objective sort should be constructed, protected and improved. These are physical, chemical, biological, interpersonal, institutional, and historical. To discover just what all these conditions may be and to provide them is the task of scientific inquiry.

Our commitment of faith requires us to apply all our resources, scientific and otherwise, to seek out and set up the conditions most favorable for the saving event of Christ to occur. This does not mean that Christ is unavailable until after all this has been done. The saving power of Christ operates with all degrees of effectiveness to the measure that required conditions are present. It is like good health. Good health has all degrees, depending on the presence of those conditions required for health. Even without knowledge of these conditions and without any intelligent action to provide them, magnificent good health does sometimes occur. Or again it is like friendship. Without knowledge of the required conditions and without any attempted action to provide them, profound and noble friendships do sometimes arise. Or it is like life within the family. At some times and in some cases the relation between husband and wife and parents and children are idyllic without any knowledge on the part of the persons concerned of what the required conditions might be for this to happen. So we might go on and speak of good government, good industrial relations, good economic conditions, and every other kind of good to be found in human life. In every case the required conditions must be present. These conditions are always present to some degree, when and if there is any good at all in human life. But this good in its various forms can be more or less, depending on the presence of the conditions required for the particular kind of good under consideration.

So it is with the saving and blessing power of Christ. It is always present and available and operative to some degree. Sometimes it rises up with transfiguring effect. All this may occur without our understanding of the required conditions and without any intelligent action to provide them. But does all this mean that we have no responsibility in the matter? Does it mean that nothing is required of us? Certainly we have responsibility. It is to discover the required conditions and then act to provide them so far as we are able.

We repeat: The revelation of God in Christ must never be identified with any set of doctrines about the revelation, not even if the set of doctrines be the truth complete and perfect. The complete and perfect truth in the form of statements about the revelation can never be more than a correct description of the essential characteristics distinguishing the event and its required conditions. The event—the transformation as it actually occurs in the lives of people in all its concrete fullness and depth—should never be confused with a correct description of the essential and distinguishing character of the event. Neither should it be confused with what humans do in providing the required conditions.

Scientific knowledge and science applied in the form of technology cannot do the work of Christ. Science and scientific technology cannot produce that transformation in the life of the individual, in interpersonal relations, in society and history, which is the kind of event here under consideration. But there is work which science and scientific technology can do and what they must do if they, along with other human resources, are committed to Christ. It is to search out, set up, protect and improve those conditions which must be present for the transforming event to occur in depth and power and scope throughout the order of society and in the course of history.

As human power increases, this intellectual understanding of the event and its required conditions become increasingly imperative. Power increases responsibility. The exercise of power either tears down or builds up the conditions required for any kind of good in human life. Therefore, if we do not know what the required conditions are and/or have no commitment to the good involved, our exercise of power becomes disastrous so far as concerns that kind of good. All this applies to every kind of good, including the good which goes by the name of the saving power of Christ. Hence, the more power we exercise, the more destructive it becomes unless we are (1) committed to the saving and transforming power revealed in Christ and (2) have sufficient knowledge of the required conditions so that we can exercise our power to provide them.

When we say that the exercise of human power must be guided by commitment to the saving power revealed in Christ, we realize that a dangerous misunderstanding is likely to arise. This statement does not mean to say that a Jew or Hindu or Muslim or some other non-Christian might not be committed to the kind of interchange which occurred between Jesus and his disciples. This saving and creative power was certainly revealed in Christ. Just what that means we have yet to explain. But one negative statement about it can be made at once. It does not mean that this saving and creative event first came into existence with Jesus. Its divine character and saving power was there revealed. To be revealed does not mean to be brought into being. To reveal means to uncover, expose, make manifest, what is already present, unrecognized though it be prior to the disclosure.

In Christ the immanent power of God to create and sustain, save and transform, is revealed in its true character, which means that it calls for one's self-giving in faith so that one may be saved. But God's immanence in human history did not begin there in Palestine with the birth of Jesus. The power of God unto salvation has always been present in human life. Otherwise human life could not have come into existence in the first place nor could it have continued in existence; and there would be no human history whatsoever. The power of God unto salvation is always present and ready to rise up with transforming might whenever the required conditions are present. The mere utterance of the name "Christ" is not one of these required conditions. There is no magic in that word. Regardless of whether one knows anything about Jesus Christ, when the conditions are present under which the divine event of transformation occurs, there it is, faithful and sure. As we said before, this does not depend upon individuals knowing the divine character of this event and what its required conditions may be.

What, then, one may ask, is the need of revelation in Christ? The need is imperative and without it there is no hope for human beings. Beginning with the age of Hellenism, Western civilization began to develop that power—political and administrative, scientific and technological—which now in the Twentieth Century has become masterful over the subhuman world and is spreading to the entire human race. Also it is increasing with accelerating speed. With power so great, humans can no longer live under the guidance of uninterpreted tradition, ignorant of what creates and saves, ignorant of what sustains and transforms toward the greater good. Our power has become too vast for that. When power reaches such magnitude, its exercise becomes fatefully destructive of the conditions of human existence and of all human good unless guided (1) by commitment to what sustains, saves and transforms creatively and (2) by knowledge of the conditions which must be protected or improved or provided by the exercise of power in order that the saving and sustaining creativity may operate effectively.

The period of rising power which led to the Western civilization of our time, now swiftly becoming world-civilization, was the age of Hellenism. It was a time when many cultures merged, pre-eminently the Greek and Roman. This merging of many cultures and many histories generated that development which has resulted in modern science, modern technology and those methods of social organization by which the activities of millions of persons can be coordinated in massive action. This is power. It has produced the bloodiest and most destructive period in human history and now threatens the annihilation of the human race.

This same period of Hellenism was also the time and place when that revelation occurred which can guide the use of this power to constructive ends and away from destruction. It was the revelation of God in Christ. Why, then, was this guidance not accepted? Why did the developing power of this world in the form of science, technology and political action go its own way while the saving power of Christ was reserved for a fellowship having little to do with the instruments and agencies of power? Such an opposition and mutual exclusion did occur, creating what Augustine called the City of this world and the City of God. Many conditions might be mentioned which brought on this division. Perhaps the condition of humans in general made it inevitable. Yet the interpreters of the Christian faith, the theologians, the representative figures of Christendom, cannot be entirely exempt from blame. The revelation of God in Christ and the continued recurrence of the saving event in the lives of people might have been interpreted in such a way as to show the vital significance of the agencies and instruments of power to the transformation wrought by Christ in human existence. At any rate this division continues down to our time. Today science is the chief source of power when applied to the techniques of social organization, to the techniques of psychological control and propaganda and to the technology of industry and war. The theologians of our time, in great part, continue to assert that Christ points to what transcends time, space, society and history while science is concerned exclusively with the temporal world. Hence, science and technology and all these instruments of worldly power have no intimate and necessary connections with God in Christ.

If this division and opposition continues between the instruments of power and the way of life in Christ, the days ahead are dark indeed. It is true that Christ opens the way to what transcends this temporal world. It is also true that science and the instruments of power are exclusively concerned with this temporal world. But the transformation wrought by Christ is a transformation occurring in human life; and human life is temporal, spatial, psychological, social and historical. Furthermore this saving and transforming event occuring in human life requires certain conditions that are temporal, spatial, psychological, social and historical. Here, then, is the place science and the instruments of power can join with the commitment of faith in Christ. They can be committed, along with all the rest of human life, to searching out and helping to provide these conditions.

The kind of liberal Christianity which prevailed forty and fifty years ago tried to overcome this breach between science and faith, but the attempt was misdirected. The liberal Christian at that time thought that scientific inquiry or philosophical speculation, either one or both, could find God as revealed in Christ in the cosmic process as known to science, or in the psychological process of the human personality, or in the course of history as explored by historical research, or in the moral teachings of Jesus and in the way he conducted his life, or in some metaphysical system developed in such a way as to bring all these materials into a single comprehensive vision. All this was mistaken because it ignored the one single, essential fact underlying everything else in the revelation of God in Christ. This one essential fact is a transformation occurring within the personality of the individual and in the relation between persons. Until this transformation occurs there is no revelation for the persons concerned and there is no saving event.

God as revealed in Christ cannot be found in the cosmic process because what we call the cosmic process is merely that structure of existence which happens to be exposed by the theories now being used by the sciences. The theories used by science in the past exposed a different structure; and the theories used by the sciences of the future will be different from what they are today, and will depict the cosmic process in a different form.

God revealed in Christ cannot be found by scientific study until one particular kind of transformation occurring in human personality and human society is distinguished from everything else. This particular kind of transformation is said to be a manifestation of transcendent being. That is true enough. But the expression "transcendent being" can be misleading because it seems to suggest that we can have some speculative or intuitive or revealed knowledge of a being which transcends this saving event of transformation occurring in our lives. This kind of knowledge we cannot have. All we can know of God is what is revealed in Christ and that is the event of transformation. The word "transcendence" should not be used unless it is understood to mean that we cannot know anything beyond what happens in human life and within the scope of inquiry based on the events occurring in human existence.

The statement just made will be misunderstood unless two remarks previously made are recalled. God is always present in human life in the sense that human existence would be impossible without the creativity which continuously lifts life to the level distinctly human and sustains it there. But this divine creativity is latent and ignored, generally, until it is revealed by rising to a level of dominance over all that overlays and opposes it in human life. This rising to dominance is the transformation here called the saving event. It is the revelation of God in Christ. After the revelation has occurred, the latent presence of the divine creativity may be recognized even where the transformation has not occurred.

The second remark should also be recalled. When it is said that "all we can know of God is revealed in Christ" we do not mean that none can know God save those who inherit the Christian tradition. This rising to dominance over counter processes in human life, which is the revelation of God in Christ, may occur outside the Christian tradition entirely. The transformation may not then bear the name of Christ. But, as said before, the name "Christ" has no magic in it. The reality is there regardless of the name given to it. And in fact, many who inherit the Christian tradition do not undergo the transformation, no matter how much they may talk about Jesus Christ and profess the Christian faith.

With this understanding of the matter it can be said that apart from Christ there is a drive toward self-destruction in human existence. This does not mean the conscious intention to destroy. It only means that when human power is used without commitment to what sustains, saves and transforms toward the greater good, this power becomes destructive of the conditions required for the continuation of human existence and for the upholding of human good. No animal has ever been so destructive of itself, of its own good and of the conditions required for its existence, as humans have been. Of course human power is also used constructively. The development of human culture has pressured us to develop our creative potentialities much more than anything else in the world. As said before, there is a divine creativity in human life that has never yet let humans go, despite our disregard of its demands. But when human power increases, a time comes when its exercise must be guided by commitment to Christ—or the point of no return is reached. Its unguided and irresponsible use to serve no ends save to satisfy current, popular desires will inevitably lead to the destruction of those conditions under which the divine creativity can continue to sustain human culture; and without the resources of culture accumulated through a sequence of generations, human life can scarcely continue.

There is much talk in modern times about a lack of purpose in American life. Our wealth and power have increased to such a measure that they require a purpose more clearly discerned and followed than was required when wealth and power were more limited. What has happened to America will happen to all the rest of the world as modern science and technology extend this wealth and power around the earth.

Wealth and power have increased so swiftly in recent years that our responsibility and action have extended far and deep into the lives of the peoples of the planet. Also our ability to satisfy whatever desire happens to possess the mind of the individual has been magnified. Under such conditions we must see more clearly and correctly what is necessary for our salvation. Above all, the old disjunction between commitment to Christ and scientific research with its application to techniques and technology cannot continue. To overcome this disjunction we must have a reinterpretation of the revelation in Christ so that the relevance of science to the Christian faith will be more apparent than it is with prevailing interpretations. Power so great must be brought into the service of Christ.

During the past few years even louder and more insistent voices have lamented our condition and the imperative need for a unifying and directing purpose. Walter Lippmann, in his *The Public Philosophy* as well as in his continuous column of comment, has been one of the leaders. But now a great chorus has arisen which says much the same thing. Editorials, articles, speeches and books all declare that we do not know how to use our wealth and power in a way that does not disintegrate our moral fiber, disrupt our social order and defeat us in our attempt to cooperate with the rest of the world when all peoples on the planet must live together with sufficient community of purpose to avoid the futility of mutual frustration.

These comments, or diagnosis of our condition, have been chiefly about America. The wealth and power we now have has brought on this disease; and ironically, all the rest of the world is now seeking this wealth and power. As they acquire the science, technology and techniques of social organization which have enabled us to achieve this opulence, their condition will become what ours is today. So this diagnosis applies not only to us; it applies to the condition into which the greater part of the human race may be moving. It is not about America particularly; it is about that plateau of achievement toward which the civilization of the human race is driving. On this plateau civilization becomes self-destructive unless it is guided by a commitment of faith that releases our constructive potentialities and guards against our destructive propensities.

The agency that drives toward this plateau where the great decision must be made—and the more adequate conception of human purpose must be discerned—is science with all its applications to industrial technology and political techniques. Since science is the driving agent, no guiding purpose or comprehensive commitment shaping the course of human life can save us unless science can be integrated into it. If the guiding purpose is, indeed, found in Christ, then scientific research and scientific technology must be a part of the life of the person committed to that saving power.

CHAPTER II:
CONFLICTING VIEWS OF REVELATION

The four theologians whose teaching on revelation we shall examine are Edward John Carnell, Paul Tillich, Karl Barth, and Rudolph Bultmann.

Carnell sums up his doctrine of revelation in these words: "Only propositional revelation can clarify the state of the sinner before a holy God."[1] His position is made very clear when he quotes—with approval—B. B. Warfield:

> Inspiration is that extraordinary, supernatural influence (or, passively, the result of it) exerted by the Holy Ghost upon the writers of our Sacred Books, by which their words were rendered also the words of God, and, therefore, perfectly infallible.

Carnell's only criticism of Warfield is that he did not defend himself in a satisfactory way when his doctrine of the infallible Bible was criticized. "Apart from the Bible" writes Carnell, "we would have no access to the redemptive events."[2] But he rejects what he calls "odious Biblicism."

> "The Bible, and the Bible alone, is the Word of God written." But we have "odious Biblicism" when we fail to see that "the written Word does not commend itself unless the heart is confronted by the living Word. Paul did not see Christ in Scripture until he met Christ on the Damascus road. The Bible is the Word of God 'out there' whether or not anyone is confronted by it; but it does not address the heart until Christ is met in personal fellowship. The living Word is the soul of the written Word."[3]

The Word of God does not reach us until "Christ is met in personal fellowship," but this personal fellowship with Christ cannot be had except by way of the Bible. One who claims to have it apart from the Bible, has nothing but a personal experience with no grounds whatsoever for calling it fellowship with Christ. Apart from the Bible people have nothing but a variety of experiences which may be called "religious experience" but without any evidence to indicate *what* is being experienced. Only arbitrary judgement

---

[1] *The Case for Orthodox Theology* by Edward John Carnell, The Westminster Press, Phila. 1959.

[2] *Ibid.*, p. 33.

[3] *Ibid.*, p. 33–4.

without evidence can call such experience "fellowship with Christ" or "confronting Christ."

Carnell asserts that "outsiders may read the Bible. But they cannot perceive the soul of Christ, for they are not in fellowship with Christ. Fellowship *knows* Christ, not *about* Christ. This is knowledge by acquaintance."[4] This is a little confusing. Ordinarily "knowledge by acquaintance" means knowledge without any mediating agency between the self and what is experienced and known. But Carnell seems to say that the Bible must always be the mediating agency between the self and Christ. What, then, does Carnell mean by this fellowship which is knowledge by acquaintance? He becomes clearer when he states, "In the one act of reading Scripture, we meet Christ in two complementary ways. First, we confront Christ's person. . . . Secondly, we receive a propositional revelation of Christ's will."

Carnell tries to make plain with an illustration what he means by confronting the person of Christ in fellowship through the reading of the Bible. He asks the reader to imagine a lover reading a letter from his beloved. The letter, when read in love, becomes for Robert the "vehicle of Wilma's soul. But," adds Carnell, "only Robert can perceive this. Outsiders may read the letter, but only love can divine the affairs of love."

Contrary to Carnell's intention, this illustration proves the exact opposite of what he wants to demonstrate. The letter can be for Robert the vehicle for Wilma's soul only if he has first had fellowship with Wilma apart from the mediation of the letter. Intimate fellowship by way of letters can occur only *after* the individuals have had the experience of responding to all the subtle and diversified expressiveness of physical presence with that abundance of meaning conveyed by tones of voice, facial expression, and body posture, along with the total concrete situation of the others person's actual existence. The actual, concrete situation in all its physical forms is often necessary to give the full meaning to the total expressiveness of the other person. Only after this background of experience has been first acquired can the written words convey the kind of meaning which creates communion in depth.

The truth about the Bible is that it becomes the Word of God in the sense of speaking to the individual with transforming power only when it is the medium of communication and profound interchange in the fellowship of Christ. By "fellowship of Christ", the present writer means a fellowship engaged in the kind of interchange which prevailed between Jesus and his disciples and was transmitted to subsequent fellowships by way of the Cross and the Resurrection. Carnell inadvertently admits that the Bible as the word of God depends upon its use as medium of interchange in such a fellowship. This inadvertent admission appears when he says that Paul first

[4]*Ibid.*, p. 34.

found Christ on the Damascus road and only thereafter was able to find him in Scripture.

Although it may be a small point, for the sake of clarity let us say that Paul did not find Christ but Christ first found Paul, a meeting which occurred by way of that fellowship of the disciples whom Saul persecuted. The kind of interchange which went on between these disciples and all others with whom they dealt was a dynamic, transforming and saving power. It was the revelation of God in Christ saving the world. It touched Saul of Tarsus; it got hold of him and would not let him go until he yielded to its transforming power on the road to Damascus.

This shows that the revelation of God and the fellowship of Christ cannot be had by way of the Bible alone. It requires the "church", by which is meant the living fellowship of those engaged in the kind of interchange which occurred between Jesus and his disciples and which was deepened and spread to many others by way of the Crucifixion and the Resurrection. The Word of God in the Bible is the creature of the church as much as the church is the creature of it. More accurately stated, the Word of God in the form of the Bible, and the living church in the form of human beings associated in fellowship, are both created by the revelation of God in Christ. This is accomplished by transmitting that kind of interchange which transforms the lives of men. No matter what supernatural and transcendent being may be involved, the interchange in this kind of fellowship is the actual event which we must try to distinguish from everything else by its essential characteristics so that we can use our power to provide the conditions most favorable for its occurrence.

Let us return to Carnell's discussion of revelation and Christian faith, for he is very helpful even though we dispute with him. He rightly denies that Christian faith is belief extending beyond the evidence. As he says, "To believe on insufficient evidence—what is that but to believe what may not be true."[5] Faith, says Carnell, requires no "leap of the will" and no "risk of the intellect" beyond any form of assured knowledge. Furthermore, he says the evidence supporting Christian belief must be of the same kind as that sustaining the beliefs of common sense.

Carnell looks to the findings of archaeology to support the truth of statements found in the Bible. He looks to historical research to assure us that events actually occurred as recorded in the Bible. Also the rules of logic cannot be violated in defending the beliefs of faith. No resort to myth or paradox or religious experience or mystical apprehension is permitted *unless* what is found in these various ways can be defended by logically ordered statements and empirically acquired evidence.

Carnell does not seem to recognize how precarious become the grounds

[5] *Ibid.*, p. 24.

on which the infallible Word of God must rest when he takes this position. Yet he freely admits the difficulties and perils of the orthodoxy he defends and lists these difficulties and perils in considerable detail.

He rejects fundamentalism in the form which he calls the "mentality of fundamentalism," while agreeing with it in the claim that the Bible is the sole authority for any religious affirmation. But he finds in fundamentalism other characteristics which he repudiates, such as the quest of negative status, meaning virtue sought by not doing certain things rather than by positive action; the elevation of minor issues to the place of major importance; the use of social mores as a norm of virtue; the toleration of one's own prejudice but not the prejudice of others; the confusion of the church with the denomination; the avoidance of prophetic scrutiny by using the Word of God as an instrument of self-security but not self-criticism. This mentality of fundamentalism, he adds, is by no means limited to those who go by the name of fundamentalists.

Carnell rejects the mentality of fundamentalism and modernism, but he also excludes teachings that are central to the Baptists, the Lutherans, the Episcopalians, the Methodists, the Roman Catholics and even the Orthodox when they set the authority of the Bible above the demands of love. For example, he says that "A glance at the church page in a metropolitan newspaper is enough to chill the heart of any cultured person. Religious claims are so contradictory, and in many cases so downright inane, that agnosticism seems to be the only honorable refuge for an educated mind. It is against this difficulty that orthodoxy cheerfully speaks to the problems of proof." He quotes at length and with approval David Hume's denunciation of religious believers, their credulity and their impudence.

After all this, Carnell in his *Case for Orthodoxy* can defend his belief in the bodily resurrection of Jesus only by saying that it is believed by millions of Christians. Yet Carnell rejects many beliefs professed by millions of Christians. Note his reference to the "inane" teaching of the churches; his rejection of modernism and fundamentalism; his approval of Hume's criticism of religious believers; his assertion that there is no truth in some of the central beliefs affirmed by Methodists, Baptists, Lutherans, Episcopalians and Catholics.

Carnell ends his book by a confession: "In the sweep of history it may turn out that orthodoxy will fail in its vocation. But in this event it should be observed that it is orthodoxy, not the gospel, which has failed." This distinction between orthodoxy and the gospel, made by the man who defends orthodoxy with all his powers, is profoundly significant. The honesty, the generosity, the humility and the forthrightness of Carnell make him preeminent among those who claim that the revelation of God in Christ is first of all a set of propositions giving us correct descriptive information about God and his ways.

This idea of revelation is contradicted at every point by Paul Tillich. To understand Tillich's interpretation of revelation, we must first see what he means when he speaks of "God beyond God" and declares that God does not exist and further insists that it is "blasphemy" to say that God exists. It is blasphemy unless one wishes to speak in the form which Tillich calls religious symbolism.

Tillich defines religion as ultimate concern. Our ultimate concern is directed to being itself or the power of being. This is so because everything depends on being. The universe, whatever happens in the universe, human destiny, all the good and all the evil—indeed, every distinguishable kind of being in existence or possibility—all depend upon the power of being itself. Since our ultimate concern is directed to what underlies and sustains everything that exists and everything that ever can exist, that concern can stop with nothing less than being itself.

The person who says that God is one kind of being, distinguishable from other kinds, is identifying God with what cannot be God, says Tillich, because every distinguishable kind of being is merely one being among others. It is limited and conditioned by these others. Such being the case, every distinguishable kind of being is more or less subject to what other kinds of beings may do. Consequently it may be broken down, remade or transformed in unpredictable ways by this action of others upon it. But God cannot be modified or changed in any way by other beings. Tillich says this because he identifies religion with ontology. The latter is concerned about ultimate being and Tillich defines religion in terms of ontology.

This exposes Tillich to a major criticism. The Christian religion is not primarily an ontology and its ultimate concern is not ontological. Its ultimate concern is directed to what can save people from their self-destructive propensities and transform them as they cannot transform themselves into the best that human life can attain. In all this theology Tillich says very little about any such actual transformation of human existence except for psychological change that might enable one to accept non-being with courage. Non-being is the self-destructive propensities. The power of being (one's ultimate ontological concern) does not deliver one from this non-being, according to Tillich. The power of being includes non-being in itself. Obviously this is so because everything that happens is an instance of being and hence is derived from the power of being. So this ontological concern for ultimate being directs one to no Savior. It gives "the courage to be," which means to accept the self-destructive propensities of existence, but nothing more.

When Tillich speaks of the "God beyond God," he means that God in reality (ontologically speaking) is beyond, and other than, the popular ideas of God. The latter are symbols. They are not God in truth. God in truth (as defined by Tillich's ontology) is the God *beyond* these symbols. These point beyond themselves to the power of being.

No limiting characteristic can be applied to the power of being because it ungulfs and transcends all limitation. To qualify being itself with any descriptive or designative or definitive term is to engage in a contradiction of terms because being itself forever transcends every possible qualification. Hence, humans can form no idea whatsoever of the power of being. Even the word "power," when applied to being itself, becomes a religious symbol, not a descriptive term. This is so because power, in the form it is experienced, is a limiting characteristic and so cannot truly apply to being itself.

God in reality, beyond all symbols, according to Tillich's ontology, is absolutely unknowable. To know anything is to be able to distinguish it from what it is not. But Tillich asserts again and again that God in reality is not any one kind of being, therefore not distinguishable from other kinds. On this account people must have symbols to refer to this unknown being. But these symbols do not describe, characterize or designate in any knowable form whatsoever this unknowable being, although they seem to do so. Persons of faith cling to these symbols because they seem to give them a knowable form of God. But according to Tillich, God, the power of being, cannot be confined to any knowable form.

Religious symbolism is a central theme in Tillich's theology. The religious symbol, as treated by Tillich, is not a symbol at all in the sense in which ordinary language is made up of symbols. Symbols in the form of ordinary language, that is to say words as commonly used, serve to describe, designate, define and relate, which means to give us knowledge of distinguishable kinds of being. But symbols in the religious sense, as interpreted by Tillich, do not give us knowledge. Symbols in the religious sense participate in what they represent. That is true if they represent being because everything participates in being. Everything is some distinguishable kind of being and in that sense participates in being itself. When the Nazis tortured and killed six million Jews, that torture and killing is a distinguishable kind of being and so participates in the power of being. The same is true of every horror and evil one can mention, as well as every honor and glory and everything in between.

When Tillich speaks of the power of being having the character of "love, power and justice," he is using religious symbols. Love participates in the power of being but so also does hate. Justice participates in the power of being but so also does injustice. Therefore, these words have no descriptive significance when applied to the power of being. They are religious symbols and give us no knowledge of any definitive characteristics pertaining to the power of being. God ontologically conceived has no definitive characteristic whether of love or hate, justice or injustice.

These comments provide the background of thought which we must have in mind when we consider Tillich's interpretation of the revelation of God in Christ. As said before, Tillich's account of revelation contradicts that of Carnell at every point. According to Tillich, there can be no system of propositions specifying the distinguishing characteristics of God and God's will for humanity. Yet that is precisely what Carnell means by the revelation of God in Christ by way of the Bible. According to Carnell, Jesus Christ is the living Word of God. We know the distinguishing characteristics of the Living Word by means of the Written Word. The Written Word of God is what we find in the Bible. In Romans and Galatians, says Carnell, we find a theological system giving us our needed information about God and God's will. The rest of the Bible does it less systematically but the rest of the Bible should be interpreted according to this system set forth in Romans and Galatians. According to Tillich, such a notion of revelation is absurd. Religion is the ultimate concern of all of us and this ontological concern is directed to being itself beyond the reach of all possible description and all possible characterization whatsoever. This theological system in the Bible may give us religious symbols with which to think about God but cannot give us any knowledge of what ultimately concerns us.

What, then is the revelation of God in Christ, according to Tillich? For Tillich the man Jesus fades out and we have in place of the man what Tillich calls "the picture" in the New Testament. This picture is not like a photograph, giving us a portrayal of the person: it is like a painting giving us the experience the disciples had in interchange with this individual. Nobody knows Jesus as he was in the actuality of individual existence under the conditions of the time and place of his life. Regardless of what Luke may say in his effort to get at the real person, the original writings used by Luke were never intended to give us an accurate description of the man Jesus and his doings. Rather they were intended to record what the writers and others experienced in fellowship with this man. In sum, the writings of the New Testament depict the transforming power of that kind of interchange which occurred in fellowship with Jesus. This is not what Tillich intends to say but it is definitely a component of what he does say.

What Tillich asserts is that the man Jesus becomes the medium of revelation because he is pictured in the New Testament in such form that when we apprehend the meaning of this picture we find that it points to the mystery of being. If the man Jesus were presented with all the limitations of human existence, there would be no divine revelation. According to Tillich, to say that the power of being could assume the form of a person is nonsense. Such a limited form of existence is the very opposite of all that Tillich says about unlimited and unconditioned being which is "God beyond God."

To use Tillich's expression, Jesus Christ is the revelation of God because of his transparency. By this Tillich means to say what has just been stated, namely, the man with all his human limitations fades away so that we see not the man but the power of being for which and in which and by which the man lived. His suffering, his rejection, his crucifixion, the apparent futility of all his striving, combined with his unwavering devotion, as pictured in the New medium through which we become aware of the mystery of being. The significance of tragedy is that it reveals what it fails to attain. In this way Jesus reveals not himself but the power of being. Mystery, not knowledge, comes to us by way of the revelation in Christ.

Here again we find in Tillich, as we found in Carnell, that he stumbles on the same basic and inescapable fact involved in the revelation. It is the transforming power of the interchange which occurred between Jesus and his disciples. This is what is revealed in what Tillich calls the picture of Jesus in the New Testament. Tillich, of course, is correct in saying that the New Testament is not a photographic representation of the life of Jesus. It is, rather, an expression of the experience the disciples had in fellowship with Jesus, the experience of being transformed by the interchange then and there occurring.

Tillich overlooks the creative, saving power of this interchange, although everything he says about the revelation of Christ is based upon it. But Tillich is not willing to rest his case on this. He is committed to a religious ontology which will not permit him to do so. This ontology drives him to say that this creative, saving power of the interchange can be called the revelation of God only because it made the disciples aware of the mystery of being itself—which cannot be characterized in any way. Or, if it did not do this for the disciples, their account in the New Testament can be a divine revelation for us only as it makes us aware of this mystery.

An inevitable question arises as to whether Paul Tillich is an atheist. One could argue that he is an atheist, not because he denies the existence of God (although he does make that denial), but because he denies that God is any distinguishable kind of being whatsoever. If Tillich said that God is unknowable because of the limitations of the human mind, but is still a distinguishable kind of being which might be known, he would not be an atheist. He would be an agnostic, not denying that God is a kind of being but only asserting that the divine kind of being transcends the limitation of human cognition. But this is not what Tillich says. He denies that God has any limiting character whatsoever and therefore is not any kind of being distinguishable from other kinds. This resolves God into nothing because "nothing" refers to the absence of all distinguishing characteristics. Indeed Tillich and his followers repeatedly say that God is not a thing. This has a plausible sound because the word "thing" often designates some material object like a stick or stone. But the word "thing" also is used to designate anything to which reference might be made. When the word is used in this sense, to say that God is not a thing is equivalent to saying God is no-thing or nothing. To have no distinguishable character is to be nothing.

Tillich, however, does not intend to be an atheist. He sincerely and devotedly strives to direct the religious consciousness beyond those images of deity which possess the human mind but are unworthy of ultimate concern and the final commitment of faith. Above all, he wants to provide a theology for what he calls the "Protestant Era." Protestantism, says Tillich, means continuous revolution in religious thought, continuous criticism and protest against the limitations, errors and evils always present in people's thoughts about God. Always we are subject to error; always our thoughts, aspirations and ways of life derived from what we think and say about God call for criticism and correction. According to Tillich, such continuous criticism and correction is precisely what is meant by Protestantism.

Tillich's theology is activated by still another profound concern, expressed in what he calls the method of correlation. Different ages, different cultures, different individuals and situations have problems, difficulties and needs very different from one another. How can we minister to all these different needs if we have a theology which limits God to characteristics of vital importance for some ages and peoples and persons but not for others? Human life, especially in our time, is undergoing continuous revolution. We cannot know what the perspective on reality will be tomorrow, or what the desperate need may be of some individual or group or situation under conditions we cannot now imagine. The minister must be able to function and to help in all of these situations. Therefore, one must first involve oneself in the situation of the individual to be helped. Then one must be able to interpret God in such a way as to meet the need of that person or that people. When God is not limited to any definable character and one is free to use any kind of symbol that is effective to meet the need, one can practice this method of correlation.

These are the concerns driving Tillich to develop the kind of theology which he proposes. These are vital concerns which strike deep into the heart of a man profoundly devoted to the service of humanity. Tillich is to be honored for this concern and for his attempt to meet it. But the danger involved in his theology should also be obvious. When God has no definable character, the minister or the church or the religious leaders are free to use whatever symbolism they think will best serve the needs of people and represent God in that form. But that makes the minister or the church or the religious leader the creator of God for all practical purposes. Tillich tries to guard against this by saying that God beyond all these symbols is being itself. But since being itself has no definable character, it can in itself provide no guidance, give no direction, be identified with no goal or purpose. The symbol, then, which is not God but serves to point beyond itself to unknowable being, becomes the only guide and stay. But the symbol is the creature of religious tradition, and religious tradition is constantly recreated by the imaginations, purposes and interpretations of people, preeminently the religious leaders. For all practical purposes this turns the priest into God, since the priest determines the correct import of the symbol.

We have already seen where Tillich stumbled over the revelation of God in Christ which can meet all the needs which so vitally and honorably concern Tillich. It is that kind of interchange which creates appreciative understanding in depth of the unique individuality of one another. It creates community which does not limit nor bind the unique individual but liberates the person to express his or her own individuality while yet abiding in mutual support, mutual appreciation, and mutual creative transformation. This is the kind of interchange revealed in the fellowship of Christ. It is God operative in human existence with power to save, because this kind of interchange, by creating this appreciative understanding of the unique individual in unique situations, is alone fit to meet the need of each different person, age, culture and situation. Yet this kind of interchange has a character by which it is distinguished from all the other kinds of interchange and all the other kinds of being opposed to it. Also it carries with it a changeless, universal moral law that gives guidance and direction and yet is fitted to every changing situation. The moral law is this: Always act in such a way as to provide conditions most favorable for the kind of interchange which creates appreciative understanding of the unique individuality of those with whom you deal.

The moral law does not say: Always have appreciative understanding of the unique individuality of those with whom you deal. This would be an impossible command, as impossible as the command to love every person. This appreciative understanding of unique individuality must be created in us by Christ. That means created in us by the kind of interchange which prevailed in the fellowship of Jesus and his disciples.

This is the revelation of God in Christ which is required by what Tillich calls the Protestant Era. Also this interpretation of divine revelation provides for the "method of correlation" and does it better than the mystery of being without the dangers involved in Tillich's ontology. Also this understanding of the revelation opens the way for the mission of Protestantism which is to protest, criticize and correct and not be bound to a final form of thought and practice held beyond the reach of criticism.

We now come to Karl Barth and his understanding of the revelation of God in Christ. Barth is opposed both to Carnell and to Tillich, though he also argues that the Bible is the only religious authority and through the Bible, which is the Word of God, we receive the revelation of God in Christ. Apart from the Bible this revelation cannot reach us. So far Barth sounds very much like Carnell. But when we come to understand what Barth means, we find that he is diametrically opposed to Carnell. Carnell insists that we get the message of the Bible by exercising the ordinary powers of the human mind. Just as we gather evidence to learn that one person is honest and reliable while another is not, just as we learn by historical research that certain events occurred in the past, so we learn what Jesus said and did, what the prophets of Israel taught and what happened to the children of Israel. The ordinary powers of the human mind and the ordinary methods of gaining knowledge are all we require, provided that we enter into fellowship with Christ when we gain this knowledge of him and of the redemptive events connected with him.

Karl Barth denies that this is the way the revelation of God in Christ can reach us. He insists that no human intellect, no matter how highly gifted, can ever find by reading the Bible the revelation of God. Only when God has chosen the individual as one whom he endows with divine grace, can that person receive the revelation. Only when God has given to the individual what Barth calls the "freedom to believe"[6] does the revelation become accessible. Barth insists on this again and again while Carnell just as insistently claims that nothing more is required than the ordinary powers of the human intellect to understand what the Bible has to say about God and Christ and the way of salvation. According to Barth the Word of God in the Bible is "inaccessible and inconceivable" to the natural powers of the human mind.

Barth and Carnell disagree just as strongly on still another point concerning the Bible as Word of God. The Bible may not be correctly interpreted even by one who has received God's grace because "we carry this treasure in earthen vessels." For this reason the individual should discuss with others who have received God's grace what the Bible reveals. The church is made up of those who have received God's grace. So, says Barth, members of this fellowship of the church should criticize and correct, suggest and instruct one another concerning what is spoken in God's word. Outsiders cannot participate because they have not the grace to believe and know and hence to learn by this interchange with one another. But in the church this interchange transforms the otherwise ordinary words of the Bible into the Word of God.

Here again Barth, like Carnell and Tillich, stumbles on what is truly the revelation of God in Christ. This kind of interchange which occurred in the fellowship of Jesus has saving and transforming power. This interchange whereby alone the Bible can be the Word of God is not an incidental reference in the theology of Karl Barth. It is basic to his entire teaching. Everything he has to say about the revelation of God depends upon the church. Yet he does not seem to recognize that this kind of interchange is itself the revelation.

Barth gives praise to God that he is one of the elect, having received the grace whereby he can believe what cannot be supported by the rational coherence and supporting evidence demanded by reason when it is not "illuminated." Those who do not have this "illumination of the reason" (Barth's own expression) and cannot accept Barth's interpretation of the Word of God, show unreasonable pride:

[6]*Dogmatics in Outline* by Karl Barth. Harper Torchbook, 1959. *passim*.

If we summarize all that opposes the acceptance of God's Word as the power of contradiction, one has an inkling of what Scripture means by the devil. Has God really said . . . ? Is God's Word true? If one believes, one will snap his finger at the devil.[7]

The devil in this quotation is the principle of non-contradiction. One who has the "illumination of his reason" by the gift of God's grace will not be troubled by contradictory statements when they seem to render unbelievable what the grace of God enables one to believe. Barth is generous enough and humble enough to say that we carry "this treasure in earthen vessels" and so may be mistaken in what we declare to be the Word of God. But no one can correct us, no one can rightly criticize us, unless that person is a recipient of God's grace and is a member of that fellowship called the church. Others, no matter how great their intellectual powers, are incompetent to correct and criticize.

Barth would be correct in this position if he said that no one, regardless of intellectual ability, can have profound intuitive understanding of the unique individuality of another person unless that person has engaged in the kind of interchange creating it. This understanding of the individuality of another is a grace given to God in Christ when Christ is understood to be the kind of interchange which creates this insight. This responsiveness to another person is not ability to formulate a statement about the other person. Rather it is ability to respond to the other in a way to meet the other's need. Such response cannot be put into statements divorced from tone of voice, facial expression and the exigencies of the concrete situation of that time and place, sometimes called the "existential situation." This kind of evaluative and understanding response to the other person can only occur in that unique situation with that unique individual when the two are engaged in the kind of interchange which creates this kind of communion. This kind of response to the other person is indeed beyond the reach of the giant intellect dealing with abstractions.

But Barth does not stop with this. He goes on to identify this grace of God with a gift enabling one to know what has happened and will happen and is now happening beyond the time and space of this world. He knows by divine grace that people shall have bodies after death although they will be made of different stuff or substance from normal bodies. He knows in the same way about heaven, which is temporal and spatial although its time and space are different from ours. He knows by the grace of God that Jesus sits at the right hand of God and will reappear when history comes to end.

It should be clear how Barth disagrees with Carnell in regard to the revelation of God in Christ. He disagrees no less with Tillich. For Barth, God revealed in Christ is a definite, knowable person. The man of flesh and blood

---

[7] *Ibid.*, p. 20.

in the actual time and place of his personal existence is the revelation of God. The eternal dwelt in this man, under all the limitations of his existence—temporal, spatial, cultural. According to Tillich, this is unbelievable nonsense. But according to Barth, the skepticism of Tillich only shows that Tillich has not received the grace from God whereby he would be free to believe what the Word of God truly teaches, that, in this man Jesus, God truly dwelt.

An important but unacknowledged presupposition is exposed in Barth's thinking when he states that the Bible does not convey the revelation to the human mind, no matter how highly endowed. Only when the mind is transformed by the grace of God can it receive from the Bible this revelation. This brings the reader to the critical point. How is the mind thus transformed so that it can discern the revealed presence of God, not only accessible to the disciples long ago, but accessible to others here and now? This transformation called grace of God occurs in the church. But the church is not merely an institution. When the church serves as the medium of God's grace, it is that fellowship where interchange, centered around the gospel message, opens the mind to God's revelation in the Bible. Therefore the revelation resides in this kind of interchange. It does not reside in the Bible by itself because, as Barth himself says, the untransformed mind does not find in the Bible the revelation. Only by way of this kind of interchange does the revelation occur. This interchange may be called preaching, provided one does not think this means some one necessarily standing in a pulpit and talking vehemently about the Bible. It is preaching only in the sense in which "preaching" occurred as Jesus sat with his disciples around the last supper before he was crucified, or as he walked with them through the fields. This kind of interchange *is* the revelation, when revelation means disclosing to the individual the actual presence and power of God in Christ operating in such a way as to save from the power of sin.

So here again we find, as we found in Carnell and Tillich, the truth about the revelation inadvertently conceded, although apparently unacknowledged. When we turn to Rudolph Bultmann, we also find in him this same implicit truth, basically involved in his teaching about the saving event of the revelation of God in Christ. In Bultmann, however, it stands out more clearly in what he calls the eschatalogical event.

Bultmann and Barth have much in common, yet on a point of prime importance they disagree. Barth states his criticism of Bultmann in *Rudolph Bultmann, Bin Vorsuch ihn to Verstehn*. The substance of Barth's criticism can be stated very briefly: Bultmann takes Martin Heidegger's philosophy and imposes it on the Scripture to determine how the text should be interpreted. This, says Barth, is exactly the reverse of the way one must approach the Word of God if one is to receive the revelation. When this is done, one imposes a construction of the human mind upon God's Word. But the whole import of divine revelation is to break down the constructions of

the human mind, thus liberating the individual God. The central theme of
Barth's entire work has been that people and God are alienated. The ideals,
the values, the philosophies, the theologies, all the constructions of the
human mind, are opposed to the way of life in God. Therefore, when a
humanly constructed philosophy such as that of Martin Heidegger, or any
other, is set up as a guide to an understanding of God's Word, the way of
access to divine revelation is blocked.

Barth admits that every human mind inevitably comes to God's Word
with some philosophy or, at least, with presuppositions, with ideas of good
and evil and with some structure of consciousness. This no person can avoid,
by reason of the human condition. But the first step to take is to acknowledge
the unfitness of this predisposition of the mind and hold it subject to
reconstruction by God's Word. But Bultmann, by taking the existential
philosophy of Heidegger as normative for interpreting the Bible, does the
opposite. Hence, says Barth, his error is profound, setting up a wall against
the transforming power of God's Word.

On this point, but on a basis somewhat different from the explicit
statements of Barth, the present writer agrees with this criticism: No pre-
established structure of the human mind should set up in such a way as to
resist the creative transformation continuously wrought by the interchange
in the fellowship of Christ. Nevertheless, Bultmann has some important
things to say and in his own manner contributes to an understanding of the
divine creativity in Christ. Also, while Barth on one point is corrective of
Bultmann, in another way Bultmann is corrective of Barth.

To understand Bultmann one must first understand a central theme in
the existential philosophy of Martin Heidegger because Bultmann makes
this teaching of Heidegger a precondition for the understanding of the saving
event in the revelation in Christ.

According to Heidegger the feature distinctly human about the existing
individual is awareness of Being and concern about Being. Being is not any
object which the human mind can know, such as the structure of the universe
can be set forth by science. It is a contradiction in terms to say that Being is
any object whatsoever which can be set over against the knowing mind.
Being overarches and unifies a person and any object which that person
knows or might seek to know. Therefore, Being cannot be an object of
knowledge because it includes both subject and object. Since Being cannot
be an object of knowledge, it can be called Nothing. In Heidegger's philosophy Being is in this sense Nothing and this is the word Heidegger uses.
Heidegger is one of the leading existentialists of our time. Bultmann and
Tillich both start with his existentialism and both make use of this philosophy
of Nothing. They treat it as the void to be filled in with a religious message.
For Tillich the message is religious symbolism. For Bultmann it is the gospel
message when this is stripped of the myths which conceal its truth.

Out of the void of Nothingness, says Bultmann, comes the Word of God spoken through Christ, telling us that our alienation from Being, which is our sin, gives Being the appearance of Nothing; but this Word from the void also tells us that we are forgiven if we acknowledge our condition and accept the message. If we make the decision to commit ourselves wholly to Christ, the void is no longer an empty void. It comes to us in love and mercy, in the form of the Word of God. To be sure, the actual world as known to science and empirical inquiry remains the same, with all its limitations, ambiguities and mystery. But that is irrelevant. The gospel message is not about the observable world nor about anything which the sciences can discover. From beyond the world known to common sense and to science, from the void of transcendant Being, comes the "Good News" telling us of love and mercy and forgiveness of sin. By the decision with which we cast ourselves upon the truth of God's Word spoken in Christ we gain what Bultmann calls the authenticity of the self. What that means shall be explained a little later.

This statement of the existential basis of Bultmann's teaching about the revelation of God is all too brief but it suggests the background against which should be seen Bultmann's famous attempt to remove myths from the gospel message so that the *kerigma* might reach us in all its purity and power. These myths have become an obstacle to the modern mind, says Bultmann, preventing many from that decision of ultimate commitment by which the saving event of Christ transforms the mind. To understand what Bultmann means by demythologizing the gospel we must have before us his definition of myth.

Myth, according to Bultmann, is any presentation of spiritual reality in the form of temporal and spatial happenings and objects. Myths make it appear that transcendent Being breaks into the order of nature and assumes the form of a happening, like a miracle. Invisible demons are supposed to operate like temporal and spatial forms of existence, causing disease and insanity. Jesus is represented as coming again on clouds in the sky. He is said to descend into hell and rise up into heaven. But this three-decker universe is foreign to all we know about the stars and planets. The mythical mind thinks of Jesus as having a body in which dwelt the transcendent being of God. The spiritual meaning of the resurrection is identified with the re-animation of the corpse of Jesus after his death. These are only a few of the myths which have been woven into the gospel.

Bultmann's objection to them is not only that they present a barrier between the Word of God and the mind; they also are ontologically false and religiously pernicious. The transcendent Being speaking through Christ does not cease to be transcendent when revealed in the Word of God. The meaning of words by which we know the forgiveness and love of another are not objects or happenings in the temporal and spatial world. To represent these communicated meanings as though they were temporal and spatial objects is to falsify the meaning of words.

Another evil results from myths when they are not purged from the gospel. This further evil appears in the form of "liberal Christianity," as this expression is understood by Bultmann and others. Since the revelation of God was presented in the form of myths and these seemed to suggest that transcendent being was immanent in the natural world, the liberal Christian sought to interpret the myth by speculative ideas about God and salvation. Thus arose all those philosophies and theologies which identified God with some kind of cosmic process, or claimed to find God manifest in nature. This completely falsifies the revelation of transcendent being as it comes to us in the Word of God. The Word of God does not come to us from anything in nature. It does not tell us about the cosmic process nor how the universe was created nor about anything within the field of scientific inquiry and empirical knowledge. Scientific knowledge about the world, psychological knowledge about the human mind and personality, anthropological knowledge about human culture, knowledge of past events gained by historical research, all this is true enough so far as it meets the tests applicable to this kind of research. But all this gives us no knowledge whatsoever of the transcendent Being which speaks through the Word of God. This message from ultimate Being, telling us that we are sinners but can be forgiven and thereby find our authentic selves in relation to Being, is not about the world of nature. The world of time and space, the world known to psychological, historical and other kinds of research is not knowledge about transcendent Being. Therefore it does not apply to the message which comes from transcendent Being.

So, says Bultmann, the *kerygma* must be accepted in its purity, free of the distortions of mythology and free of the falsifications imposed on it when it is confused with scientific knowledge about the natural world. Also it must be freed from philosophical speculation about what lies beyond the reach of scientific testing. All this must be wiped away so that the Word of God can reach us with its true and full meaning, thus enabling us to accept it with a decision of the total self. Only by way of such a decision can the saving event of God's revelation reach us and transform us into authentic selves. The decisiveness with which we must commit ourselves to the Word of God in Christ is prevented if we become entangled with questions about how this message is related to scientific knowledge.

Perhaps Bultmann's most mature statement about the revelation of Christ is to be found in his Gifford Lectures, published under the title *The Presence of Eternity*, with the sub-title "history and eschatology." The question he seeks to answer in this book might be stated thus: What is the true historicity of humanity? His answer is that the true historicity of humanity is achieved in the eschatological event. But this event does not occur at the end of time in a cosmic catastrophe as pictured in some places in the Bible. The eschatological event means the culminating end of history; but this culminating end occurs whenever an individual brings his or her total self into action with all its resources. This is what Bultmann calls decision. In making such a decision we gather up the past so far as it has entered into our lives to make us what we are and give life a direction for the future which it would not have had if we had not made that decision. In this sense and in this way, past history culminates in an event which transforms the past and creates the future, because the past takes on a new character when it is gathered into the making of this kind of decision. So also does the future. In a sense and to a degree a new world is born by such a decision.

In making such a decision, the individual is free from the past and from former decisions, not in the sense that they cease to be the individual's past experience, but their significance is transformed by this kind of decision. That is to say, a future is created which the past could not have created without this decision. In that sense, the past is no more, meaning that the past no longer can produce the kind of future that it would have produced without that decision.

Bultmann is fond of stating his case in paradoxes that are confusing because they seem contradictory. For example, in making the kind of decision just mentioned, says Bultmann, one transcends history while still being in history:

> It is the paradox of Christian being that the believer is taken out of the world . . . and that at the same time he remains within the world, within his historicity. To be historical means to live from the future. The believer too lives from the future; first because his faith and his freedom can never be possession; as belong to the eschatological event they can never become facts of past time but are realized over and over again as event; secondly, because the believer remains within history. In principle, the future always offers to man the gift of freedom; Christian faith is the power to grasp this gift. The freedom of man from himself is always realized in the freedom of historical decisions.[8]

Faith and freedom cannot be possession because they are achieved only in the event of making the kind of decision above described. After this decision is made, the event of making that decision is past. Since faith and freedom were only in the event of making that decision, the individual no longer has faith and freedom after the event has occurred unless he or she makes another decision of the same sort.

What is meant by saying that human freedom is freedom from self? It means that in making the kind of decision mentioned, the past of the individual is integrated into a new form so that one is not oneself as in the past but is a different self by reason of this decision. Also one's future is different from what it would have been if one had not made that decision. In this sense the individual is "free from self", that is, from one's past self.

In the kind of decision just mentioned, the individual not only achieves freedom but also what Bultmann calls "authentic self" or "genuine life." The

[8] Bultmann, p. 152.

person also achieves true historicity. By this is meant that a future is created out of the past which would not have been created apart from the person's decision. Thus one becomes a creator of history and not merely a creature of history as one would have been who merely yielded to the drift of events. Now this freedom, this authentic self and genuine life, and this true historicity cannot be achieved by one's own strength and will. It must be given by the grace of God and this grace is given in Christ. So says Bultmann. What does this mean? According to Bultmann, it does not mean that it was given once for all in the life of Jesus. It is given here and now in the eschatological event. The eschatological event of Christ happened two thousand years ago, and it happens again and again whenever the decision of freedom is made. It is made in Christ when it is made in response to the preaching of the gospel. The decision of freedom, says Bultmann, cannot be made in any other way because Christ reaches us only in our response to preaching.

If "preaching" as Bultmann uses the word merely means someone is standing in the pulpit and earnestly expounding the Bible centered in the gospel story, then plainly it is not true that the decision of freedom and the authentic self never occur except when one is listening to a preacher. But the statement can take on truth if by "preaching" is meant the kind of interchange creating the kind of fellowship Jesus had with his disciples. As said before, the consequences of this kind of interchange often ripen in solitude when the integration of what one gets from the other completes itself in such a way as to create a new and different self. One can call this kind of interchange "love" if one wishes and Bultmann mentions love as necessary for this freedom to occur which is also the authentic self and the historicity of the self given by the grace of God.

It remains to explain what Bultmann means by "the presence of eternity" in his book by that title. This again is paradoxical language, unnecessarily confusing. Bultmann quotes Erich Frank in a comment that mirrors Bultmann's own view:

". . . to the Christians the advent of Christ was not an event in that temporal process which we mean by history today. It was an event in the history of salvation, in the realm of eternity . . . in an analogous way, history comes to an end in the religious experience of any Christian 'who is in Christ' . . . For although the advent of Christ is an historical event which happened 'once' in the past, it is, at the same time, an eternal event which occurs again and again in the soul of any Christian."[9]

Now if "eternal" used in this quotation meant "not temporal," the expression "eternal event" would be not merely paradoxical but a flat contradiction of terms, such as "round square," because events are necessarily temporal. But if we interpret the expression by its context, "eternal event" in

[9] Erich Frank, quoted in Bultmann, *The Presence of Eternity*, p. 153.

Christ is an event having two characteristics. First, it occurred not only in the fellowship of Jesus but again and again in later history where individuals are gathered in a like kind of fellowship. Second, it is "not an event in that temporal process which we mean by history today" because that temporal process which we mean by history today is a sequence in which one event follows another without that kind of creative transformation which we have seen occurs in the fellowship of Christ. In this kind of interchange, there is a transcendence of time and history when this means that the past takes on a new character relative to the present. This occurs because the past of one unique individual, being different from any other, is communicated to a second individual. This second individual also received the same from the first. After being thus communicated, these two pasts, each radically different from the other because of the uniqueness of the individuals, are integrated in the personality of each of the two. Thus a new kind of past comes into being, namely, the sharing by each of the past of the other so that each assumes responsibility not only for what one has done and been but also responsibility for what the other has done and been.

This shows how interchange in Christ transcends time and history by creating a new past and a new future which is different from "that temporal process which we mean by history today," to quote again the word of Erich Frank. At the same time it is true historicity because the individuals become creative of history and not merely pushed around by a process over which they have no control. Also it is an eschatological event in the sense of being a culmination and a new beginning.

It should be noted that this kind of interchange and this kind of event cannot occur unless the true uniqueness of individuality is brought forth in the individuals concerned. Normally, individuals conform to a pattern which inhibits the uniqueness of individuality. In such case they do not communicate the past that is different in each; rather they communicate that conventional pattern which is the same for all. In such case there can be no creative transformation of past and future by integration of pasts very different from one another. Since the uniqueness of individuality must come forth in the kind of interchange that creates freedom and authenticity in the eschatological event, the interchange must be of such sort as to create in each participant a profound appreciation of the unique individuality of the other.

So here again we find in Bultmann what we found in Carnell, Tillich and Barth, when the teaching of each is carefully analyzed and the pre-suppositions exposed, whether or not they are conscious of the pre-suppositions entailed in what they say. As each presents his case, we find implicit in the discussion the same truth. The revelation of God in Christ occurs in a kind of interchange which rose to dominance over all else in the fellowship of Jesus and can rise to dominance over all else in the fellowship of Jesus and can rise to dominance again and again when individuals are joined in the same kind of fellowship by meeting the required conditions. It is the grace of God in

Christ because it cannot be achieved by purposive striving beyond meeting the required conditions. When these conditions are present, the new creation occurs. This integration of the diverse pasts of unique individuals creates a future which the individuals could not foresee, imagine, or intend so long as the future depended on the separate past of each individual. But when the unique past of each is integrated with the past of the other through the free and full communication of uninhibited and unique individuality of each to the other, a new future is created out of this new past. All this is given by God's grace because it could not be determined by the individuals, nor imagined by them, prior to this kind of interchange, because they did not have the kind of past making possible the anticipation of this kind of future and this new being of the self.

Sin, says Bultmann, is one's resistance to this kind of creative transformation of the past, of oneself and of the future. It can occur only when the individual commits to God in Christ to have past and future controlled not by oneself but by God when we understand that God is revealed in this kind of interchange.

With this understanding of the revelation of God in Christ, derived from the study of the outstanding theologians of our time, from the Bible, and from all that we know about humans in history and in social relations, we shall go on to examine how this revelation is related to science.

CHAPTER III
THE SAVING EVENT

Our study of what these outstanding theologians say about the revelation of God in Christ indicates that this revelation reaches us in the form of a kind of interchange. This being so, the task for science in relation to the Christian religion is to search out and provide the conditions most favorable for this interchange to occur. Scientific language and scientific forms of thought do not themselves enter into this interchange which awakens the individual to wholeness of being in communion with others; evocative words are used to express that depth and fullness of the total self which comes into action with this interchange. Intellectual abstractions are only incidental, whether the communion occurs in the presence of other people or in solitude. As previously explained, periods of solitary meditation and worship are a necessary part of this interchange.

With this understanding of the central feature of the Christian faith, we can now proceed to examine the ways in which science can be applied to the service of Christ.

One objection often made to the participation of science in matters spiritual is that science is based on sense experience. Yet science is no more based on sense experience than reading the Bible which requires sense experience of written words and ceremony, or the communion of friends where the expressiveness of each must be observed. It is probable that more sense experience is involved in spiritual concerns of this sort than in the communication and acquisition of scientific knowledge. Science in many of its forms uses mathematical symbols which require the minimum of sense experience for the maximum of meaning. Einstein expressed his cosmic picture of relativity with three letters combined with the symbol for equality and the sign for multiplying a number by itself. Scientific knowledge is not about sense experience any more than public worship is about sense experience, although sense experience is involved in both. The only instance when science is *about* sense experience is in that very limited and specialized field of psychology where sense experience is studied. Compared to the whole of science, this is microscopic.

Scientific inquiry can be applied to the service of God in Christ in two ways, provided that this revelation is identified with a kind of interchange as here proposed. First, it can seek to specify, as accurately as possible, the essential characteristics distinguishing this kind of interchange from everything else. Seeking to specify as accurately as possible is what we understand science to be. The sciences are distinguished from one another by *what* they seek to specify.

But science is not only the endeavor to specify as accurately as possible. It is also the endeavor to discover under what conditions predictable events will occur. Hence it is the task of science to ascertain under what conditions the saving event of Christ will occur. If any conditions at all are required for the occurrence of this event, then these conditions can be sought and specified. It is universally acknowledged in the Christian religion that certain conditions are required. One of these conditions is that the individual come into vital association with the fellowship in which this transforming event takes place. Another condition is that the individual recognize the need to be transformed. This is called confession and repentence of sin. A further condition is that the individual accept as the ruling concern the life-giving interchange in Christ which delivers from fragmentary and self-destructive forms of existence. While these conditions are universally acknowledged in the Christian religion, we need to know them with more accuracy than is common. Without this more accurate specification, intelligent action cannot be applied to meeting them.

This knowledge which science might provide will not of itself open the way for the power of Christ to change human lives. Knowledge without passionate commitment of the total self is futile when the knowledge is about transformation of the total self. If the self is not committed in its wholeness, so far as that is possible, all the knowledge in the world about what is required for change in that wholeness will not bring on the change. If the self is not given to what transforms the self, the self will not be transformed. This shows the correctness of what Bultmann says about decision. It also shows the radical difference between the event in which the individual self is transformed and the other kinds of events with which science deals.

The events with which science ordinarily deals do not involve the total existing self. They are not "existential;" instead the events with which science ordinarily deals are objective and impersonal. We seek knowledge of them and seek to control them in order to use them to serve our own endeavors. All this is changed when it comes to the saving event in Christ. Here the event is not anything we can use to promote goals. Here the event is the transformation of our ownselves along with our goals. When this difference is ignored between the instrumental control of events by science and the existential event of our own transformation, the enterprise of science in Service of Christ is corrupted and the entire undertaking is misdirected.

The saving event of the interchange which is Christ in our midst requires commitment of the self in its wholeness. But this wholeness is precisely what the self lacks until it has been given wholeness in the interchange of communion. Hence we cannot commit ourselves in wholeness to this communion when we have no wholeness to commit. The very communion itself must create it in us.

The same difficulty applies to the goals of endeavor when we seek to provide the conditions under which the event of Christ will occur. In dealing with other events by scientific control of the conditions under which the events will occur, the events are controlled to achieve pre-determined goals. But in the event of Christ the goals themselves must be transformed. This reverses the order of scientific control: instead of the event's serving the goals, the event radically transforms the goal. This transformation of the goal by the event is not unknown in science, as can be seen by the event of a new discovery in science, sometimes transforming the way of human life. Nevertheless the use of science to set up conditions under which predictable events will occur is the use of science to achieve pre-determined goals. If this were attempted in providing conditions for the transforming power of Christ, it would be self-defeating. The saving event could not occur under such conditions.

This might seem to be an insuperable obstacle in the way of bringing science to the service of Christ; but the difficulty disappears when we penetrate further. The Christian religion has long taught that the transforming event of Christ can occur only after Christ takes the initiative. Christ must first begin to transform the individual, restoring a measure of wholeness and giving new goals, before the individual can even begin to try to commit himself or herself. Otherwise stated, the kind of interchange prevailing in the fellowship of Christ must first initiate the transformation in the individual before the individual can begin the practice of commitment. The same point is made by asserting that commitment of the individual to Christ is a gift of God's grace. Some measure of wholeness must be given and some transformation of goals must occur before the individual can have any wholeness to commit and can seek the goals of life which are followed in the fellowship of Christ.

But all this does not prevent those who are committed to Christ from seeking the conditions most favorable for this to occur. Those already committed to Christ can seek a better understanding of the conditions and procedures by which people can best be brought into that relation with the fellowship of communion which initiates the transformation that leads to their own endeavors to commit themselves more fully.

When research is not applied to this problem, one or other of two alternatives is likely to happen. One alternative is that the sect will continue to practice its rituals and procedures because they are hallowed by tradition. Tradition has sanctified them, given them the character of the holy, so that we who practice them are distinguished from all others as God's people. But the question still stands: Do these forms provide the conditions most favorable for the transforming event to occur in human lives? If the affirmative answer to that question is not to be an expression of ignorant prejudice and pride, it must be based on observation of consequences. If this observation is made by seeking accuracy of specification distinguishing the transforming event, and by striving for the most reliable knowledge of required conditions, we have a case of science in service of Christ. If one prefers to use the term "empirical" inquiry rather than science, so be it. The point is that inquiry be directed (1) to identifying the distinguishing characteristics of that transformation whereby the individual attains greater wholeness of being and freer, fuller, deeper communion with other persons; and (2) to discovering the conditions most favorable for the occurrence of this change in the individual and in his or her way of life. How scientific knowledge applies to the problem of attaining wholeness and transformation of the individual will be more fully discussed and illustrated in the latter part of Chapter VIII where the work of Erik Erikson is examined.

If science or (empirical inquiry) is not brought to the service of Christ in the way just mentioned but is still used by the Christian religion, it will be used to find methods of propaganda and "public relations" to increase the numbers attending church, persuading them to "buy" what the church has to offer and to make larger contributions of money to the work of the organization. In this way one may build a large and powerful church and religion may prosper all over the land. But this has nothing to do with the saving event. It may be the "Christian religion" but it is not the presence of Christ. Furthermore, when this happens the church becomes one more of the powerful organizations of our civilization, each promoting a special kind of good and competing with other organizations to win the devotion of people to itself for what it has to offer. This brings us to one of the major problems of our civilization—exposing the destructive propensities in human life when not transformed and saved by the event of Christ. The imperative need of bringing science to the service of Christ will be more clearly seen if we examine this problem with care.

The most striking characteristic of our civilization, distinguishing it from every other period, is the enormous power of different organizations competing with one another to control and dominate human life. This power has been given by scientific research and scientific technology. These organizations, each striving with great power to shape the life of humanity according to its own regulations, comprise many areas. Most prominent among them are government, industry and institutional education.

Over and above these organizations internal to each nation are the international organizations that strive with all the power that research and technology can give them to determine the way that the human race should go. Most notable among these are communism and Western democracy. The relation of Christ and science to the struggle between communism and the West will be discussed in a later chapter. Here we shall consider only the competition going on for dominant control over human existence within our own nation.

In the United States, government, industry and institutional education all compete for control over human life. Of course, more specialized agencies doing the same thing might be mentioned, such as organized labor; but to keep the problem within manageable proportions, we shall examine only government, industry and institutional education in this context. While we shall be looking at our own nation chiefly, the same problem in much the same form pervades all Western democratic nations.

Government, industry and institutional education each provide a special kind of good that is indispensable under modern conditions. But it is a special good, or more accurately a partial or relative good, which is not sufficient for an individual's wholeness of being. Government is good in contrast to its alternative which is anarchy; but when it dominates the whole of life and subjects every other kind of good to its control and service, it becomes an evil. The same is true of industry and of institutional education. Each has a good which we need but never is this good sufficient in itself. Not even a perfect synthesis of the good of government, of industry and of education is sufficient for the whole person. In addition one needs love and friendship, the spontaneous, intuitive responsiveness of each to other, not regulated to serve the state or industry or education, but good because of the appreciative understanding of one another which it creates and the wholeness of being in each which it helps to create or recover.

To the measure that government dominates and controls everything in human life, the individual is reduced to a fractured fragment. The person becomes a system of reactions under the control of the regulator called the government. The same is true when industry or the "free market" or any other specialized agency dominates. When neither government nor industry nor institutional education exercises supreme control but all compete with one another to regulate the reactions of the individual, the condition of the individual is no better. It may be worse. It has sometimes been said that we have freedom if industry and education each have sufficient independence from government so that each of the three can resist undue dominance of the others. This may have been true once but it is not true under conditions prevailing today—which brings us to the most dangerous and critical problem of our civilization.

Today government, industry and institutional education have the power and the means to pervade the whole of human life to a degree far beyond any other time. This power and this means is given by scientific research and scientific technology. Even a person walking alone in the woods or driving a car through lonely desert and mountain will be listening to political propaganda or industrial advertisement or institutional education or entertainment on the radio. The entertainment one gets has become institutionalized largely in service of the market to sell goods. This listenting in solitude to the powerful agencies seeking to dominate and control and shape human life is only a faint suggestion of the pervasive power exercised by government, industry, and institutional education. A large part of all the resources of scientific research and technology are given over to increasing this pervasiveness and this subtle, irresistable, hidden control that reaches the individual beneath the level of conscious resistance. We are not now referring to the so-called "hidden persuaders" although they are included. We are not referring to any special gimmick or to any cynical or sinister use of a special device. Regardless of good intention and noble purpose, the whole system of power used by government, industry, institutional education and other agencies to shape the thoughts and feelings, sentiments and impulses of the individual can be called a system of hidden persuaders.

The point is not that what these agencies try to do is evil in itself. Of course much evil is done by evil persons with intent to do evil. Every person does evil at times. Sometimes one can help it and sometimes one cannot. But we are not now speaking of the evil in the system which might be corrected in such a way that the system would then be good. We are talking about the evil in the system as a whole, the evil pervading our entire civilization. This is what we must now try to make plain.

There are many specialized goods, relative, partial and contributary to the good of human life as a whole. But the good of human life as a whole cannot be had unless there is wholeness. Wholeness means integrated individuality not broken down into automatic reactions without unifying purpose. This wholeness can be had only when there is that kind of interchange which creates appreciative understanding and concern for the individual and not merely for a person's reactions externally regulated. This kind of interchange and this kind of wholeness in communion, we have said repeatedly, is the revelation of God in Christ.

Now this wholeness of the individual could not be broken down by government, industry and education in times when these agencies lacked the pervasive and all penetrating power they now have to subject the individual to their control. This does not mean that the agencies in other times were good. Rather the evidence seems to the contrary. So far as their power could reach and so far as concerns the function they were supposed to serve, the government, industry and education of other times were probably worse than today. Even if we suppose that our government, industry and educational system are the best ever, our civilization is still moving toward catastrophe if the individual is being reduced to a system of reactions externally regulated. The evil is the breakdown of wholeness and of that communion with others which creates, restores and sustains this wholeness. The evil is that government, industry and education provide partial, special kinds of good that become evils when not contributory to this wholeness and to this communion. When this wholeness and communion are broken down by the pervasive and irresistible power of these partial goods, the individual is reduced to reactions under the control of these goods. One becomes a system of reactions and not a total individual human being. This, of course, is a matter of degree. It can be more or less. But the more effectively these partial goods seduce and falsely satisfy, and the more pervasive and powerful the agencies supplying them, the more complete will the breakdown of individuality become.

A system of reactions cannot love. Love requires a whole individual with that person's personal resources brought into action to appreciate in fullness and depth the whole individuality of another. A system of reactions can love when love means erotic play. It can love when it means the coordination of one system of reactions in one individual with the reaction systems of others in such a way as to provide comforts for the family, or entertain guests, or have a jolly time, or keep the wheels of industry going, or win a political campaign. One system of reactions can help another system to get it out of trouble, even to save life. Better yet are automatic mechanisms that eject the pilot from the falling plane and open a parachute, or a tank that makes the lungs breathe, or a drug that kills the deadly virus, or an automatic alarm informing police of a burglar. Automatic reactions externally regulated, whether those of a machine or of a human organism, can do a great deal of good of the kinds just mentioned. But these goods become evils when they do not contribute to the good of the individual at the level distinctly human. The difficulty some people have today in distinguising between automatic thinking machines and human persons is significant. Many of us are reduced to a system of reactions approximating those of a machine and this reduction is brought on by living for goods which are unrelated to creating wholeness.

If such is the condition of our civilization, we ask: How did we get this way? The answer is not difficult to find. We got this way because all the power created by scientific research and scientific technique has been given to the agencies providing partial goods while none of this power, or very little, was given to providing the conditions under which the supreme good of wholeness in communion can be had. As these powers of the partial goods became ever more pervasive, ever more insistent, ever more dominant over all else, the one great good, without which these partial goods become evils, was crowded out.

It was crowded out partly because it was not clearly distinguished. Traditional doctrines, ceremonies, rituals and myths were almost the only designators for it and these were not sufficiently accurate and precise to make the needed distinctions when subtle techniques of persuasion and transformation were applied to bring the individual under control. This crowding out of the supreme good had another cause as well. This second cause was an accident in the historical development of the Christian religion. When modern science began to develop, a bitter controversy arose between science and the traditional doctrines of the faith. This controversy has today largely died out but the breach still persists. Science is today accepted by the sophisticated leaders of the Christian religion. In its own field science is beyond dispute but—and here the trouble lies—its own field is distinctly separate from the field of faith. All manner of interpretations of the Christian faith have been developed to show how science and Christ can co-exist without interference with one another and even extend help back and forth over the abyss of separation. Science is not so interpreted, nor is the Christian faith so conceived, that science can be integral to one's commitment to Christ. The consequence of this is obvious. All of these agencies can be equipped with the ever growing power acquired through scientific research, but Christ cannot be. Hence these agencies pervade and dominate and control human life to the exclusion of Christ. This will continue and become worse if research is not put to the service of the saving event. This is the predicament of our civilization today.

Let us now look at this problem of our civilization by examining separately the three agencies of industry, education and government. The one thing for which scientific research is *not* being used in industry is to discover and provide conditions within the industrial plant and in other relations which might meet the demands of Christ. The suggestion that this might be done will sound absurd to many for several reasons. For one, it is often thought that Christ belongs to the church and has no essential connection with industry. The second reason it sounds absurd is that Christ has not been interpreted in such a way as to show how the divine transforming event might enter into industry. In general it has been thought that the only connection Christ can have for industry is by way of moral ideals and these are often thought to be irrelevant. The third reason for thinking the suggestion absurd is that Christ has not been interpreted in a way to show how scientific research might find out how to provide conditions more favorable for wholeness and communion of individuals.

Not only will the suggestion sound absurd. It will also sound naive because, so it is said, management will use this kind of interchange so far as it can be brought into industry as a device for controlling the workers and increasing productivity and profits.

The last statement is true, except for one provision which we have stated before and must repeat again and again to avoid this very misunderstanding. It is true that knowledge of how to serve Christ will not result in that service unless there is first commitment to Christ in the sense of giving first priority to the saving event. For this reason we introduced this entire subject by pointing to the first condition that must be met. This first condition is to find ways by which people might be led to make this commitment, with the understanding that Christ must take the initiative in producing the first steps.

Now let us turn to the alleged absurdity of this suggestion that scientific research might be applied to finding how to provide conditions in the industrial plant that would be more favorable for the kind of interchange that creates more wholeness and communion than now prevails. Two facts relevant to this question should be noted.

First, industry management is coming to recognize that the most important problem in industry is the human factor of relations between management and the workers, between different levels of management, between management and organized labor, between workers in their relations to one another when at work, and between management and the officials of government. The problem in all these cases is to find how to have that kind of interchange in which each individual will bring the resources of his or her whole individuality into action (1) to get the viewpoint of the other not only with regard to the work but also in regard to the unique individuality of the other, and (2) to be able to integrate these diverse views and achieve the depth of appreciative understanding of one another so that all can work together in unison with continuous reconstruction of the system derived from insights developed in this way. Management now recognizes that automatic reactions externally regulated are not sufficient. Extensive discussion of the "organization man" shows how widely this evil is recognized. In fact, this problem of interpersonal relations is actually being discussed from many angles in the journals and books and conferences where problems of management are considered. The problem is widely recognized to be vital and of first importance to industry. It certainly has not been translated into the problem of serving Christ. Neither has it been conceived in that perspective nor with that profound human and religious significance which it must have to be carried into the Christian commitment of faith.

We are not suggesting that this problem of interpersonal relations as conceived by management has as yet any religious significance nor that it can have until it takes on a different character. We are only trying to show that the most vital and perplexing problem for industry today, recognized to be such by outstanding industrialists and counselors, is of such a sort that Christ, properly interpreted, is relevant to this problem. We are trying to show that Christ is not exclusively a concern for the churches but can be and should be a concern for industry, when Christ is so interpreted as to show the relevance of the saving event to the enterprise of economic production.

This problem of interpersonal relations also exposes a second fact that indicates the relevance of Christ to industry. Industry can reach its maximum productivity only to the degree that the parties in the several different relations above mentioned do have the kind of interchange that brings the whole self into action and in the communion of appreciative understanding of one another. No matter how remote is the possibility of this kind of interchange extending through all relations, there is every reason to believe that even now some individuals in industry are sufficiently committed to Christ to have this kind of interchange with one another. Professors and church leaders sometimes seem to think that industrialists are morally inferior to them-

selves. Such prejudice is absurd, of course, because people committed to
Christ can be found in all walks of life; and there is no reason to think that
they are fewer in industry than among university professors and church
leaders.

The important point here to be considered, however, is not that interchange in Christ can bring to the maximum the productivity of industry,
although that is an important consideration when we ask the relevance of
Christ to this institution. More importantly, to the measure industry applies
research to finding the conditions in the industrial plant under which the
interchange in Christ can occur, industry will help to save our civilization
from the chief danger that threatens it, i.e., the reduction of individuals to
systems of reaction more like machines than like fully developed persons.
Christ alone can save our civilization from this fate when Christ means that
kind of interchange which creates wholeness of being and communion between individuals.

Our civilization is dominated by industry, which is what we mean when
we say that it is an industrial civilization. That is the reason that Christ in
industry is a vital problem for our civilization. But industry cannot be so
conducted as to open the way for Christ to exercise some measure of control
in the industrial plant unless the saving event is so interpreted as to show its
relevance to industry and also to show that scientific research can be applied
to the problem of finding the conditions under which interchange in Christ
can occur in the conduct of industrial production.

In all this the transcendence of Christ must be recognized. Christ is
transcendent first in demanding priority over all other goods, goals and
interests in human life. The reality of Christ in the form of interchange
creating wholeness and communion demands the priority of transcendence.
Just as soon as this saving and creative event is subordinated to some ulterior
end, it ceases to have its creative and saving power. My whole self cannot be
given to this kind of interchange, nor can it create wholeness in me, if this
event is not accepted as supreme and all important above all else.

The second sense in which Christ is transcendent is that this event
creatively transforms the individual so that goals are changed. Obviously no
event can serve the goals we bring to it if it transforms our goals. Christ is
transcendent in the sense of carrying us through a sequence of transformations by which our humanity is being created. As Albert Camus and others
have said, we are not yet fully human but our humanity is in process of being
created. Transforming events in Christ occurring in sequence, under favorable conditions, expand the range of what humans can know and control, can
appreciate as good and distinguish as evil. Above all they increase our
capacity to enter into profound communion of appreciative understanding of
others over barriers of hostility and estrangement and diversity. Thereby the
individual attains a more profound understanding of self and of others.

But all this transcendence does not exclude the actual, present occurrence of the event in human existence. Unless it is actually operative in our lives, it cannot be transcendent in the sense of transforming us as we cannot transform ourselves by our own ideals, purposes and aspirations. Secondly, unless it is an actual event occurring in our lives, it cannot be transcendent in the sense of commanding the absolute commitment of all our resources to its service because the most powerful of our resources, namely, science and scientific technology, cannot be fully put to the service of anything unless it be an event occurring when required conditions are present.

We now turn from industry to the problem of government. Government like industry seeks to pervade, dominate and control human life. Sometimes government is the greater power, subordinating industry; sometimes industry subordinates government to the service of industrial production; sometimes the two balance one another to prevent the undue dominance of either.

It is sometimes claimed that this balance of the powers, each restraining the other, is the best possible condition. This is, however, a serious error. This check, balance and restraint of one another is nothing but stultification and weakness of the whole, unless this balance can be made to serve a greater good. But then we must know what is this greater good and how the balance can be made to serve it. If all the great powers resist and obstruct one another, then what power will serve this greater good? Obviously none, unless these powers in balance do themselves serve the greater good. This demonstrates the futility of trying to solve the problem of our civilization merely by keeping the dominant agencies in balance and mutual restraint.

Also one must always ask: What agency will do this work of balancing by shifting its weight from one to the other of the agencies seeking to dominate all others? Will not this agency that does the balancing be the one supreme and all-dominant agency, controlling and regulating what the others do? If so, we must ask again? What will this agency try to accomplish? Will it merely check, balance and restrain, so that no agency can do anything very effectively, or will it seek a good beyond all these other agencies? And what is this greater good? Is it the so called "free market," released to dominate and control all else by this check and balance of other agencies?

Generally an affirmative answer is supposed to be given to the last question. If so, we are being told that our civilization is to be saved by the free market rather than by Christ. This seems to be the hidden pre-supposition in the minds of many. It is the consequence of industrial civilization where the production of economic goods dominates the minds of people so completely that no other good can be recognized as equal, much less greater, in value. This illustrates and demonstrates the point we are making, that industry pervades and subtly shapes our minds until we react automatically to increases of economic goods and higher standards of living as though these had priority over all else.

The balancing of competing interests to check their undue dominance is said to be one of the responsibilities of government. The argument here presented is to show that this cannot save our civilization from its self-destructive propensities unless this balancing is done in the interest and service of a greater good. This points ahead to further responsibilities of government.

If a government is at all democratic, it has the responsibility of arousing the people to an interest in public affairs and to assuming responsibility for the values in their civilization. If the people are apathetic and indifferent to the problems which must be solved to uphold and improve the life of the individual in the prevailing culture, the government will not and cannot uphold these values. Even the highly centralized control of a dictatorship cannot function as a government if it does not have a party, made up of millions of persons who identify themselves with their civilization and its goals and assume personal responsibility for them. No democracy can maintain itself as a democracy, regardless of the voting mechanism, if large numbers of people do not identify themselves with the good to be achieved in the social order and by means of the social order, so that this good becomes their own personal good.

This participation of many people in the affairs of state and this personal responsibility of each individual for the good of the civilization can be accomplished in only one way, by that kind of interchange between individuals by which each acquires the interests and perspectives of the other and each undergoes that creative transformation by which these diverse interests and perspectives are integrated into his or her own individuality. Only in this way can each individual gather into his or her own life the life of all and give this life to them in the communion of a culture that is creative and profound.

Here we see the relevance of Christ to government, just as we saw this relevance to industry. Our government is losing its democratic character and the power to win the world to a common good for all because the research employed by the government is not devoted to this problem. The problem is to discover those conditions under the control of government which might be set up or improved under which this kind of interchange might occur between each and all, so far as this is possible.

Until people are won to commit themselves to Christ when Christ is understood to be this kind of interchange, the saving event of this transformation will not run strong and deep and wide throughout the lives of many people. But when the problem of government and of industry is recognized to be *this* problem, and when research is devoted to it in the way mentioned, many more might be won to this commitment and the event of this creative transformation might run much stronger, deeper and wider than it does now.

The problem and responsibility of government can be viewed from still another angle.

Government must have supreme power of control. It must monopolize the use of violence by prescribing when and how violence shall be used, by what officials and for what ends. Under these conditions it must have the right to kill. Government must have power of this kind to maintain social order. If any agency under its jurisdiction has more power than the government, social order cannot be maintained or, if it is maintained, this other agency with more power than the ostensible government will be the real governing agency. How can the government excercise power so overwhelming, with legal right to coerce and kill, and at the same time provide freedom and justice for the individual?

This question requires an understanding of what is meant by freedom and justice. These are large words with many meanings. Also they are frequently used without any clarity beyond a vague sense of virtue and nobility accompanying their utterance.

Freedom of the individual requires, first, that the individual be free of extreme inner conflict that prevents effective striving for other goals. People in this condition tie themselves in knots, so to speak. Freedom requires that one be liberated from this inner bondage in which one part of oneself opposes, suppresses or diminishes the effectiveness of other parts. This is the condition previously designated as fracturing or fragmenting the individual. The opposite of it is wholeness of the individual, a wholeness which is the inner condition of freedom.

Freedom is sometimes called free will. But the will is nothing other than the whole self in action as opposed to some fragment of the self in action with the rest of the self holding back and resisting by inertia if not by active opposition. Thus free will is the individual acting in wholeness of being.

Freedom requires this inner condition, but it also requires a social relation. The social relation of freedom is that in which diverse individuals and groups have that measure of appreciative understanding of one another and the capacity to integrate into the purpose of each the view-point of the other, such that each can act without undue frustration by the other. The highest degree of freedom in this social relation is in an intimate friendship where the good of the other activates each individual as much as the individual's own good. This does not require that the two be alike. Rather this relation perhaps reaches its deepest level of communion and fullest freedom when the two are very different from one another but complementary, as between the sexes.

If this is freedom, then fullest freedom is found in that kind of interchange which is the revelation of God in Christ because this creates both wholeness of the individual and deepest communion between individuals. When the word "love" is so defined as to mean this kind of interchange, then this interchange in Christ is love. However, it is better to think of love as the product of this interchange rather than identical with it. This interchange begins between people who at first do not love. It transforms them creatively so that they come at last to love in this sense. In other words, human love does not create Christ but Christ creates this kind of love in human lives.

The word "Justice" is also confusing until we settle on some one definite meaning adequate to the problems of human living. Justice of this adequate kind is not separate from love and freedom. It is the course of conduct which must be followed if people are to live in that relation characterized by freedom and love in the senses above stated. Justice is that distribution of goods and services, that adjudication of rewards and punishments, and that shaping of public policy which best serve to provide the conditions under which all persons involved have equal opportunity to engage in the kind of interchange which creates freedom and love.

If freedom, love and justice be as stated, then freedom, love and justice can prevail only to the degree that people are under the control of Christ.

With this understanding of terms, we come back to the problem of government. If our analysis of the problem is correct, government can combine maximum power with freedom and justice to the measure that its power is used to provide, uphold and defend those conditions most favorable for interchange in Christ. The government cannot do this unless it can know with some degree of accuracy and reliability what these conditions may be.

The only way to know what conditions are required for the occurrence of an event is to observe what happens under controlled conditions. In the exact sciences, the conditions must be controlled to a very high degree and the observations must reach maximum accuracy. But outside the exact sciences this control of conditions can have varying degrees of completeness and the observations different degrees of accuracy. When the findings of research are applied to the practices of agriculture, industry, medicine and education, this completeness of control and this accuracy of observation fall far short of the demands of exact science. Nevertheless, this rough application of scientific inquiry has vastly increased the power of agriculture, industry, medicine and education to accomplish what they try to achieve.

If science in this form is applied to discover what conditions subject to control of government are more favorable for the interchange which creates freedom and prescribes the demands of justice, then government guided by this knowledge might promote freedom and justice more effectively than in any other way, provided that the administrators of government are committed to this kind of interchange.

To avoid misunderstanding we must repeat: Scientific knowledge cannot bring Christ into industry or into education or into government unless people practice in public and private the rituals of commitment by which the whole self is brought more completely under the control of Christ. No matter how correctly scientific research might specify the conditions required for Christ to enter into industry, education and government, nothing would come of it without this commitment. Knowledge, skill and techniques cannot do it unless the individuals concerned are themselves committed and constantly recover this commitment and deepen it by worship and dedication. It is the responsibility of the church to provide these practices of commitment, to perfect them, to induce people to practice them in public and in private, not only once a week but every day, and to practice them recurrently in every time of need. Without the church as leader in this commitment, scientific research and scientific knowledge can be of no avail in the service of Christ.

On the other hand, however, these practices of commitment, provided and promoted by the church, cannot be very effective amid the mighty agencies equipped with the power of science, unless science, the instrument of power, is also brought into the service of Christ. Yet the church and the fellowship of faith are indispensable. Nothing said in this discussion of the part which science should play in the Christian religion should obscure the vital importance of the church when it fulfills its proper function.

We have looked at industry and government to see what relevance Christ might have to these agencies now powerfully extending their control over human life. We have sought to know not only the relevance of Christ but also to learn if research might be applied to provide conditions in industry and in government that would make Christ more relevant to saving our civilization from reducing individuals to a system of reactions controlled by industry and government but without freedom and without power of individuality to exercise reciprocal power over these agencies.

We now turn to ask the same question concerning institutional education. Research is being applied with increasing intensity to education to discover the conditions and procedures under which education can be more effective in developing the kind of mentality and the kind of person most needed. With more people being subjected to institutional education, continuing for a longer time under its discipline with increasing rigor of application and more effective methods, institutional education will be increasingly powerful in determining what kind of being a person is to become.

Alvin C. Eurich pleads for more organized research to be given to education and bases his argument on what research has done for other undertakings:

> . . . in agriculture we have a long history of experimentation and the application of new methods to meet new conditions. State experimental stations were attached to land-grant colleges in 1888. At that time it took almost half of our gainfully employed to raise food for the nation. Today it takes about 8 per cent and an enormous surplus continuously confounds us. The record is phenomenal. But where would we be today without the experimental stations and the extension services that carry the results of investigations to our farmers?

> Similarly in industry, development programs have proved so profitable that we regularly plow back a percentage of profits for research and development. One of our major corporations proudly states that it has more than 9,000 people working on new developments.

> In medicine and health we have large corps of investigators who spend all their time planning for the future. They have been so successful that

about 90 per cent of the drugs prescribed today were unknown twenty years ago.[1]

As director of the Fund for the Advancement of Education, Eurich is not writing on the behalf of agriculture or industry or medicine. He is urging the establishment of a Commission on Educational Development, the purpose of which would be the following:

(1) Sponsor new experiments designed to provide higher quality education with due regard for efficiency and economy.
(2) Disseminate information about new developments not only within the state but throughout the country.
(3) Promote the adoption of such new developments as have been tried and found successful; it would also issue an annual report and recommend necessary legislation.

Eurich cites numerous instances of research and experiment applied to education which have greatly increased its effectiveness in certain schools and localities. By use of what has been discovered in research, some high schools have students at time of graduation superior to the graduate students of some colleges and universities. The comments by Eurich on research applied to education and what should be done about our schools are relevant to the problem we are considering. Education is not anything the teacher can do for the student. The whole problem of education is to provide the conditions under which that interchange will occur between student and teacher and between the students with one another which does two things: it arouses not a fragmentary part of the individual but brings the individual with all his or her resources into action to respond with appreciative understanding to teacher and associates and, secondly, integrates into the wholeness of one's own individuality what one thus gets from others.

Of the conditions which must be provided for this kind of interchange to occur, the most important is the commitment of the teacher. To the measure that the educator's whole being is lifted and carried and continuously transformed by this kind of interchange with the students, a person is a good teacher. Of course other conditions are also required, but commitment to creative and transforming interchange is primary. It has been shown that scientific research can be applied to discovering and improving the conditions under which this educational kind of interchange can occur with far greater effectiveness than under other conditions.

If education be the kind of interchange just mentioned, and if the saving

---

[1] "New Strategy for American Schools," by Alvin C. Eurich. *Saturday Review of Literature*, Sept. 3, 1960.

event in Christ also be of this sort, then the problem of applying scientific research to education is not far removed from applying it to Christ.

There is, of course, a difference between interchange in the fellowship of Christ and interchange in general education, although education can be conducted in such a way that the saving event of Christ actually occurs. There is a difference, however, between education where Christ is present in power and where this is not the case. In general education where Christ is not dominant, the primary goal is to achieve mastery of some special field of accomplishment or, if not some special field, then to master the resources of the prevalent culture so far as possible. Where Christ is present, the primary goal is to be transformed by this very interchange itself rather than to make it the means to some other end such as mastery of the prevailing cultures. Where Christ is present, the goal is to become so transformed by this kind of interchange that one shall live under its dominant control, not for the sake of the culture nor to master some special field, but simply in order to live thus in Christ.

When Christ is present in education, we learn history in such a way that we identify ourselves with it and it becomes our own personal history. We learn English literature in such a way that when great literature reveals the human condition with all its shame and grandeur, hope and fear, horror and glory, we identify ourselves with the condition of humanity so that we find all this to be true of ourselves as people who gather all these lives into our own lives and give our lives to them. The same is true when we study social problems or mathematics or physics; these are for us not primarily utilities we can use. They are strivings and achievements and thoughts of other persons which we can share with them and thereby live their lives merged into our own lives and our lives merged with theirs. This is the great communion found in Christ.

If it be true, as here stated, that education is a kind of creative interchange, and if Christ also be a kind of interchange, and if the interchange in education can assume the form of the interchange in Christ, as just indicated, and if research can find and demonstrate the conditions under which this kind of education can rise to dominance, we have the answer to the question we are asking. That question, of course, is: "How can scientific research be applied to education in service of Christ?"

To sum up: Industry, education and government become increasingly powerful by means of science. With this magnified power each seeks to dominate and control the whole of human life. But each seeks to direct human life to ends different from the others. Not one of them can seek the good of the individual in the wholeness of being unless its power is directed to the service of Christ. But this they cannot do except by providing the conditions favorable for the saving event to occur. This in turn requires that they know what these conditions are. Such knowledge must be obtained by scientific observation and experiment. This is the relation of science to the Christian religion.

One may ask, why in our time is science needed to find out the conditions under which Christ brings salvation when science was not required to do this in the time of Jesus and in other times since then? The answer to this question must be clearly understood if the indispensable part of science in the Christian religion is to be recognized and accepted.

In the time of Jesus and in other times prior to the Seventeenth Century, science had not begun to reconstruct the entire order of human existence in thought and action, in sentiment and devotion. When the conditions of human existence are being changed extensively and profoundly, the conditions which once made possible certain ways of life will no longer be present. Hence the way of life dependent on those conditions cannot continue unless the required conditions in the form available in the new situation are searched out and provided. Never has human existence undegone such swift and radical change of conditions as during the last three centuries under the impact of modern science and technology. This applies to the relationship of parents to children; it applies as well to health and friendship and all other interests of human life. So long as scientific technology did not disturb and radically change conditions, human life went on for better or worse without knowledge of the conditions required to have wholesome food, pure water, good family relations and all the other necessities of human life. Life developed in adaptation to the conditions provided by nature and modified by traditional methods. But when these conditions are swiftly and profoundly changed by science, we must know to a measure not previously demanded, what conditions must be present for health, for family life and all the other needs of human existence.

This applies also to Christ and the commitment of faith. So long as conditions were not greatly disturbed, and so long as we did not have the power to change them radically, it was not possible and it was not necessary to know by means of science what conditions must be present for the saving power of Christ. Now all this has changed. Our power is enormously increased so that we can and do change almost all the conditions of human existence. The conclusion from this should be obvious. When this happens, the exercise of this power must be guided by knowledge of the conditions required for the saving power of Christ. If this knowledge is not sought and used to guide the exercise of power so great, these required conditions will disappear and along with them will disappear the way of life dependent upon them.

How disastrous for human life can be the swift change brought on by modern technology, when there is no knowledge and no concern to protect or recover the conditions of well-being, is demonstrated in Africa today. The tribal life is broken down, family relations are torn apart, and most of the other conditions previously sustaining interchange of person to person have suddenly disappeared. Mental and social wreckage ensue. Whether it be the tribal life or the life of the fellowship in Christ, certain conditions must be present. When these are broken down and taken away, the blame should not be put upon science and scientific technology per se. The blame should be put upon the failure to apply science and its technology to the problem of searching out these required conditions and then protecting them or modifying them in such ways that sustaining interchange can continue between husband and wife, between parents and children, between groups, classes and races. Above all is needed that kind of interchange which creates wholeness and communion.

This is the reason for saying that the Christian religion must not only accept science as good and right in its proper place but must absorb science into the very heart of the Christian faith so that commitment to Christ means commitment of science to the service of Christ. Science must be seen to have as much Christian significance as anything else necessary to human existence.

With this understanding of our problem, some further defense will be made of our practice of referring to "interchange in Christ" and not to the man Jesus. Quite naturally we picture Christ as the man Jesus because the transforming power of this kind of interchange occurred in his fellowship. But a further fact pertaining to this matter must now be emphasized.

Historical developments have lifted to a mountain peak the fellowship which the man Jesus had with his disciples. On this distant peak we cannot see the interchange as it occurred in the subtle forms of expression between the individuals concerned. To experience this interchange as it occurred between Jesus and his disciples, it would be necessary to hear the tone of voice, to see the expression of the face and the look in the eyes, to have the experiences preceding the words spoken then and there, and to have the experience of the total situation, because all this gave the depth and uniqueness of meaning to those words spoken in that living context. But this living context in the unique concreteness of that time and place can never again be recovered in the fullness and power of that fleeting situation. More important still, interchange of this kind involves a mysterious intuitive apprehension of the meaning expressed by the total individuality of the other. This is far more than a matter of words. Sometimes a silence conveys it more profoundly than words can ever do.

All this demonstrates that we cannot experience the interchange that occurred between those unique individuals amid the social and historical conditions of that time and place because these can never again be brought into existence. They are gone with the wind, never to return.

Since we cannot experience the interchange as it occurred then and there between Jesus and his disciples, and between the disciples three days after the Crucifixion, we symbolize this interchange by retaining an image of the man Jesus. This is inevitable and quite correct provided that we do not misdirect our commitment to the image. The image of the man Jesus that we happen to have in mind has no transforming and revelatory power except as it symbolizes the kind of interchange which does have this transforming and revelatory power today, as it had with Jesus.

This saving event occurs in our lives today not by return of the man Jesus either in the flesh or as a ghost. It occurs in our lives when the same kind of interchange occurs that occurred in the lives of the disciples engaged in communion with Jesus. On this account we say that the present living Christ is the transforming power of this kind of interchange.

There is another reason for emphasizing this interchange. Interchange overarches and overcomes the opposition between subject and object, between self and other person, between the individual and society, between one generation and the next, between one race, people or culture and others. Most important of all, it overcomes and transcends the estrangement between the far past and the living present. By interchange from person to person and generation to generation, this transforming power of Christ can be here in our midst even now, when required conditions are present, as it was when the man Jesus walked with the disciples. It can be with us as it was when the resurrection occurred. By this kind of interchange the past comes to life again and creates for us a present that we could not have if that past had not occurred; and out of this newly created present a new future is born which could not be ours if the past had not been what it was with Jesus and his disciples.

We cannot recapture that past in any other way because communion cannot be recovered by any description of past events nor by any doctrines about them. In communion we understand one another not primarily by descriptive statements but by wordless intuitive responses. The persons we know best are not known by any kind of statement about them. We know them because we are able to respond to them in the way that meets their need. In many cases words can be utterly incompetent, presumptuous and foolish in such communion. One who knows another only in the form of verifiable statement describing the other does not know the other at all after the manner of Christ, where a silence, a tone, a touch, a posture, a deed, opens the gates of understanding beyond the reach of words. This is the depth and the mystery, the power and the glory, the tears and the music, and the long, sad sweet memory through the years, of that communion which is the word of Christ in human life.

If all this be true, then it is plain that the revelation of God in Christ with its saving power can never be had by way of historical knowledge about the man Jesus, nor by any Biblical statements about him, nor by any theology or philosophy or ontology about God or Christ or Being. Only in the form of this kind of communion does the event of interchange bring us the revelation of God with its saving power. On this account we speak not of the man Jesus but of the living Christ in the form of an event, occurring when required conditions are present.

We speak of blessedness to be found in the life of Christ. But despair also has its place. Despair, as here understood, is consciousness that one cannot attain what makes life worthwhile. One becomes aware that no resource available in or outside oneself, so far as one can see, will enable one to have what alone can justify the suffering and the struggle of existence. When one cannot attain what makes life worthwhile, life is not worthwhile. This is despair.

When despair comes upon a person who has not learned to practice commitment to Christ, it may drive that person to drugs or suicide. More commonly it causes one to engage in activities to distract the mind and conceal from consciousness the recognition of the predicament. Perhaps many people spend their lives doing things to cover over and conceal despair that would otherwise overcome them. How many people live this way, we do not know. Psychological studies seem to indicate that it may be true of a considerable number.

For us who seek above all else to bring our total selves into the way of Christ, despair is an opportunity. It breaks the barrier of self-sufficiency. It drives us to bring ourselves more completely into the keeping of Christ because there is other way to live if we are to be honest with ourselves and not resort to the evasive device of concealing from ourselves the realities of our condition. So we turn to more intensive meditation and more earnest practice of those rituals and symbols which long practice has taught us to use to bring ourselves more completely under the control of the interchange that creates deeper concern for the wholeness of being in ourselves and in other persons. This enables us to find support beyond the limits of self-sufficiency. Beyond these limits we find a life more buoyant because it is sustained by deeper levels of being than what had sustained us when despair overwhelmed us.

Perhaps the point can be illustrated by something much simpler than the life of faith. One who does not know how to swim will struggle to keep one's body at a higher level in the water than the specific gravity will support. One may succeed in doing that with much exertion; but in time one becomes exhausted, gives up in despair, and drowns. But one who knows how to swim will sink to that level in the water where the weight of one's body is upheld by the water. Sustained in this way one can swim for a long time without exhaustion. But to reach this level of support the beginner must pass through the period of despair. One must despair of one's own ability to hold oneself up. Only then will one trust the support of the water.

There is a way of life surmounting every ill and leading on by creative transformation to a scope and fullness of appreciative consciousness we cannot now imagine. But this destiny cannot be found this side of despair.

Neither can it be found the other side of despair unless the individual learns to merge life with the creativity of Christ as the soaring bird with outstretched wings is lifted by the rising air. But this merging of one's life with the creativity of Christ cannot be learned once and for all time. Self-sufficiency creeps up and takes possession of us again and again. So we must break free of it again and again by returning to that practice of worship which loosens the constraints of self-sufficiency. Often we cannot do this until despair comes again. Thus despair has its liberating function in the life that seeks to merge itself in the creativity of Christ.

CHAPTER IV
CHRIST AND CHRISTIANITY

Christianity is the form in which Western culture has received the living Christ. The doctrines, the rituals, the institutions, the symbols, the ideals, the practices of Christianity have all been shaped by Western culture. They have not been shaped by Christ alone, but by all the influences entering into this culture. Such being the case, it should be plain that Christ can work in human life with very different doctrines, rituals, institutions, symbols and ideals because ours are by no means the pure and perfect and final expression of the living Christ.

Our tendency to identify Christ exclusively with this Christianity of ours is one source of hate, suspicion and other forms of ill will directed against us in many parts of the world. Our arrogance exposed by this claim arouses resentment. Again and again a prominent Christian leader will espouse a set of doctrines, ideals and practices and declare without qualification: This is Christianity. Other Christian spokespersons equally well equipped will set forth another body of doctrine opposed in certain vital features with the first. These persons should say, This is my attempt to understand Christ. Instead they assert: This is Christianity. This propensity to conceal the fallibility of one's own personal views about Christ behind the facade of the great name of Christianity has given a false turn to the doctrines which seek to interpret Christ. The false turn is that, in many cases, the discussion centers on the question "Who represents the truth of Christianity?" It should be directed to the question, "What is the living Christ?"

In Chapter II we saw how diverse and conflicting are the forms of Christianity now dominant. Only by ignoring the question, "What is Christianity?" and seeking only to know what is Christ, could we find any identity beneath the argumentation and opposition separating these several Christianities.

Much interest has arisen in recent years in the study of the different religions of the world. This has its value, but the study often ignores the question, "How can we identify in the life of any individual or fellowship the saving event of transformation?" The word "Christ" has been used in such a way that people tend to identify that name with a doctrine or with a man who once taught a doctrine. But Christ can be a transforming power for us only in the form of a transforming event. With this in mind, we recognize that Christ incognito may be present in the lives of individuals and fellowships professing other religions than Christianity. The same point is made, and correctly made, when it is said that the presence of Christ may be missing in the lives of individuals and fellowships professing the Christian religion. The important thing is not to profess the Christian religion but to commit oneself to the saving power of Christ.

When people ask, "Does my religion have the truth whereas others do not?" or "Do all the religions have the truth divided among them in various mixture?", they are posing a question that leads nowhere. The urgent question is "What is the saving event of creative transformation?" As our civilization, and perhaps all the civilizations of the world, move steadily toward the potential of self-destruction, we must focus on the control issue and not on peripheral matters.

The history of Christianity has shown a great diversity of forms ever since the first century. The lives of different individuals, sects and groups professing the Christian faith have been and are most diverse. This heterogeneous mass issuing from Hellenism comes to us through the channel of the institutional church which carried it through the Dark Ages and down into the Middle Ages. It all bears the name of Christianity because the church which conveyed it to us gave it that title. The torture and burning to death of thousands of witches was once a devout form of Christian practice. Many a person with dark skin has been mistreated and even killed because Christianity demands the supremacy of the white race.

Must Christ always and everywhere bear the marks of our culture before we can recognize the way of deliverance from the human propensity for perversion and self-destruction? May not Christ rise in power in forms very different from our culture? As said before, the doctrines, rituals and ideals of our culture are not the pure expression of Christ. They are at best the forms in which our culture apprehends the saving event of Christ. In other ages and in other cultures other forms may better serve to lead people to commit themselves to the transforming event.

If it be admitted, as I think it must be, that the prevalent forms of Christianity have no monopoly on the saving power of Christ, a serious question arises: How can we know that it is Christ if the event does not bear the features by which Christ has always been recognized in the forms of the Christian tradition?

This is a very serious question and if not answered correctly can have fatal consequences, not only for Christianity but for the entire human race. Also, it strikes at the very root of the problem we here have under consideration, namely the problem of science in its relation to Christianity.

The doctrines of Christianity have been formulated to guard against the error of accepting something as being Christ when it is not. But these errors have been the ones arising in our tradition, and the doctrines have been shaped in terms of our forms of thought. These errors are not the ones likely to arise in other traditions very different from our own. Such being the case, the doctrine of historic Christianity which developed to distinguish Christ from what opposed Christ would not serve this purpose when the questions to be answered about the way of salvation are not the questions we would ever think of asking. Under such conditions the doctrines which may have guided us to Christ might guide others away from Christ.

This problem of distinguishing what is truly Christ from what is not has been, and is now, one of the most serious. All the great controversies and heresies have been on this issue. The various sects and major divisions of Christianity today are divided on it. These schisms and controversies indicate that the problem has not been solved satisfactorily, at least for our time. Worse still, these major divisions show that some have lost the way to Christ. The ecumenical movement may have virtues of its own, but if for the sake of harmony it overrides and ignores the vital problem of distinguishing what saves one from one's stunted, perverted and self-destructive forms of existence, it is creating a fatal illusion. There is a way of deliverance from the monstrous evils that threaten and corrupt. Nothing is more important than to find and follow that way and distinguish it from ways that lead to perversion and destruction. The tendency to put this question aside so that all branches of Christianity can unite in mutual support against developments rejecting Christianity would be exactly the right thing to do if Christianity were itself what saves. But Christianity cannot save us; only Christ can save us. Christianity includes all those individuals, sects and divisions professing to follow Christ while designating very different things when they use this word. Christ is not every sort of thing and every way of life followed by anyone who happens to proclaim acceptance of Christ. In this age of confusion, we must know the way of life by some other mark than the conventional forms of confession.

This question cannot be ignored in the modern world where powerful agencies are shaping our lives, distorting, misleading, destroying, creating illusions and fascinations and stampeding masses of people without regard for where they are going.

If Christ and none other is the way of salvation, we must be able to set forth evidence concerning the way of Christ which is convincing. To be sure, as said before, mere intellectual demonstration concerning the way of salvation will not induce a person to follow it. Other means must be used for that. But if these other means are used to lead people away from Christ, thinking that this other way is the way of Christ, the fatal error has been made. Intellectually demonstrable distinctions are necessary in this age of confusion, no matter how much these distinctions must be supplemented by the religious symbols used in the commitment of faith.

It has been said that love is the mark of the work of Christ in human life. But, as noted before, this word is far too vague and multiform in its meaning to be a guide. Bruno Bettelheim has devoted his life to children who have been given up as "hopeless cases." He has worked to restore them to an acceptable way of life. Also he heads an institution with a staff of workers all engaged in this undertaking with considerable success. He has written books to demonstrate that "love is not enough" to nurture children in a way to save them from serious delinquency and even derangement. One can always counter by arguing for various definitions of "love." But that is exactly the point at issue. At least Bettelheim has shown that what most people think is love in its most worthy form is "not enough" for the proper nurture of a child.

The word "love" may be quite adequate for the use of lovers in communion, because this kind of interchange does not want, and could not use, accurate designation. In this relation symbols which evoke and express the depth, fullness and wholeness of personality are needed. Such symbols, non-cognitive but profoundly expressive, exceed any designation of which we are capable.

The point we are trying to make is not that accurate designation is better than symbols which evolve and express without designation. On the contrary, nothing is so vital and nothing attains so great a good as the interchange where individuals express themselves most fully and are most profoundly appreciated in the wholeness of their being with non-cognitive but profoundly expressive symbols. But symbols with accurate designation are needed for another purpose, to specify some distinguishing characteristics that enable us to know when this profound communion occurs. If we are unable to distinguish this kind of event from others, we may provide the conditions for the occurrence of an event which we think is this when it is not.

Introspection cannot solve this problem. Many have thought that they were in Christ when they were not. Many have believed that they loved profoundly when they were subconsciously infected with malicious hate. All available evidence seems to indicate that individuals can be quite mistaken when they judge introspectively that they have experienced the saving event. Self-deception in this matter is not at all uncommon. This we know from the studies of psychiatry and clinical psychology. Some of the most horrible evils have been perpetrated under the illusion that one was with Christ.

Here, then, is our problem. It is one that science must help us solve, in that a solution demands an inquiry that calls for accurate observation and precise specification.

Four different methods have been used by Christian leaders to distinguish true statements about Christ from false ones. These four can be given the names of reason, religious experience, tradition and Biblical faith. When reason has been used to distinguish the way of Christ, it has generally been reason apart from the data of observation. It has been reason used to develop a coherent system of propositions based upon premises chosen because tradition happens to contain these premises. The coherent system thus developed has not been tested by applying it to all relevant data accessible to observation. This use of reason is properly called rationalizing, which is no more than a device for defending a belief accepted on the grounds of tradition and not by the tests of observation.

When this use of reason was found to be misleading, some Christian leaders turned to what they called "religious experience." There was neither clarity nor agreement concerning the characteristics distinguishing authentic religious experience from other experiences falsely so called. Indeed there could be no clarity or agreement on this because "experience" is the most vague word that could be used. One kind of experience is distinguished from other kinds by specifying the object of the experience, or some structure defining it. Scientific experience is distinguished by the method of inquiry used and the kind of objects experienced. So also aesthetic experience, the experience of love, of hate and all the other kinds are distinguished by indicating the object or specifying the structure. Hallucinations, delusions, errors, and insanities are all experiences. Many a person has given the name of "religious experience" to one or more of these. Drugs, orgies and illusions can produce ecstasy and this ecstacy has sometimes been called religious experience.

One cannot know what one is experiencing unless one can specify some structure in the experience and show that it is the structure of some continuing form which others also can experience under the required conditions and which the individual can identify when these conditions are present. While appeal to religious experience was once the way in which many Christian leaders tried to distinguish Christ from mistaken claims about Christ, most sophisticated leaders today have discarded this approach because of its unreliability.

A third attempt to distinguish true statements about Christ has been appeal to a tradition. It is claimed that if a body of tradition can be traced continuously back to Jesus and his fellowship, and if this stream of tradition has been authenticated in each generation by those specially chosen for this purpose, we have the standard required. The Roman Catholic Church pre-eminently has made use of this method. While other divisions of Christianity may not base themselves upon tradition with the consistency and careful discrimination employed by Catholicism, all divisions of Christianity obviously inherit the Judaeo-Christian tradition and are powerfully shaped by it. But this tradition contains contradictory statements and conflicting practices along with demons, witches, apparitions, the practice of torture and much else. No one can accept all of it. Therefore, some standard other than "being in the tradition" must be used to distinguish what shall be accepted and what rejected. No one can escape the tradition into which one has been born; but one can and does select from the total body of it. As soon as criticism, interpretation and selection are applied, we are back again where we started: By what test can we distinguish that selection, interpretation and criticism of tradition that gives us the saving event of Christ?

If one answers this question by saying that the truth is found in that one line of tradition which can most surely be traced without a break back to the fellowship of Jesus, we still have the question: What particular element or feature thus traceable gives us the truth? Is it the unchanging form of a ceremony or a certain style of garment worn or certain words used or certain ideals proclaimed or certain doctrines professed? Or is it a certain kind of event transforming human life?

No question is more important than this: What analysis, selection and interpretation of the Christian tradition gives us the truth whereby we can *here and now* distinguish in our lives the actual presence of Christ and not be misled into identifying Christ with what is anti-Christ?

A fourth way in which it is claimed that we can distinguish Christ in the life of today is by means of the Bible. Present day theology, recognizing the errors of past theology in appealing to reason, to religious experience and to tradition, is now taking its stand on "Biblical faith." But the Bible is composed of words and sentences which must be interpreted by the minds of people. What meaning the human mind at any time is able to derive from written words depends upon the resources of experience one brings to the interpretation, the organization of one's personality, the ruling interests which govern one's thinking, the demand laid upon one by office and associates.

Today the highest attainments of scholarship are applied to the study and interpretation of the Bible to discover as accurately as possible what the words and sentences in the Bible might have meant to the persons who originally wrote the book and used these words and sentences in the profession of their faith. This study centers on the words and sentences used in the fellowship of Jesus, including the epistles. Of course, the Old Testament is also relevant.

When we come to this study of the Bible, we are immediately confronted by diverse and conflicting interpretations of it, as we saw in our discussion of Carnell, Tillich, Barth and Bultmann in Chapter II. These four are by no means the only disputants over what the Bible informs concerning Christ; but they are good representatives of the controversy. All these persons are scholars of highest attainment, people with powerful intellects, equipped as few have ever been to find the truth by studying the text of the Bible and all other sources of information bearing upon the problem. Each of these persons has an impressive division of Christian leadership siding with him against the others. Each is an earnest, devoted Christian sincerely seeking the truth. Yet the disagreement between them runs deep and wide. They cannot all have the truth.

Now disagreement is not fatal. Rather the criticism and correction of one another engendered by disagreement is one of the chief ways of weeding out error and finding the truth *provided that the disputants follow the same principles of inquiry and share the same presuppositions concerning what to seek*. But when they do not follow the same principles of inquiry and are not even trying to find out the same thing, the disagreement cannot arouse the kind of criticism, correction and interchange leading to fuller truth.

In case of the four scholars examined, there is no agreement on the principles of inquiry nor on what to seek when they seek Christ. For Carnell the principles of inquiry demand that one use the ordinary powers of reason to discover in the Bible those propositions which correctly describe past events. The goal of inquiry is to get correct information about the divine presence in the man Jesus.

For Tillich the revelation of God in Christ can never be found by way of propositions correctly describing past events. The goal of inquiry is not to find the divine presence in the man Jesus but rather to look entirely beyond the man Jesus to the power of Being. Furthermore, this revelation is to be had not by propositions correctly describing anything, but by religious symbols which represent what can never be described in any way.

For Barth the principles of inquiry concerning God in Christ demand the repudiation of all the natural powers of the intellect. Only when natural powers of reason are "illuminated" by the grace of God can we find God in Christ. The goal is to have "the freedom to believe" that the man Jesus with his flesh and blood, his ways and words, is identical with God.

For Bultmann the principles of inquiry demand that we get behind the myths abounding in the Bible and find beyond them not any set of true propositions nor even religious symbols which, for Tillich, convey the revelation. Rather, what we must seek to find is an "eschatological event" which repeats itself down through subsequent history when the gospel is preached under required conditions.

Plainly this kind of disagreement cannot be fruitful. It does not open the way for mutual criticism, correction and suggestion because the individuals do not share the same principles of inquiry; and what one seeks to discover is not at all what the other is seeking.

Besides this radical and unfruitful disagreement among those who seek to understand the revelation of God in Christ by studying the text of Scripture, there is another difficulty even more serious. The difficulty pertains to the kind of meaning conveyed by the words and sentences used in the fellowship of the disciples with one another after the crucifixion; the words used by Jesus with his disciples; and the words used by the great prophets. These words conveyed a meaning which can never be discovered by ascertaining the conventional meaning these words had in the common usage of the culture prevailing at that time. Scholarship can discover this conventional meaning, approximately. But this is not the meaning which the words had when used by Jesus and the prophets and the disciples in the fellowships which formed about these individuals. This brings us to a distinction of utmost importance in seeking to know Christ, one which was stated before but which must now be repeated relative to the problem of interpreting the Bible.

Meanings determined by common usage miss the point entirely when words are used in a fellowship to express and to evoke concern for the individuality of each in the wholeness of being. This kind of meaning is determined by the uniqueness of the individuals then and there engaged, by the uniqueness of their relation to one another, by the uniqueness of the total situation, by the tone of voice, the expression of the face, the posture of the body, the entire expressiveness of the actual existing person. The meaning is finally determined by the intuitions aroused in each with these intuitions creating communion in depth and wholeness.

Obviously this kind of meaning attached to words is not at all the same as the common conventional meaning where there is no attempt to understand individuals with appreciation of the mystery and depth of being in unique individuality.

The meaning which words have in the kind of interchange just indicated is not primarily designative nor descriptive. As said before, it is expressive and evocative. Furthermore, when words are used in this way, we do not have doctrines or descriptive statements; we have an event in which individuals are transformed into wholeness of being and in profound communion. We have an "eschatological event" when that expression means a culminating goal of human existence, casting off the conventional forms and causal sequence which reduce human beings to functions of the system grinding on like a machine.

This brings us to a critical decision to be made: When we seek God in Christ, are we looking for propositions that are true? (Carnell) Are we looking for symbols that point to the power of being? (Tillich) Are we looking for statements which are true propositions but known to be such only by the grace of God? (Barth) Are we looking for a transforming event which can only occur when the gospel is preached? (Bultmann) Or are we looking for a transforming event which occurs whenever the required conditions are present but without binding ourselves to the claim that preaching the gospel is the only required condition, unless "preaching the gospel" means the kind of interchange and communion above indicated?

If we answer the last question in the affirmative, we can establish the principles of inquiry to be followed when we seek Christ. We can also agree on the presuppositions concerning what we seek when we seek Christ. The principles of inquiry are those by which we seek to discover the conditions under which this kind of event occurs. In general this is what science always tries to do, the different sciences seeking to know the conditions under which different kinds of events occur.

The transformation wrought in the lives of the disciples by participation in the fellowship of Jesus indicates that in their association the kind of interchange occurred which creates concern for the wholeness of being in one another. We know this because we know that this kind of transformation occurs when individuals are able to enter into this kind of fellowship and participate in this kind of interchange. This we know from ancient wisdom; we also know it from the studies of clinical psychology, from psychotherapy and the intensive studies of interpersonal relations conducted in clinics, institutes and elsewhere.

In actuality, this kind of interchange is the living Christ whenever and wherever it occurs. It is the revelation of God because its occurrence in the fellowship of Jesus with saving and transforming power has been revealed to subsequent history by way of a continuing fellowship in which recurrent events of this kind appear. This kind of interchange with its saving and transforming power is not the work of the man Jesus, nor of any of the participant individuals, because it transforms them each and all as they cannot transform themselves. Therefore, it is not the man Jesus but God revealed in the fellowship of the man Jesus. For this reason the great theologians have always distinguished between the man, the human nature, and God revealed by way of this man.

This kind of interchange is not the work of a collectivity and cannot occur in collectivism. It is a kind of interchange which magnifies the uniqueness of the individuals concerned, restoring them to wholeness, to freedom and to communion at depths which ordinary social relations do not permit. In the world as it exists with all its pervasive evils, this restoration of wholeness with all its constructive potentialities is never complete and perfect. But in the event of Christ it can be approximated to indefinite degrees.

Increasing numbers of people are finding that the old symbols of the Christian faith are unfit for their use and new ones are developing rapidly. Many of these new symbols—communism, Nazism, nationalism, capitalism arouse passionate devotion and can lead to a martyr's death as did the Christian symbols of old. But these are not the symbols of Christ. They generate strivings that conflict with one another and may lead to irreparable disaster.

So we come again to our question: What descriptive statement confirmed by objective evidence can show amid all these conflicting commitments the one wherein Christ is found? Some of these commitments are practiced in the name of Christ. Especially is that true of certain forms of nationalism. The ordinary way of distinguishing commitment to Christ is to note if Biblical language is used; and especially if the people state that Christ is what they serve above all. Again if the people make use of Church services and conform to the accepted moral customs of what we call our Christian society, the worship is said to be of Christ. But surely these are not sufficient to distinguish the way of salvation.

It is the mission of Protestantism to lead the way to new forms and doctrines when the old forms no longer direct our devotion to Christ. But

Protestantism will lead away from Christ, not to Christ, if it has no other means for identifying Christ except Biblical language, the traditional forms of the institutional church, and the doctrines which have symbolic power but no descriptive truth.

Is Protestantism equipped with the kind of knowledge required to distinguish Christ from what is not Christ? Without this equipment Protestantism cannot fulfill its mission in a time of swift and radical change such as modern life is undergoing. To acquire this distinguishing knowledge, Protestantism should pursue psychological and social studies to dintinguish the kind of transformation in organization of personality, in interpersonal relations and in human development generally which make for wholeness of being.

This suggestion is completely misunderstood when it is thought that this kind of knowledge will of itself bring about these transformations. To repeat over and over again: No knowledge of any kind will by itself bring about this transformation. Only the transforming event of Christ can accomplish this change. But we have responsibility in the matter and to shirk it will be fatal. Our responsibility is to do what we can to provide the conditions most favorable for the occurrence of this transforming event. To do this we need the kind of knowledge just mentioned.

Protestantism, so long as it is true to its Protestant character, cannot confine itself to any one changeless set of doctrines or other religious symbols and practices. It cannot assume that any single set is always the best for every age and culture, for every individual and situation. If the transforming power of Christ could be identified with the magical power of some doctrine or ceremony, then we should hold to that always and everywhere. But if Christ is an event not dependent upon any single doctrine or ceremony, then the revelation of God in saving power cannot be identified with any of these. The problem then becomes to provide the conditions for the occurrence of this event and not merely transmit a doctrine or a ceremony. This opens the way for practical resourcefulness and empirical knowledge in service of Christ. In this way Protestantism might come to the rescue of those people who are caught in a storm of change where new symbols are rising to mislead the commitment of faith.

A further mission of Protestantism, in a time when other cultures and peoples outside the tradition of Western culture are swiftly rising to dominance, is to carry to them a commitment to Christ without those wrappings of Western culture which alienate peoples now striving to cast off subservience to the Western world. Most important of all, it is the mission of Protestantism to undergo the radical change now occurring in all forms of life throughout the world and still be able throughout this change to show the way to Christ. It should be able to do this even if the period resulting from this change should be called "post-Christian." Indeed, many religious leaders are now giving it this name. But with adequate equipment of knowledge and with recognition that Christ and Christianity are not identical, this can be done. Christ can reach us in a "post-Christian world" even if in such a world Christ should come incognito.

All the peoples of the world seek scientific knowledge as soon as they have enough education to understand its character and value. This kind of knowledge can pass through the barriers set up by diverse cultures because it is abstract. But scientific knowledge does not extend down into that wholeness and uniqueness of the individual. The abstract nature of this knowledge renders it unfit for religious commitment and for communion because it does not and cannot arouse and direct the deeper levels of existence. It cannot bring the whole self with all its resources into action. Scientists may bring their whole selves with all their resources into action when engaged in research, but this wholeness of commitment is not induced in them by psychological knowledge nor knowledge about their commitment. It is induced by the fraternity of scientists combined with whatever other conditions may be involved, depending on the individual scientists. In any case, worship and commitment, to be genuine, must bring the wholeness of our existence into action so far as that is possible. This requires language fitted to the culture, the group, the period of history and the unique individual. It cannot be done by scientifically accurate statements about this kind of commitment and its required conditions. Consequently scientific knowledge can never be a substitute for the doctrines and rituals and other forms of religious symbolism.

Misunderstanding on this point is so deep and pervasive that it has generated a prejudice, difficult to overcome in the minds of many, against any use of language about religious commitment which does not carry the potency of religious symbolism. So long as this persists, we flounder and blunder in seeking Christ when undergoing radical changes in our culture and in the organization of personality. Also we become involved in hate, fear, suspicion and bitter conflict between diverse cultures because each uses a different symbolism for its commitment and does not recognize any kind of religious knowledge which can pass through the barrier set up by these different forms of symbolism. It is true, as said before, that the symbolism of commitment and communion must be different for different cultures and different ages and, to some measure, for different individuals. But this very diversity requires a kind of knowledge by which the same identical Christ can be distinguished as operative throughout this diversity.

The concrete immediately experienced realities reaching down to the roots of human life cannot be reduced to descriptions of any kind. This is true of love and friendship, of profound aesthetic experience, of hate and fear and horror, of ecstacy and sacrificial devotion and of much else in our lives for which we have no words at all. So also the actual, operative presence of Christ creating and transforming us down to the roots of our being cannot be reduced to structures described by any form of science whatsover. Nevertheless, while Christ cannot be *reduced* to a set of structures scientifically described, certain distinguishing features of the saving event might be known with descriptive accuracy sufficient to guide intelligent action in serving Christ and in recognizing this even beneath the forms of diverse systems of symbolism.

Once scientific inquiry gives reliable knowledge concerning the indispensable healing and saving power of Christ in a form of knowledge that can be universally communicated and accepted as true because of supporting evidence, then each individual and group and culture and age can develop its own symbols suited to its own experience and need, without fear of having lost the reality of Christ amid all this change and diversity. Then each can be blessed and guided by the intuitive awareness which no science can ever provide; and this can occur without danger that this innermost kind of experience will lead into vagaries and illusions. The observable characteristics of behavior identifying Christ will guard against this danger.

The human way of life is distinguished by far-reaching constructions of imagination. Science is one of these constructions. It consists of theories, often mathematically formulated, which are applied to data selected from the massive fullness and depth of existence. The data are selected to conform to the theory and the theory is shaped to give that pattern to the data which can guide inference and action in a way to solve the problem under consideration. But these data, together with the inference and action they guide, are superficial compared to the wholeness and depth of existence. Existence is like the ocean in the mystery of its deeps. Science glides over the surface; it does not truly penetrate the mystery.

Not only science but also art and the aesthetic forms of experience require constructions of the imagination which are then applied to existence. But in art and aesthetic experience, the purpose of the construction and its application to existence differ from that of science. The purpose of scientific construction is to guide inference and action superficially but expansively to the farthest reaches of space, or to the ultimate microscopic levels, or through the intricacies of society or the human mind and personality, or backward into the past or forward into the future. The purpose of scientific construction is to achieve the widest range of accurate generalization about existence. The purpose of artistic construction is to achieve the most complete concrete wholeness in depth of perception. The great works of science are designed to guide the thin thread of inference over the surface of innumerable events. The great works of art are designed to guide perception to the fullest apprehension of the concrete wholeness of some event.

Still another construction of imagination is the system of moral order and idealism. The system of moral order is designed to regulate the conduct of people in relation to one another and in relation to the rest of existence so that human life can develop its constructive potentialities.

Another construction of imagination is philosophical speculation and philosophical analysis. Technology is also a creation of human imagination designed to control events in service of human purpose. So also are government and industry. All the diverse forms of human culture are the works of human imagination by which events are distinguished and ordered in such a way that they can be (1) controlled, (2) evaluated, (3) experienced in their concrete wholeness. The last mentioned, number three, is represented by art and aesthetic experience, by love and friendship, by self-awareness and communion.

One way of distinguishing human life from all other forms of existence is to say that it is existence shaped and directed by the works of far-reaching imagination. Imagination soars beyond the surge of existence to construct imaginary forms and then applies these forms to the surging flow of existence to select and organize what is relevant to these forms. The form thus constructed may be scientific theory, artistic design, moral ideal, technological device, political policy, industrial purpose, family order, friendship, love and communion between persons.

What is the relation of Christ to all this? Christ is the creative transformation of the individual person and of the culture whereby the reach of human imagination is expanded either to bring more events under human control or to perceive, evaluate and more profoundly experience the concrete wholeness of events.

Whenever the reach of imagination is extended, it transcends what we were able to think, do, feel or intend before this further extension was created. Obviously we cannot imagine what lies beyond the reach of our imaginations. The reach must be extended before we can even so much as intend what is imagined after the extension has occurred. Therefore we cannot, by exercise of imagination, extend our reach beyond the limits of our capacity to imagine. This is a tautology but needs to be emphasized in this context to show that we cannot ourselves expand the reach of our imaginations until after we have been creatively transformed in a way to imagine what we could not imagine before. This creative transformation is what we have found throughout this writing to be the revelation of God in Christ.

The limit of human imagination is progressively extended from infancy. It is also progressively extended in the development of human culture. The expansion of scientific theory and technological control are the most obvious examples. More important still, although not so obvious, is the progressive creation of language, when language means not merely the multiplication of words and combination of words but rather the multiplication of meanings and the expanding scope of meanings. This progressive creation of language is the progressive creation of human imagination. It is also the progressive creation of the human level of existence. It is also the creativity of Christ.

People can intend to have the reach of their imaginations extended, but they cannot cause a new idea to come into their minds when no intimation of that idea has ever reached them before. People can put themselves under conditions where a creativity not directed by themselves may create the new theory, ideal, intuitive insight of love or other innovation, previously beyond the scope of their imaginations. But they cannot intend what that further reach of imagination will disclose until it has been revealed by this added comprehension of their minds.

This progressive creation of the compass of imagination is the progressive creation of humans, because this exercise of a wider ranging imagination is what distinguishes humans from everything else. Without this exercise of imagination, the biological organism is only another subhuman animal, excepting that it is unfit to survive without the sheltering and feeding devices of a culture.

What people do with their imaginations after they have been extended is their doing. It is human creativity. But the creation of this extended imagination is not their doing. It is divine creativity. Scientific research conducted within the limits of human imagination is the work of people. It is human creativity. Devising a new technology within the limits of human imagination is human creativity. Producing works of art within the limits of the reach of human imagination is the creative work of people. Shaping the policy of government within the limits of human imagination is human creativity. The same is true with the organization and management of industry. So also with moral ideals or with appreciative understanding of fellow humans. And the same is true with everything else human beings do. What is done within the limited reach of imagination is human creativity. It may be monstrously evil or grandly good. *But extending this reach of human imagination so that people are able to do greater evil and greater good is the divine creativity.* It is the progressive creation of the human level of existence with consequent increase in responsibility for distinguishing the evil from the good, with consequent increase in responsibility for choosing the good and opposing the evil.

What, then, is this good that people should choose? The good is any condition or action which provides for the divine creativity to extend the reach of human imagination and thereby continue the creation of the human level of existence and bring it to a higher level of responsibility and to a higher level of dominance over the unformed surge of existence. The evil is any condition or action which obstructs the divine creativity in extending the reach of imagination, or reduces the reach already created.

Why is this the good and this the evil? It is so not because individuals may happen to want to have this extended reach of imagination. Some want it; many do not. This extended reach of imagination is good in the sense of being the constitutive good of human existence. It is what constitutes human existence. It is what distinguishes the human from every other kind of animal and gives to human life its dominance, its power, its moral responsibility and its religious aspiration. Religious aspiration is distinguished from every other kind of aspiration in seeking to undergo creative transformation beyond what can now be imagined. Therefore, those who oppose this good of the divine creativity, or do not want it, are rejecting the distinctive level of human existence. Those who do this thereby demonstrate a failure to find what makes the very existence of the human level good, no matter how great the suffering and no matter how great the self-destructive propensities in it. People who have never been able to experience this good are thereby rendered incompetent for evaluating the good of human existence.

According to some, the good is what any individual happens to want or choose. Of course value can be defined in this way and there is no objection provided that other ways of distinguishing good and evil are also recognized to be legitimate. Good and evil have many dimensions. Those who find their good in one dimension may regard other dimensions as irrelevant. Nevertheless, there are other dimensions in which other people find their good and their evil. People who cannot recognize this diversity in the dimensions of good and evil are suffering from provincial blindness.

People who have found the good of the divine creativity in Christ and commit themselves to it, have found a good that is indestructible so long as there is any human existence at all because, as said before, it is constitutive of human existence. This does not mean that everything in human existence is good. Far from it. What tends to destroy human existence, or hinders its further creation, is evil. A great deal going on in human life has this destructive character and on that account is evil.

Yet those who have found the good of the divine creativity running through human life, creating anew in every infant the expanding reach of imagination, have found a good extending far beyond their own existence. It extends throughout the whole range of human history, because the divine creativity is always present in human life, even when overlaid and suppressed by counter activities and destructive drives. This total expanse and depth of good becomes the good of those who identify themselves with it by final commitment to it. It is a good that can reach as high as the utmost soaring flight of human imagination ever to be attained in human history. It is a good that can reach as deep into the concrete fullness of existence as aesthetic experience, art and love can ever extend. This is the good of the creativity of Christ. It stands comparison with any other kind of good that any person may ever choose. The great saints have proclaimed it and many a simple person has lived by it without words to tell about it. It is the secret of the blessed life but a secret only because it is so difficult to articulate. To some persons it seems to be utterly unintelligible.

Nowhere except at the human level of existence does this divine creativity rear the constructions of imagination so high in the form of theory and moral ideals, nor penetrate so deeply into the concrete fullness of existence in the form of aesthetic experience and communion between persons. Four distinctive characteristics of the human being provide for this divine creativity whereby a person is made the child of God as nothing else can be.

The first of the four is the use of that kind of sign, otherwise called language and other symbols, carrying meanings which can be expanded indefinitely in their range of comprehension. This range is not tied down to the local situation so closely as is the meaning attached to the signs used by lower animals. Indeed the meaning of signs used by humans are not tied down at all if "tied down" refers to some known limit beyond which the meaning cannot reach. There is no known limit to what people might think about, imagine, emotionally respond to, by the use of language and other symbols. As said before, the extension of meaning which human signs can carry at any one time is limited by the reach of human imagination at that time. But when people give themselves over to the divine creativity of Christ with final commitment of faith, and at the same time apply all the relevant resources of science to search out and provide the conditions under which this creativity rises to dominance over all else, there is no known limit.

The possible height and depth of the reach of what can be made accessible to human experience, of good to cherish and of evil to avoid, cannot be known until creative transformation exposes them.

So this first distinctive feature of the human being can be stated thus: A human is a biological organism functioning with signs capable of carrying meanings that can be expanded indefinitely.

The second distinctive characteristic of the human being, whereby the divine creativity can expand the range of imagination indefinitely, is equally essential. It is a sexuality that can bind male and female and parent and child in close bonds of intimate fellowship and communion continuously through many years. This is essential, both for the child and for the adults, because this sexual bond with its intimacy breaks down the protective devices, the fear, the suspicion and other barriers that sensitive human beings set up against that kind of interchange whereby one individual can acquire from others what the other has experienced of good and evil and make this one's own. As we have seen before, this is the way the divine creativity expands and deepens the range of good and evil, of beauty and love, of knowledge and ideals. The sexual bond between man and woman and parent and child provides an intimacy beyond any other and thus opens the way for the divine creativity *provided that* the individual in the wholeness of being, including sexuality, is committed to the divine creativity.

Without this close bond with some caretaker, if not with parents then with foster parents, no child can undergo the continuous creative transformation that enables him or her to enter into deep communion with others. The parents also need this bond with the child and with one another. Hence, without sexuality binding individuals in intimate union to create responsiveness and break down protective devices, the expanding reach of imagination could not be created as it has been and as it continues to be.

This does not mean that human sexuality is always practiced in such a way as to serve the divine creativity in human life. An individual is always liable to turn against Christ in all areas. Refusal to commit oneself to the divine creativity applies not only to sexuality. It applies to scientific research, the major theme of this writing. It applies to government, industry and all the arts and forms of human interest. But human sexuality is fitted above everything else to hold parents and children together long enough and intimately enough and in communion deep enough to rear the human level of existence as could not be done without this sexuality. Perhaps sexuality more than anything else has opened the way for the progressive creation of humanity for evil and for good throughout all the generations of history. This creation of humanity in Christ through history is the meaning of history, as we shall shortly explain.

The third distinctive characteristic that makes the human being the peculiar creature of divine creativity in Christ is the capacity to communicate meanings that are shared to form a culture.

The fourth characteristic by which one can be progressively created in Christ with reaches of imagination beyond any known limit must be examined with care. It is the human capacity to transmit meanings through a sequence of generations, each generation adding, subtracting or otherwise modifying the range and form of human imagination. The sequence of generations operating in this way is called human history.

History as here understood is not merely past events. Nor is it our knowledge of past events gained by historical research, although this is a part of what is meant. But history is the transmission to the present and on to the future of the consequences of events which have occurred in the human past. This transmission is accomplished by the kind of interchange which creates the human level of existence. It is the kind of interchange by which the form and reach of experience had by one person is acquired by another so far as it can be (1) communicated by use of language and other symbols and signs and (2) integrated into the experience of the receiver and thus expand the range of what one can experience as good and distinguish as evil.

In the same way that this interchange occurs between individuals, it occurs between one generation and the next. This is the creation of history. This kind of interchange creates human language progressively through the sequence of generations, when required conditions are present. Also transmitted and modified by this kind of interchange are habits, techniques, skills, ideals, laws, institutions and everything else developed in the human past. Of course a very large part of what was created in the past is not transmitted. Much is lost because the interchange by which the consequences of past events might be transmitted is suppressed and obstructed by counter processes. For example, the practice of slavery reduces the kind of interchange which transmits the creations of past events. This is so for two reasons: Slaves are not allowed to have that freedom and fullness of interchange by which their minds might acquire and transmit the heritage of the past; also, they cannot transmit even what they do acquire because they cannot participate in the interchange of the ruling group. What is said of slaves applies also to all people who are exploited and deprived of access to the culture of their time.

Oppression and exploitation reduce the capacity to transmit the resources for human living created by past events. Many kinds of interchange which are not transmissive of these resources, but obstruct their transmission can be found in every society. Devotion to gadgets and trivialities, gossip, automatic mechanism of social control, deadening bureaucracies, military organizations, stupifying rituals, hate and fear—all this and much else in every society can reduce to a minimum the kind of interchange by which the consequences of the past and the new creations in the present might be progressively accumulated and transmitted from one generation to the next. The social system of Sparta could not accumulate and transmit to the future such an abundance of the consequences of the past as could the citizens of Athens. To the measure that this transmission from past to future is reduced to a minimum, history moves toward its own extinction. To the measure that this transmission is magnified in volume, history moves toward dominance over all that might bring it to an end. This is true when history is defined as transmission of the consequences of past events to the present and on to the future.

Consequences thus transmitted through a sequence of generations can be of two kinds. First, they may be of such sort as to reduce the capacity of each generation to acquire and transmit what the past has produced. Transmitted consequences of this sort may take the form of continuous war, slavery, exploitation of the many by the few, poverty, sickness, illusions which waste the resources, ideals perpetuating practices by which individuals treat one another as utilities rather than as persons, and much else of this sort. Such consequences transmitted from past to future tend to extinguish the process of history. On the other hand, the transmitted consequences may be of such sort as to enable each individual to gather up more of the cultural consequences of the past and communicate them to others. Transmitted consequences having this character would be a form of art which interprets profoundly the vivid and varied experiences of individuals so that these experiences become communicable; a body of knowledge such as science and methods of control such as technology which are communicable; a social order where power and prestige are gained by engaging in the kind of interchange by which one integrates into one's own person the needs and interests of the many and expresses them to others with such efficacy that these others also become living embodiments of the far ranging interests of society and the cultural accumulations of history.

This second way of transmitting the consequences of past events to the future makes one increasingly the creature and the creator of history, while the first of the two does the opposite. To the measure that the second way becomes the ruling purpose of human life, history becomes the embodiment of human purpose; and human purpose becomes a vision of horizons expanding with the sequence of generations.

History becomes inceasingly creative of the individual, and is increasingly created by the individual to the measure that interchange between individuals enables each to understand the other and does it in such a way that what each acquires from the other becomes a part of oneself, thus progressively creating one's own mind and personality.

Due to the first of the two ways of transmitting the consequences of the past to the future, the greater part of all that happens in human history beats down, limits and obstructs the creation of the human mind and the development of its constructive potentialities. Nevertheless, history could not come into existence, neither can it continue, without creating the human mind in every individual who participates in history. This is so because the consequences of past events at the level distinctively human could never reach the present except by way of human minds created in each generation by what that generation received from the past. Therefore, the creativity creating these minds is the same identical creativity which creates history. All the values of human life, and all increase of these values depend upon accepting this creativity as the purpose of human history. That means that the purpose of human history is to increase the effectiveness of that kind of interchange which creates appreciative understanding of one another, so that this understanding of each for the other will be more comprehensive, profound, and correct. To the measure that this kind of interchange becomes the purpose of human life, it will become the purpose of history, because it creates and sustains the ongoing of history.

Immediately one hears the cynic scoffing and contemptuously asking "Do you think that this kind of interchange will ever be the accepted purpose of human life?" The answer to that question should be direct and final. It might be worded thus: Only the coward and the weakling demand assured success before being willing to promote the greatest good in human life. To undertake such a project and fail in the undertaking is better than to succeed in doing mean and little things.

This reference to failure must not be misunderstood. One who is committed to the creative interchange in Christ never fails in one sense of the word "failure." What such a one seeks and finds in Christ is not primarily an ideal possibility to be actualized. It is an actual, operative creativity present in one's own life and in others. Furthermore, in this communion which is

Christ, the shame, the failure and the ignominy experienced elsewhere take on positive value because these are a part of the individual's total self and this total self in this communion is appreciated and understood as precious. Often failure, shame, and ignominy are the obverse sides of what is of greatest value in the individual person and can be recognized as such when this communion occurs.

Also it is not a rare thing in human life for this interchange of communion to be accepted as the purpose of human existence, although it may never be verbalized as such. Whenever true lovers have communion that is genuine, this is the purpose of their existence and is so accepted although no intellectual formulation of such a purpose may occur. Whenever individuals gather for no other purpose than to seek and find appreciative understanding of one another, this is the purpose of existence for them. How frequently this occurs it is hard to say, but surely it must happen at times in the lives of most people. Hence there is nothing fantastic or starry-eyed in claiming that Christ in this sense can be accepted as the purpose of our existence.

Yet the drift of human life toward its own extinction is always with us and, so far as we can discover, has always been present in human existence. Life distinctively human is highly unstable; it wobbles, sometimes toward its own elimination, sometimes toward its fuller development. One of the chief dangers of our time is an apathy due to a sense of futility in all we undertake. This springs in part from lack of vision of anything sufficiently great and good to make it worth risking failure in the endeavor to promote it.

Not only does the creativity of history magnify constructive human powers, it also increases destructive power. However, the descriptive term "destructive" does not distinguish one kind of power; it dintinguishes one way of using power. Any kind of power can be used either constructively or destructively. Also it is not paradoxical to say that power is used constructively when directed to the destruction of what prevents creative interchange. It is also used constructively when it sets up, sustains and protects the conditions which must be present for the most effective operation of creativity. This requires science and technology as well as personal commitment to Christ as the creativity of history.

Human life being what it is, one can imagine that the only way of access to the greatest good is by dedication to it combined with failure to achieve it. Certainly success would be better. But human life may be so evil that any success in the form of popular favor will be corrupted by the greedy, the arrogant and the cruel who make use of successful development for their own ends. Many a new venture of high promise has been corrupted in this way, Christianity itself being the outstanding example. If this is the truth about human life, the noblest good can retain its virtue only when success is so limited and failure so great, in spite of utmost effort and sacrifice, that the corrupters are not attracted to it. Perhaps the only way to protect the glory of human existence from the exploiters is to make ignominy, suffering and very limited success the only way of access to it. This may be one meaning of the Cross of Christ extending its shadow over the whole expanse of human history. When the greatest good is to be had without sacrifice and without shame, the greedy and the arrogant may enter and corrupt it by their participation.

Whether or not this is always true, it has sufficient measure of truth to demonstrate that the greatest good ever to be found in human life must be found by dedication to it, regardless of success or failure. When assured success is made the precondition for accepting it, the glory and the blessedness depart because of the way in which the good purpose are turned to evil ends.

All this applies to that purpose implicit in every human person, which is also the purpose of society and history. The purpose is implicit rather than explicit because it scarcely ever is acknowledged and allowed to take control of human life. Yet it is the purpose of human existence in the sense that it progressively creates human existence through history when required conditions are present.

Of course history is not itself a mind, having a purpose. Neither does "purpose of history" here refer to an over-all pattern to be found by searching the events of the past. Neither does it refer to a cosmic or supernatural mind overruling the events of history in such a way as to produce a predetermined outcome. "Purpose of history" here refers to the creativity revealed in Christ which creates the human level of existence progressively by expanding the reach of human imagination in height and depth. This creativity does it by way of a kind of interchange creating the human level of existence in each individual, beginning with the new born infant. This human level is created in the infant by communicating to the developing child by way of the parents and others the resources for human living that have been acquired in the past. Thus is history created in each generation.

This creativity—which is the purpose of history in the sense of creating history—is not the totality of all events nor any pattern found in this totality. Nowhere can this creativity of history be found so clearly and so unmistakably as in the developing personality of the child through interchange with persons who embody the consequences of the human past. The chief of these consequences is the human language with all its meanings.

A society so organized that each individual can adopt a purpose for his or her life which merges with the purpose of society and history will surely prevail over every other kind of society. Nothing can stop the spreading dominance of such a society because of the powerful motivation it gives to individual action, and because of the massive power of the concerted action of millions working with a common purpose. Nothing in the human world can prevail against such a society so long as people believe that the purpose of history is truly the purpose as interpreted by that society and as served by individuals who accept it. The spreading dominance of such a society can only be stopped by exposing the error in its interpretation of the purpose of history, insofar as it involves error.

Nothing can expose the error in a society so organized with individuals so motivated if its interpretation of the purpose of history approximates the truth to some degree and if opposing societies present no better interpretation of purpose but merely come with scepticism, denying that history has in it any purpose whatsoever. The enthralling glory of identifying one's individual purpose with the purpose of history is too great to be given up by the attacks of scepticism unless some better interpretation of the purpose of history is presented and adopted by another society.

People in the Western World have no agreement among themselves concerning any purpose actually operative in history. The most powerfully influential voices either deny that any purpose can be found or else ignore the question entirely. To be sure, many theologians claim that a divine purpose overrules the course of history; but they admit that it cannot be found either by the study of history or by analysis of the processes of human existence. A purpose so conceived, admittedly beyond history, but not supported by substantial evidence found either by study of the human past or by analysis of human existence, can never give to human action the vast importance which it acquires when it can identify itself with a demonstrable creativity actually creating and sustaining the movement of history.

There is only one conclusion to be drawn from this fact about the Western World. Either it can find an interpretation of the purpose of history better supported by evidence than any other and can organize society to serve that purpose or else it is doomed to give way to the spreading power of a society organized to serve a purpose interpreted in such a way as to persuade the human mind.

The Western World has based its appeal upon freedom. But the appeal of freedom has no great power in it unless it is freedom to serve a cause of such transcendent importance that it enthralls the mind and arouses the last devotion.

Freedom is precious only when it opens the way to something grandly significant. Freedom taken by itself merely opens the door. But what is beyond the door? If you merely repeat, "Freedom," all you have is another door to open. But what does it open to? You repeat, "Freedom." That only leads to opening doors endlessly with nothing attained save more doors to open. Such a prospect has no powerful appeal. Freedom to be of great value must lead somewhere. But where? Until that question is answered, the proclamation of freedom defeats itself. Until the Western World can find in history a vision of expanding horizons, the freedom it offers turns back on itself and leads nowhere.

Why has the Western World not found a purpose in history supported by enough evidence to persuade people generally that it can lead them on generation after generation? The answer to that question should be plain. It has not found such a purpose because it has not searched where it can be found. No purpose for history can be found by searching the human past. It can only be found by analyzing the living present. It must be found here and now by exposing that creativity which creates the human mind by transmitting the consequences of past events to the present and on to the future. This cannot be discovered by studying the human past because the subtle and complex process of interchange between living persons, as previously explained, can be experienced only in the present. That tone of voice, that facial expression, those words spoken here and now in a living context which give to them a meaning they never again can have, those deeds intertwined into a complexity of living creativity, all this sinks into oblivion forever beyond recall when the years have rolled them into the past.

Autobiographies and intimate personal letters which are also works of art, together with those works conventionally labeled works of art, may help to bring to us some sense of the divine creativity operative at the time those works were produced. But even this creativity, arising out of our interpretation and appreciative understanding of lives long past, is in the present. It is not the creativity which actually operated in those lives which we now reproduce in living form. It is the divine presence operating here and now to create appreciative understanding of those who lived long ago. It brings into our own lives the drama, the tragedy, the beauty, the blessedness and the horror of the story of humanity, but it does it now. It is operating in our lives here, bringing the past to life again in us.

Since the purpose of history is the creativity of the living present, it cannot be found by studying the past nor by foretelling the future. Neither historians nor prophets can tell us what it is. Since historians cannot find it, so long as they keep within the limits of their specialized competence, they will always deny that history carries a purpose. Of course, they may not keep within these limits. They may dream and speculate as Toynbee and others have done. These dreams and these speculations may help us to interpret the present but they do not tell us about the past.

Since the historians are forbidden by their specialized competence from finding any purpose in history, those who turn to them to be informed about it will receive a negative answer or else a speculation not supported by the findings of pure historical research. This explains the failure of the Western World to find a purpose for history which can be widely accepted. The failure results from looking to the historians to agree among themselves concerning what this purpose is. If some one other than an historian suggests what this purpose might be, we look to the historians to tell us if they find in the human past what has been suggested. The answer they give is always in the negative because this purpose can never be found in the past. So we assume that there can be no purpose in history. Some accept a theology of history which does not rest its case on what can be found in history but requires us to look beyond history. Such a view can never be widely accepted; and, even if it were, it would not solve the problem of finding a purpose which can be identically the same purpose in the life of the individual, in society and throughout the actual process of history. The purpose of history is found by way of the revelation of God in Christ. Christ must be found in the present, as we have tried to demonstrate again and again.

Another illusion concerning purpose in history has blinded the endeavor to find it. It has been sought in the form of some social structure rather than in the evanescent creativity of the living present. It has been sought in the form of the state, as by Hegel; or in the form of economic production and distribution, as by Marx; or in the form of cultures, as by Spengler; or in the form of civilizations and a universal church, as by Toynbee; or in the form of the church interpreted to be the body of Christ, as by M.C. D'Arcy; or in the form of a Kindgom of God or other transcendent being beyond history, as taught by Niebuhr, Tillich, Berdyaev and others.

No structure, whether immanent in history or transcendent beyond history, can give us the purpose in history when the structure is taken by itself alone. Certainly the creativity of history must have structures in which to operate; but the structure are incidental to the creativity and, as this creativity passes from age to age and culture to culture, it will cast off old structures and take on others. For this reason the purpose in history can never be identified with any structure except as some structure can be found which is intrinsic to, and inalienable from, the creativity itself. None of the structures above mentioned seem to be of this character. It is the creativity itself and not its structure alone which is the purpose of history.

It is not difficult to find the development of social structures throughout the human past. Especially is this true of those structures called the technologies and the economies. Consequently, if we seek for the purpose in history by studying the relics and records of the past, this development of structure is what we find. For this reason all who seek to find purpose in history by studying the human past will identify it with this development of structure, if they find anything at all which they call this purpose. For reasons stated, all such development of structure, when labeled purpose of history, is an illusion.

When creation of the human mind in community by way of creative interchange is identified with the purpose in history, this creation is not *necessarily* progressive except during infancy and childhood. It must be progressive in the early years or the infant would never acquire a human mind and history could not continue by way of that individual. Also creativity *can* be progressive from one generation to the next. Creativity will be progressive when scientific research is joined with personal commitment to the creativity of Christ. For reasons already stated, the developments of history today are probably regressive instead of progressive. This will continue until people learn to bring their scientific research into the service of

Christ. In other ages this was not required because in other ages science with its applications was not the dominant power in the world. Today it is. When people allegedly commit themselves to Christ but do not commit the mightiest power at their command, they have not met one of the primary conditions required for Christ to rule.

Next to scientific research and its applications, perhaps the ruling interest in the Western World today is sexuality. The Christian religion has been reticent and reluctant, even stumbling, in committing the fullest development of sexuality to Christ. When the two driving forces of our age are not given to Christ, how can we hope that the creativity of history can be progressive? This is not the fault of Christ. It is the fault of the Christian religion. This is the reason for the plea here made to distinguish between Christ and Christianity.

To the measure that we give ourselves fully with all our resources, including both our science and our sexuality, to the creativity of history, we become the creators of history as well as the creatures. To the measure that we do not give ourselves with all our resources to the creative transformation in Christ, our stature as creators of history is diminished because we do not transform the present and shape the future as we might.

The late Albert Camus, when accepting the Nobel Prize, expressed the chief contribution made to history by the artist which is also the chief contribution made by every person. It is to communicate what people have experienced so that all can share it so far as possible. All persons do this more or less, not in the form of art, but in the way they express themselves at times, if they are honest and generous. Thus do we become a community living a life of pain and beauty common to us all because even the ugly and the drab take on a precious quality when tenderly and deeply felt by one who sees the ugly and the drab against the background of the individual who displays these qualitites. The shame, the tragedy, the horror, the heroism, every form of experience, when communicated to form the story of life we all live together, are the substance of history and give to human life its blessedness.

Camus writes: "To me art is not a solitary delight. It is a means of stirring the greatest number of men by providing them with a privileged image of our common joys and woes . . . This is why true artists scorn nothing. They force themselves to understand instead of judging . . . the silence of an unknown prisoner subjected to humiliation at the other end of the world is enough to tear the artist from his exile . . . not to forget that silence, but to relieve it, making it re-echo by means of art . . . constructing his work without shame or pride within sight of all, constantly torn between pain and beauty, and devoted to extracting from his dual nature the creations he obstinately strives to raise up in the destructive fluctuations of history."

It is not success; it is not pride and honor. It is the story imaginatively grasped of all the qualities of human experience, gathering us into a community and growing in volume as the generations pass, which gives to life the depth and greatness of its common good. This is the purpose which we can make the purpose of our history and thereby overcome the destroyers, as only the meek can do.

CHAPTER V
HUMAN MATURITY

In *The Phenomenon of Man* Pierre Teilhard De Chardin, like many before him, traces the evolution of life up through human history and finds that certain stages of development are prerequisite to later stages which then ensue. When conditions required for a later stage have been established, a very different form of development may arise, based on these prepared conditions. The whole expanse of human existence, and the life which developed long before humans appeared, can be divided into such stages.

During the thousands of years when we were food-gatherers, we brought forth our greatest achievement. This is language. It is greatest because all else distinctively human depends upon it. Then came the second stage in the evolution of human life, beginning with farming in the neolithic period, passing on to the rise of the city with civilization, and continuing down to our time. The most conspicuous achievement of this period, which can be called the period of civilization, has been the increase of three forms of power: Economic power to produce goods and services in ever increasing quantity; political power to organize the collective action of increasing numbers of people; and military power to conquer, destroy and defend.

As language was a necessary prerequisite to later developments, so increase of power in the three forms mentioned has been necessary to prepare conditions for a very different kind of development. After language has been created and highly developed, and power has been increased to the magnitude of our time, a new problem arises. It is how to use this power in a way to develop more fully the constructive capacities of human existence rather than to degrade and destroy them.

Perhaps the chief significance of the twentieth century is one that is little noticed: The self-defeating character which has begun to appear in the increasing power to produce goods, organize collective action and conduct war. The three forms of power have become self-defeating in the following ways. Increasing power to produce goods and services becomes self-defeating when the increase of these goods threatens unemployment and dangerous economic depression or inflation; when it involves enormous expense to store the unused surplus produced; when it causes vast waste of time and energy and material given over to inducing people to buy what they do not want; when it requires built-in obsolescence to keep the wheels turning and the country prosperous; when it diverts millions from constructive thought and action in the effort to consume the ever increasing abundance of goods.

The following comments by Barbara Ward indicate the extent that our increase of economic wealth can affect American society:

> Wealth has always meant, above all else, elbow room and choice, and history is strewn with the wreck of individuals and groups and classes who used this elbow room to make frivolous and ridiculous choices—playing at shepherds and shepherdesses with Marie Antoinette, jumping horses over recumbent peasants with the Esterhazys, drinking champagne out of chorus girls' shoes with the rampant Edwardians, doing the year-long round of beaches, yachts, and night spots with today's cafe society.

> But if a whole nation acquires wealth beyond any earlier human dream, it, too, can opt for the trivial temptations of the rich. The modern moralists see in tail-fins and mink earmuffs more than the virtuosity of the ad men. They see a society corrupted, as so many rich groups have been corrupted in the past, by a scale of choice that exhilarates and bemuses and finally extinguishes all sense of the proper ends of man.

The ominous point in this quotation is not that great wealth has corrupted the small groups who have gathered to themselves the wealth produced by the social system of which they are the beneficiaries. This has always happened since economic power was great enough to produce such abundance. What is ominous is that today for the first time in the history of the world economic power has become so great that almost all the people may, before a great while, have this elbow room for trivial choice. Up to this time the serious business of life for the vast majority has been to acquire, first, the necessities then the luxuries. But we are approaching a time when there will be enough productive power to enable people to choose some ruling purpose beyond an increase of wealth. If they do not do this, if they continue to make the production and consumption of goods the ruling purpose after this is no longer a vital need but a self-defeating endeavor, the degradation and perversion suggested by Barbara Ward will ensue. Worse than that, people who make the consumption of goods the ruling purpose of life lose the capacity to undergo that creative transformation of the mind by which the reach of imagination is extended. Rather the reverse sets in. The reach of imagination shrinks toward the limits of the subhuman. This means that the human animal becomes less and less subject to divine creativity. The bond uniting one with God becomes weaker and thinner. One becomes less and less a child of God and more and more a subhuman animal.

Here, then, is the urgent question: What shall be the ruling purpose of

---

[1] "The Great Silence in the Great Debate" by Barbara Ward, p. 26, *New York Times Magazine*, May 8, 1960.

life for the majority of people when this majority no longer is required to give any great amount of time, energy and thought to the production of goods? When thus liberated from the constraint of this purpose, what shall that more comprehensive purpose be?

The second form in which civilization has increased human power is political. Political power becomes self-defeating when the organization becomes so massive that it reduces the individual to a function of the system. In such case the individual cannot develop the potentialities of individuality. The increase of political power becomes self-defeating in another way. When its increase engenders hate, fear and suspicion between nations having this power—and also between those who have it and those who are relatively weak—the increase of political power becomes self-defeating. When the increase of political power increases the threat of war and creates growing fear and anxiety in the citizens, it becomes self-defeating. The same consequence ensues when the multiplicity of powerful national units, without a superstate to control them, brings on anarchy. Again the increase of political power becomes self-defeating if the formation of a superstate imposes a system of control more oppressive to individuality than the national units were before the world-wide organization developed. When subordination of the individual to a mere function of the ruling system reaches such extreme degree that the individual loses all sense of responsibility and becomes a demonic tool of the state such as occurred in Nazi regime, political power becomes self-defeating. The same is true when the political unit becomes so massive and unwieldy that no one seems able to control it as it rolls on toward universal annihilation. When the increase of political power reaches these dimensions, it becomes self-defeating.

Much the same can be said of military power. It also becomes self-defeating when it can no longer be used in self defense or in conquest without exposing its own people to irremediable disaster.

So we reach the conclusion: The period of human history when the increase of these three forms of power was the chief accomplishment is a period now coming to an end. Of course no such transition from one kind of development in human history to another can occur in a day or a year. It generally takes several generations if not several centuries. Nevertheless, we are in the midst of such a major change in the form and content of what shall be the primary accumulation as the generations pass. In the future it will not be power as it has been during the centuries of civilization up to this time. This does not mean that power will cease to develop. It does mean that it cannot increase unless it is subordinated to the service of something else beyond accumulation of economic goods, increasing numbers organized for collective action and military might.

Language did not cease to develop after civilization began; but it became subordinated to the service of increasing power in the forms just mentioned. So it will be with power in the next stage of human development now beginning. Power can increase only if it is brought under the control of a greater good. This is so because, otherwise, increasing power will destroy itself. There may be no next period in human history, because power may not be subordinated to the service of a greater good and so will soon bring history to an end. But if human history continues, the increase of power in the three forms must serve a kind of development different from that of the past. By different from the past we mean different from the mere increase of economic goods, the increase of political control and the increase of military power without further purpose beyond these three in mutual support of one another. These three are good insofar as they prepare the conditions and resources for a more comprehensive and beneficent purpose. As language represented the first stage, so power represents the second stage, in the historic development of human life. But now it is time to pass on to the third stage.

What will be this greater good which the accomplishments of past history have now made it possible for organized society to promote? The answer to that question can be found by analysis of our present situation as created by these past developments.

The chief source of our troubles today is that our power has increased beyond the scope and control of our sense of right and wrong, of good and evil. We do not have the capacity to appreciate that form and magnitude of positive good which would enable us to control and direct the use of our power. Our power dominates and controls our sense of values rather than our sense of values controlling our use of power. Our predicament can be stated in the cliché: Our power has become too great to be controlled by our sense of values.

Such being the case, the only thing that can save us is to increase our capacity to evaluate and live for a good so great and so profoundly shared by all humanity that we can all unite more or less effectively to use economic, political and military power to serve it. This would reverse our present condition in which our power so impoverishes or subordinates our sense of values that it will either degrade us or destroy us entirely. Only by thus expanding and deepening our vision of what is good, and distinguishing it from what is evil, can we enter the next stage of human development for which the past has been a preparation.

This brings us to the next question. How does one increase capacity for discerning deeper levels of good? By "deeper levels" is meant those values capable of sustaining a more comprehensive system of other values. How does one undergo that transformation by which vision of what is good and distinction of what is evil become more comprehensive and more profound?

There is a way of learning from one another which creates the vision of greater good. It should be carefully distinguished from the interchange creating ordinary language and the interchange creating power.

Vision is created when individuals are aroused by interchange not merely to express their ordinary likes and dislikes, not merely to communicate what is ordinarily called their values, not merely to reveal how they evaluate this and that. Vision is created when individuals are aroused by interchange to express what they value most when all the resources of the unique individuality of each are brought into action; when this vision of each is communicated to the other and integrated into the other's vision to expand and deepen it and make it more comprehensive. When this occurs not only between two people but continues from one to the other and between each and all in a fellowship, a vision of good may be created which gathers into its compass more of the concrete fullness of existence, and more of the valuable possibilities of existence, than any vision before its time.

We have already noted that this is the kind of interchange which occurred between Jesus and his disciples and continued among the disciples after the resurrection. In consequence we know from the records that St. Paul began to sing and shout for joy over the vision that had come to him. Others in this fellowship have been singers and shouters, including St. Francis. The disciples went forth to all the world preaching the gospel and the gospel was the communication of a vision. This vision may have had much mythology in it, but it was rooted in the concrete fullness of actual existence in the form of communion (or love) for one another and for all others.

This creation of vision has occurred in the past in the case of rare individuals and fellowships under very unusual conditions. We are entering a period of history when this creation of vision must become one of the major concerns of society if our wealth and power are not to drag us down to lower levels of self-destruction. This can become a concern of society only when there is sufficient economic abundance to liberate people from the struggle to obtain the necessities and when there is sufficient political control to liberate them from the anxieties and struggles of trying to protect themselves from war, social disruption and that wild destructiveness which breaks out in individuals when they feel the frustration and futility of existence for lack of vision. Since these are the requirements for any extensive concern with the creation of vision, it is here claimed that history had to pass through the first two stages, creating language and power, before this could be a major concern of society.

The kind of interchange that creates vision cannot occur unless required conditions are present and these conditions must be discovered and provided by research. This is a social problem, a psychological problem, a biological problem and a problem of organic chemistry. It may be that changing the chemistry of some human organisms (or all human organisms) will increase capacity for this kind of interchange.

Of course, all this is speculation; however, it does not seem unreasonable considering what is being discovered in the field of organic chemistry.

Providing all the conditions we can discover does not mean that this kind of interchange will inevitably occur. The complexity of human individuality is so great, and the constant change in the psychological ingredients of personality is so marked that we can never be sure that all the subtleties of required conditions are present. We do not suggest that people are like machines, automatically performing as predicted when conditions are right. Even if vision was always created when specified conditions were present, this performance would still be an extreme contrast to the performance of a machine. The difference is that the machine produces what is predetermined by the mechanism. The creation of vision is a new creation, the content of which could never have been imagined, much less predicted. Freedom is precisely this kind of creative transformation. More arbitrary unpredictable behavior is not freedom. But the new creation of vision beyond the reach of human imagination up to that time, created by the unique individuality of two or more persons integrating their diverse visions into a total vision that never existed before is the highest attainment of freedom.

With society organized and resources applied to provide conditions most favorable for it, this creation of vision in a fellowship of faith might continue through a sequence of generations until the growing vision became the chief accomplishment of that period of history.

Poetry and drama and all the fine arts would have an important part to play in this. But the creators and carriers of the vision would not all be artists by any means. There is a kind of unpremeditated, spontaneous ex-pressiveness of the total individuality in communion which at times can surpass all the fine arts in communicating a vision. Great preaching does this and so do many simple persons in moments of great love. Further, this kind of interchange creating vision, when sufficiently extensive, will create a language fit to communicate vision of the great good. The kind of language used by us today, when creation of power is the chief concern, is designed to regulate behavior and direct efficient action. In ancient times the Roman language was like ours in this respect while the Greek language was better fitted to express vision.

We do not predict by this that the next period of history will be devoted to the creation of vision. We have stated that our economic wealth and our political, technological power will drag us down to triviality, folly and de-struction if the creation of vision does not become a major concern in the period of history into which we are now moving. We have mentioned the part which the fine arts and the language must play in the creation of vision. But most important is a commitment of faith to what creates vision. Such a faith must be guided by a better understanding of the revelation of God in Christ than the common practices of the prevailing forms of Christianity have provided.

When it is said that vision is created by the kind of interchange arousing in each a profound appreciation of what the other values most, one may ask: Suppose the other person values most what is evil? The answer to that question is of first importance. No matter how evil may be that which the other person values most, the profound appreciation (evaluative) understanding of the person and the evil is a great good. The evil is not good; but the appreciative understanding of the person in the wholeness of being is one of the greatest goods. The evil persons here under consideration are you and I. We become transformed from the evil to the good precisely by this kind of interchange. If the kind of interchange creating appreciative understanding of one another can only operate between the good people, our case is hopeless. but Christ came to save sinners.

The problem of providing biological necessities, economic abundance and the instruments of power is not yet solved for all peoples. Millions on earth are still on the verge of starvation and suffer other ills of the body which scientific knowledge, technological power and good will can remove. Also innumerable and dangerous defects of the social order cry for correction in all parts of the earth, in the most prosperous countries as well as in the most impoverished. Therefore, our statement should not be misunderstood when it asserts that the ages are past when priority was given to the struggle to obtain the necessities, the economic abundance and the instruments of power. At times and places and in many undertakings, these ancient goals must still be the ruling concern because they are necessary prerequisites to other goals.

But the distinctive feature of our age is that we are beginning to see that these instrumental goals will become self-destructive if they are not made to serve other goals towering above them. This can be called a mark of maturity. These further goals can no longer be left to the chosen few, the good people, so to speak. They have become imperative for all people, as the goals of food and health and shelter have been in the past. This does not mean that every individual in the past sought food and health and shelter as the primary purpose. Many in the past had food, health and shelter provided for them because society was so ordered. We have come to the time when in like manner society itself must be so ordered that these further ends of human existence, rising beyond the instrumental goals, can be served. If this is not done, our magnified power cannot be used constructively. When power so great is not used constructively, it inevitably becomes destructive; and its destructiveness becomes so devastating that human life cannot continue indefinitely with its misuse.

Another characteristic feature of our time is exposed in the rise and spread of existentialism. In a sense existentialism indicates that we have reached the status of maturity without yet attaining the understanding and the vision required to exercise the responsibility accruing to maturity.

If the substance of existentialism could be reduced to a few statements, it might be worded thus: The depth and concrete wholeness of individual existence is always vastly more than any definition nor characterization of human personality which the human mind can formulate. This existence in its wholeness is always more than any ideal or purpose or function or form of action to which the individual may commit. At least this is true so long as the individual lacks authenticity, and this lack of authenticity is the chief concern of the existentialists. To be authentic is to be committed with the wholeness of one's being. People in our civilization lack authenticity, say the existentialists, because they can find nothing fit to engage them in such a way as to bring the total self into action. Striving for more wealth and power cannot engage the total self any more because in our civilization, as previously stated, these goals have become self-defeating.

Since the existence of the individual with all its potentialities is always more than any character one assumes or any way of life one follows, these suppressed potentialities generate anxiety. One form of this anxiety arises from the casual indifference with which the individual assumes whatever character the social situation demands and whatever goals one undertakes to follow. Since these do not truly engage the individual, they are a false self. To use Sartre's expression, they are "bad faith." Since this character and this purpose are superficially acquired, they may be cast off at any time. The individual feels this rebelliousness and it creates anxiety as one does not know what one will do or become.

This is one form of anxiety of which the existentialists speak. There is another and more mature form. It can be expressed in questions and statements like these: Who am I? What am I? What is the purpose of my existence? Does it have none? Then why do I live? Life is meaningless when there is nothing to live for. The goals I profess and the character I display are shams. The character which I thought was myself, and the goals which I thought were sufficient, I now see were those of immaturity. They were the play-acting of a child. I must find something greater, vaster, more comprehensive. But have not found it and there seems to be nothing of the sort unless I arbitrarily throw my whole self into some undertaking for no other reason that I decide to do it.

This failure to find anything great enough and good enough to command total commitment is what the existentialists mean when they speak of confronting nothingness. Nothingness can be identified with death only when there is nothing one can serve of such sort that one's death along with one's life can be of value because of the contribution one's death can make to the cause for which one lives and dies.

Finding nothing that can engage the total self in this way, both in living and in dying, the existentialist says that life is meaningless; it is absurd; it has no justifying structure, goal or good. Since there is no direction, purpose or way of life fitted to bring the total existence of the individual with all its potentialities into action, the individual is forced to live under the constraint of imposed goals and forms which are alien in that they cannot absorb and satisfy individuality. In this condition the individual is said to be alienated. Camus is never wary of condemning it. Perhaps his most powerful denunciation of this condition is in *The Fall,* the last book he wrote before he was killed in an accident.

The spread and impact of existentialism in our time indicates that many feel that the goals and way of life which have dominated our civilization up to this time are unfit to meet the demands of human existence. This is a further mark of maturity in the negative sense of having outgrown the goals that once seemed sufficient. Maturity in the positive sense would be to find a goal sufficient in value and magnitude to engage all the powers of maturity. But maturity in the positive sense has not yet been reached, if it ever will be. This is the age of human maturity in the negative sense just indicated.

Existentialism is not new, if by that is meant that no one in the past ever held similar views. But it seems that existentialism today has a wider appeal and stronger impact than in the past. Also the regions where existentialism is widely influential are regions where economic abundance and the instruments of power have been achieved sufficiently to reveal their unfitness to comprehend and direct the potentialities of human existence. And the areas where existentialism prevails are those regions where the increase of wealth and power begins to show its self-defeating character. All this seems to indicate that civilization has reached a point where creation of vision has become a necessity.

When wealth is widely distributed, it does not even serve the purpose it once did of giving the marks of superior rank to those who possess it. It is said that Sweden has provided its people with more of the conveniences of modern civilization more widely distributed than any other country. It is also reported that in Sweden there is more suicide, more crime, more juvenile delinquency and mental illness than in any other country. This seems to indicate that the potentialities of existence in the individual demand something more than modern civilization can provide; and when this something more is not forthcoming, these aberrations occur.

This is the human condition at the age of negative maturity with power greater than we ever had before and with the responsibility pertaining to such power. But we do not know what to do with this power nor how to meet the demands of our responsibility. It is an awkward and dangerous age. But a question is being asked, earnestly and urgently, about the purpose of human existence. Existentialism is one way the question is asked. Such an age as this, profoundly disturbed by such a question, is a time of promise as well as peril.

Arthur Koestler has an article with the heading "Post P.H." meaning fifteen years post Hiroshima. He suggests that dropping the bomb on Hiroshima marked a new stage in the development of human existence analogous to what is called maturity in the life of the individual. By maturity Koestler means that we are now responsible for our own continued existence. Heretofore the manner of our life and our continued existence depended upon our adaptation to natural conditions and the kind of social order established by tradition. Today the gigantic power symbolized by the bomb enables us to master, control and shape our culture. Instead of being sustained by our civilization, we must now sustain it. The continued existence of humanity depends henceforth upon the way we use our power. In the past we could hate and fight but did not have the power to destroy the conditions of our existence. Now we have that power. As children can fight with one another without great danger to themselves but when they reach maturity and carry weapons, they become exceedingly dangerous if they continue to do so, in like manner the human race has reached maturity with the power of nuclear fission and fusion.

The human race now also has the responsibility to regulate the population of the earth. Likewise the fertility of the soil and the other resources of the planet can be consumed to leave a barren earth unfit for human habitation unless we assume responsibility for the conservation and proper use of these resources. Heretofore the earth could replenish as fast as people could consume. Human beings might exhaust the resources in one region but could always move on to some other unexhausted part of the planet. Now the whole globe is in human keeping and we can exhaust its life-giving qualities. We also now have the science and power to conserve and replenish these resources by applying research to this problem combined with proper use of technology, the arts of social organization, administration and education.

Not only the earth and its resources but also, and more important, the kind of mentality people shall have can now be shaped by propaganda, by the kind of entertainment provided, by political action, by methods of social manipulation including terror, by institutional education and moral guidance. The human mind has always been shaped by the prevailing form of culture more than by anything else; but now techniques and arts are being acquired by which the form of culture is more under the control of deliberate choice. Of course people cannot plan to change the culture in ways beyond the reach of the imagination which that culture permits them to have, but whether or not the consequences are planned and anticipated, political control, scientific research, education and other methods shaping the human mind, can radically change the content and form of a given culture. Hence the responsibility of people for their own mentality is in our time.

In seeking for a purpose to guide the use of such power, certain considerations are imperative. The purpose must provide for the widest diversity of individuality and culture and race, because all humans, both present and future, are now connected in one society, the fate of which is to be determined by the use of this power. The purpose must also provide for the development of new systems in the future beyond the reach of our present imagination, because what we do with power so great will determine the conditions of human existence for the indefinite future. This is the kind of decision we must make concerning the use of our power. It is the kind of decision humans must make when they reach maturity.

This decision is not one that we can avoid. If we refuse to decide, we shall nevertheless be establishing a way of life by drifting into it—and it may be a way of death. This is the consequence of what we do, by choice or otherwise, when all people are in one package and when power is so great as it is today. If our power is not yet great enough to have this fateful consequence, it soon will be. The issue is not alone that of our continued existence or extinction, although that is involved and comes first to mind. Just as serious, perhaps more serious, would be a continued existence so mean and miserable that it would be better not to live at all than to continue in such degradation.

If we seek in Christ to find the way of life, we do not look primarily to an ideal. We look to an actual kind of interchange going on in human life which can become more or less dominant over counter processes when required conditions are present. The first thing to note about this kind of interchange is that it creates, to the measure conditions permit, the most profound appreciative understanding of the unique individuality of one another across the barriers of diversity, estrangement and hostility. Therefore, it is not a choice of one way of life to the exclusion of other ways; rather it is a decision for what provides for the greatest diversity of ways and the indefinite transformation of human existence. It even provides for estrangement and hostility provided only that the way be kept open for the kind of interchange which creates understanding of the interests of the other party.

On the other hand, this way of life is not permissive in the sense that it permits everything. No possible way of life can be of that sort, even when people profess it. The way of life in Christ demands with rigor two basic requirements. One is that this kind of interchange be given priority over all else. The second is that the resources of our civilization, preeminently our science, be devoted to finding and providing the conditions under which this kind of interchange can be most effective.

No other conceivable way of life provides for so much difference in belief and practice, so much transformation in the social order, so much change in the views of the world and of people. No other possible way of life can provide for so much creative transformation of human beings and our world, expanding the range of what can be known, controlled, appreciated as good, distinguished as evil, understood about ourselves and other selves. It does not even require that all people undergo this kind of creative transformation or seek expanding ranges of experience, provided that appreciative understanding of these diverse choices be maintained.

There is one major objection to choosing a way of life for all people, not only for today but also for the indefinite future. The chosen way will exclude other ways which other individuals, peoples, cultures and ages might find better fitted to them. But if we choose the kind of interchange mentioned, this objection does not apply. Certainly every way of life must set up limits beyond which people cannot be permitted to pass. Without such limits rigorously enforced, the continued existence of the human race is impossible. Also, without such limits, diverse ways of life will so obstruct, harass and impoverish one another that none can be lived in the form that is preferred. Mere permissiveness is not enough. But a way of life can be chosen which provides for the greatest possible diversity and transformation without mutual destruction and without harassment and impoverishment of the opposing ways. More positively stated, in this way of life diversities sustain and endow one another with greater value through their conflicts and oppositions as well as in their harmonies. This is so because conflict can be a powerful stimulus to inquiry and understanding of one another when the value of integrated diversities has been found to be progressively creative of human existence.

The problem of civilization at maturity, meaning the responsibility imposed upon people to choose a new and different way of life for the human race after eight thousand years of increasing power, can be viewed from another standpoint. To get this view before us, we need to look again at two features characteristic of a developing civilization. We have looked at these two before but will now consider them in that relation to one another which exposes the problem of civilization at maturity.

These two features are (1) the expanding reach of the constructions of imagination in the form of science, technology, moral idealism, art and religious symbolism and, underlying this, (2) the widening community without which these constructions cannot arise or increase their scope. The development of these constructions requires community because they can arise and increase only when the suggestions, findings and innovations of many different individuals widely scattered in space and time can be brought together by communication and made accessible to each individual engaged in rearing the structures of civilization. The constructions of civilization have never been able to rise very high when this kind of communication was narrowly limited. The wider, freer and fuller this kind of communication among inventive minds, the more rapidly and loftily have these constructions been reared. For example, before modern methods of communication and transportation were available, civilization rose most rapidly around the Mediterranean because the rivers and seas in that region provided means for this kind of interchange over wide areas and between different centers of developing structures of thought.

This wide and free interchange is the social condition that makes possible the continuous expansion and diversification of knowledge, art, technology, morals, religious symbolism and the various forms of social organization entering into a civilization. The more numerous and diverse the sources of information and suggestion reaching the individual, provided that one can absorb them into one's own individuality to form resources peculiar to oneself, the higher can be reared the constructions of civilization.

As civilization advances there comes a time when specialization can be a barrier to the communication required to enable individuals to bring forth new solutions for new problems and thus release the inventive powers on which the rise and growth of a civilization depends. There is one corrective for this obstruction to communication brought on by narrowing specialization. If the specialized fields of inquiry and the specialized functions of society can be directed to providing the conditions under which interchange can increase community at that level where individuals are not specialized, that is, between individuals as wholes and not merely between individuals as functions serving a specialized field, then the specializations will not impair community at the level where it sustains and satisfies human life. Also, in such case, the specializations will not become uncooperative because they will be cooperating to sustain and magnify this community which the specialized functions are serving. Direct communication between the specializations may fail. The techniques and technical language of one may be unintelligible to others; but since they have a common good to serve, and since the specialists are not only specialized functions but also individuals in communion with other individuals at the level of the community they serve, the technical unintelligibility will not be a barrier to communication at the level where it is most important. The specialized techniques and language can always be translated into the values of the common good which all seek to serve, since that would be the purpose and the utility of the technicalities and specializations.

In every society individuals have specialized functions, but over and above their functions they can be individuals with an existence not contained in the function they serve, if in addition to their specialized associations they also participate in a community which fosters this wholeness. Such a community is one where this wholeness is appreciated and understood by reason of the kind of interchange that prevails. The purpose of the specialized functions should be to provide the conditions needed for this kind of community fostering wholeness. When this is reversed, when individuals are so completely subordinated to the specialized functions that nothing is served within reach of their interest save only the ever-repeated round of functions, the society ceases to have any value for the individual's wholeness and one ceases to be a whole individual. One becomes a fragmented part of a human being. One loses authenticity, to use the expression of the existentialists.

Here we have two contrasting demands which must be met by every civilization. One is the performance of functions which must be increasingly specialized as civilization advances. The other is the recognition and nurture of individuality in community. The two demands must be met in the sense that no civilization can survive indefinitely if either demand is excluded.

When conditions change, as they always do, the specialized functions must be redirected and amplified by innovating insights in order to do what the changed conditions require. These insights must come from individuals who are more than functions of the established system. When individuals have been so completely subordinated to the functions of a system that no resources of individuality are available for the solving of problems beyond the routine performance of the established function, no innovating insights will arise to suggest new ways of action when changed conditions require it. Every society must have a bureaucracy in the sense of people serving specialized functions, but the word "bureaucracy" has come to be associated with individuals who have lost their capacity to solve problems requiring innovating insights. This incapacity is due to deprivation of individuality by reason of subordination to the routine demands. When this occurs the individual becomes incapable of imagination beyond the limits of established ways of life. Or, if imagination continues, it assumes the form of irrelevant dreams by which the individual escapes in fancy from the dull routines of life, thus releasing suppressed potentialities but in such a way that they cannot serve society or suggest ways of dealing with actual situations when these call for action different from the established routine.

This conflict between the performance of specialized functions required by every social system and underlying these functions, the sustaining community nurturing the potentialities of the whole individual, is one cause for the decline of all the highly developed civilizations. "Decline of a civilization," as the expression is here used, means that the constructions of human imagination such as knowledge, technology, art, methods of social organization and control, become incapable of the innovations required to deal constructively with changed conditions. Also in the sequence of generations these constructions are not communicated fully from one generation to the next. This incapacity to communicate results when individuals are suppressed to functions of the established system so that they no longer have any appreciation for what the system as a whole is intended to serve. What the system should serve is its purpose. When its purpose cannot be communicated, intelligence cannot be applied to its problems, nor can its value be appreciated. When this condition ensues, we have what is here called decline of the civilization.

As civilization becomes more powerful, and hence more difficult to control, this danger arising from subordination of the individual to a function of the system becomes increasingly acute until, in the age of human maturity, it will be fatal for the entire race if not corrected.

As we have seen all along, there is a kind of interchange which nurtures wholeness of individuality in community. The service and maintenance of this kind of community in which all might participate outside their specialized functions and associations, might be the purpose of the entire social system and of the civilization taken as a whole. This is not true of our civilization in the day of its negative maturity. In general we sacrifice interchange of whole individuals for the sake of greater efficiency in the performance of specialized functions. Power has been sought by making the system of specialized functions increasingly dominant.

The problem is one of establishing the right relations between two kinds of interchange which we shall distinguish by calling one "functional interchange" and the other "individual interchange." In functional interchange the participants treat one another as functions of a system, disregarding everything in the individual except what pertains to the individual's function. In individual interchange the participants treat one another more or less as whole individuals. Perhaps these two kinds of interchange are never entirely exclusive of one another. Perhaps there is always some recognition of individuality when treating another as a function in a system. And perhaps there is always some recognition of function when treating another as a whole individual. Also there is never complete and perfect recognition of all the potentialities of the individual. But these two extremes can be approximated to various degrees.

As a member of the managerial staff of a corporation, one can treat oneself and one's associates as nothing more than functionaries of the managerial order. One who has been reduced to such a function has been called "the organization man." Scientists in their capacity of specialists serving the function of their specialization can reduce themselves to this function and interact with one another and with other people in no other capacity, or at least approximate this condition. People engaged in labor can be treated by others, and might view themselves, merely as functions of industrial production. Members of the military organization may treat themselves and be treated by others simply as functions of the fighting machine. All this is a matter of degree to be sure. As said before, perhaps no human being ever becomes in his or her own eyes and in the eyes of others a simple function of an operating system and nothing more. But this can be approached.

The faculty of an educational system and the students might all interchange with one another almost exclusively as functional members of the educational system. Members of a bureaucracy in the government can work like automatons under the control of push buttons. So also can presidents and kings, executives and administrators. All resources of individuality not exercised in serving the function assigned to the individual may shrivel and die for lack of recognition and exercise. Or these potentialities may be suppressed and seek outlets in ways unfitted to serve either the function or the community of individual interchange. Even members of a single family in their capacity of parents and children can be reduced to serving the several functions of the family in such a way that the wider interests and potentialities of the individual members are ignored and not allowed to develop.

The consumers in an industrial society may conduct their lives as though their existence had no other purpose than to consume goods and services. The economists and the industrialists in such a society may treat everyone as having the function of consuming what is produced so that prosperity can continue, unemployment be avoided, profits increase and the power of the industrial system be magnified. Rivalry with some other system, such as communism, might intensify this development of specialized function to the exclusion of individuality.

The point of all this is to show that throughout the five thousand years since the rise of the city, power has been increased primarily by subordinating individuals to the functions of a social system, and this development has culminated in the Western civilization of our day. Perhaps in many cases there was no other way to increase the power of the system except by analyzing the undertaking into clearly defined functions and then allocating individuals and groups to these functions, with conditions enforced whereby these individuals and groups give their whole lives to these functions with little consideration for any other potential of human individuality. This is the way, in general, that civilization has succeeded in magnifying power.

The horror and cruelty that has played so large a part in the story of civilization is due in part to this reduction of individuals to functions of a system. In order to make the system operate effectively, individuals reduced to functions drive themselves and are driven in disregard of their human individuality. When the individual thus reduced to a function deviates from the demand of the function assigned, that person is killed, tortured or otherwise mistreated because the function must be served, not the individual human being. When two opposing systems fight one another, the individual members of the opposing system are not viewed as human beings. They are functions of the system which must be destroyed and so are destroyed with the system.

Christianity has often been accepted and lived as a system of belief and practice while individuals belonging to this system have been treated as having little other value save as functional members of this system. Consequently when individuals deviated from the demands of this system, they were tortured, burned to death or otherwise killed without mercy, the killers doing this with a profound sense of moral righteousness in so doing because Christianity as a system of belief and practice must be sustained and its power over the individual and over society increased. Tens of thousands of so-called witches, sorcerers, heretics and other foes of the system have been slaughtered, maimed, cast off by friends and relatives, dying in utter loneliness, often believing themselves to be forsaken by God as well as by humanity. This is the consequence of identifying Christ with Christianity when Christianity is a system of belief and practice reducing its members to the functions of the system in order that the system can have the power to control human lives, to order society and direct the course of history.

This reference to Christianity as a system of belief and practice is not intended to suggest that Christianity has been worse than other systems. Rather many other systems, as previous reference to Nazis indicated, have been worse. Any system whatsoever, religious or otherwise, becomes an evil when it excludes or reduces to a minimum the kind of interchange revealed to be the presence of God in the fellowship of Christ wherein the whole individual is recognized and nurtured by concern for his or her individuality.

Also it is not here intended to suggest that human life can dispense with systems. Religious systems, political systems, economic systems and many other systems are necessary to human existence. In addition, individuals must maintain these systems by serving as functional members of them. Functional interchange is necessary to sustain human society and all the values society can carry. The problem is not to eliminate functional interchange; the problem is to make it serve individual interchange.

Thousands of years of civilization have endowed us with a vast increase in the instruments of power designed for functional interchange. It has not endowed us with nearly so much understanding and appreciation of the ways and means for providing conditions under which individuals can recognize one another in wholeness and bring the resources of individuality into action beyond the limits required for the performance of assigned functions. By reason of the accumulated instruments of power, both the human individual and the subhuman world can be remade and fitted to serve the functions of the system; but in this process the wholeness of individuality in community can be lost. When a civilization follows this line of development, the more dominant, all-inclusive and powerful the system, the less likely it is that individuals will have the resources out of which can arise the correcting and transforming insights needed to save the system when such correction is required to meet new conditions. The very power and efficiency of the system in reducing individuals to its service deprive them of resources of individuality independent of the system. But precisely these resources are required to generate insights leading to required changes when the system begins to drive toward its own destruction.

Here we see the fatal weakness and cause of downfall of every civilization which for the sake of power magnifies functional interchange to the neglect of individual interchange. Put in theological language, this is the judgment of God upon civilization when it develops in this way. It is revealed to be the judgment of God in Christ because in Christ the nurture of wholeness is the chief concern.

There are two very different standards by which any culture, civilization or social system can be judged. One is internal to it, the other transcendent. The transcendent standard is not confined to any culture or any system. It is not confined to any but it is internal to all.

The internal standard (but not the transcendent) judges the culture or other system in terms of its efficiency as a coherent working order. By this standard a proposed course of action is judged better or worse, right or wrong, by whether or not it upholds the coherence and mutual support of all the other activities in the established order. Such a standard for judging better and worse is called relative because it is relative to the culture under consideration and does not apply to any other culture. The philosophy teaching that no standard should be applied to any culture except one meeting the internal demands of that culture is called relativism. This view that all valid standards are relative to the culture or social system, and that it is wrong to apply any standard to the culture which does not meet the internal demands of the system, is widely held today among philosophers, social scientists and educated people generally.

A serious error is made when one claims that all standards and all values are relative to the culture. The argument throughout this chapter has been directed not only to showing the error of this view but also to demonstrating that this way of judging better and worse when it is the only standard used, must inevitably lead to disaster. The practice of using such a standard and excluding every other has led to the downfall of every civilization and today is dragging us down. In the past there was always a way for the human race to return from the disasters of this practice because the whole human race was never before involved in any one civilization and power was limited. Today the consequences of relativism will be much more serious.

What is this other standard for judging good and evil, which is not relative but absolute, which is not limited to any culture or system into which the whole human race might be drawn and in which all individuals might conceivably be reduced to assigned functions so completely that all would be content to live their lives within the confines of the functions assigned to them provided that they had all their biological desires satisfied and were entertained lavishly with fanciful and sensuous entertainment? What is this other standard transcendent to, and critical of, every possible system that can ever be achieved or imagined?

We have already answered this question many times. This standard can be stated first in the form of a moral command, then in the form of a religious command. The moral command is this: Always act, so far as possible, to provide conditions most favorable for that kind of interchange which creates concern for the wholeness of each individual involved and thereby fosters the development of the constructive resources of individuality beyond the confines of any function in any system. The religious command is like unto it: Commit yourself, body and mind, with the wholeness of your being, to what operates in the interchange creating concern for wholeness in one another and nurturing the potentialities of this wholeness. This command, both moral and religious, combined into one can be stated thus: Thus shalt love the Lord thy God with heart and mind and soul and body, and thy neighbor as thyself.

The matter can be stated in other words by saying that no system can ever satisfy the demands of human individuality in its wholeness because this wholeness is always breaking free of the established system and reaching after wider ranges of good to be appreciated and evils to be distinguished, structures to be known and technologies to control these structures. All this requires more or less continuous transformation of every system, not merely to make it more efficient, but to remake it so that it opens the way for this expansive development of human personality, for human culture and for the fuller realization of human destiny.

This does not mean that systems in themselves are evil nor does it mean that we can disregard the standards internal to the systems by which their functions and their efficiency can be judged. These are necessary but they should be subordinate to the absolute standard.

Human beings, to the measure that their individual wholeness is not fractured, are made not for any system, organization, civilization or culture except as these are designed to serve something on beyond them. So long as human beings are confined to any system, they are caught as in a prison. Since human potentiality always transcends the limits of any system, it has become popular to say that humans are made for Transcendence. But "Transcendence" is often conceived as entirely negative in its meaning. In such case it means what is on beyond whatever may be under consideration; but "being beyond" tells us nothing about what it is. Attaching a capital letter to the word adds nothing any more definite. We are made for transcendence provided that we supplement this negative statement with the further specification that we are made for Christ when Christ means what creatively transforms the human mind, including our imagination, so that we can comprehend and evaluate what we could not before. In Christ this kind of transformation can go on indefinitely. This is transcendence but with some positive information attached to the word.

What transforms us after the manner mentioned cannot be any ideal because ideals are what the human imagination at any one time is able to comprehend concerning ideal possibility. This limitation in our comprehension of ideal possibility is what must be overcome and in Christ it is, progressively, when required conditions are present. For this reason no ideal can be the absolute standard, not even the ideals said to be contained in the teaching of Jesus. The ultimate standard can be nothing other than the demands of the living Christ in our midst.

As said before, this kind of interchange calls for continuous and intensive study by all the relevant sciences, so that we can better understand its demands. This study by the sciences will develop a language about Christ different from the language of devotion. It will be an objective and universal language so that people in different cultures and living in civilizations arising in the "post-Christian era" can commit themselves to this saving event. This kind of language and this kind of knowledge about Christ are needed in our time as they were never needed before.

The language of traditional Christianity is the language of one system; but Christ, we repeat, cannot be confined to any one system. We who live in the traditional system of Christianity must have the devotional language of that system. But people who live in a very different system must have the devotional language fitted to that system. People living in all these different system, cultures and traditions, should be able to commit themselves to the saving and transforming event which occurs when required conditions are present. On this account we need to have two kinds of language to refer to Christ. We need the objective and universal language to communicate about this saving power across the barrier of diverse cultures and ages. But we must also have the devotional language suited to our own age and culture.

The argument of this chapter has been to show that Christ, and the individual committed to Christ, cannot be confined to any system. That includes the system called Christianity. To be sure, if Christianity means commitment to Christ, then indeed we cannot get beyond that. But without the knowledge provided by science and without its language, we cannot speak and we cannot recognize the living Christ outside our devotional language and rituals of commitment. We have come to the time when we must be able to transcend these limitations, and science provides the means for doing this.

This difference in the two ways of approaching Christ is analogous to the two ways of approaching our child or friend or husband or wife or other person whom we love with devotion and self-giving. If we are to be helpful in providing conditions favorable for their well-being, we must have objective, empirical knowledge to deal with their health, if that is the difficulty, or to deal with financial troubles, or political or whatever may be in the conditions of their existence which need to be provided or changed. This kind of knowledge and this kind of language we must have if we are faithful to our commitment as husband or wife or parent or friend.

But the other approach is equally important, and in this other approach scientific knowledge and scientific language cannot help us except by providing favorable conditions. In this other approach we respond with wholeness of being to the wholeness of being in the other; and for this there is not descriptive language and never can be, because all descriptive language refers to abstractions, never to the concrete wholeness and depth of unique individuality.

There is a second need for the objective knowledge and language of science to supplement that of devotion. Devotional language and the self-giving of commitment can be used entirely apart from the actual being of Christ; and the individual who has thus strayed from Christ may never discover this tragic error if there is no objective descriptive language subject to empirical test by which to demonstrate the error and show the way back.

This need for science to supplement prayer and ritual, music and poetry and the many forms of religious symbolism, becomes most imperative in the time of maturity. This is so because all the cultures and peoples of the world must be able to use the devotional language rising out of their diverse histories while at the same time they must commit themselves to what creates a community including us all; and it must be a community of concern for the wholeness of the individual. Otherwise we cannot be saved from either one of two evils. One of these evils is annihilation; the other is the degradation of individuals to button pushing automatons serving the specialized functions of a planetary social system managed by a ruling group with unlimited power.

If we are to be saved from this fate in the age of maturity, science must be applied to the service of Christ to supplement the poetry, the music, the ritual and the private practice of religious commitment.

CHAPTER VI
WORLD COMMUNITY

Any considerable change in the social order of any people on earth today makes a difference to all other people. As soon as such a change begins, or seems imminent, the attention of the whole world is immediately focused on that spot. All nations and all large associations recognize that they have common problems. If community is defined as this kind of interdependence and this interest in one another, then a world community now exists. But in this community the major divisions hate and fear one another. Opposing forms of society are unable to trust any commitment made by the other. They constantly threaten war to the point of mutual annihilation, employ spies and promote hidden designs intended to weaken and, if possible, eliminate one another. This is, of course, not the kind of community we want, and it cannot continue indefinitely. It will either destroy itself or change into a different kind of world society.

Another kind of community is often dreamed—and in small groups it can be attained. It is one sustained by the sharing of common interests due either to a single unifying tradition or to some purpose which all seek to achieve cooperatively. No complex community can rest on this base when it is made up of millions of people with diverse and opposing interests, with different histories and mentalities. Obviously no world community can be an association of like-minded people such as this. Common interests and unifying purposes enter into large communities at times and to varying degrees and extents. But these are not pervasive enough nor strong enough to uphold the community of New York or the United States or the alliance of Western democracies, much less the community of all nations and peoples.

This brings us to the third kind of community, the most common kind. Here people are bound together by institutions which direct the consequences of behavior in such a way that when individuals or diverse groups seek what is beneficial to themselves, the consequences of their action automatically serve the interests of other members of the community. For example, when the institution of public education supports the community, it is of such sort that when the individual or local group seeks the kind of education that is personally beneficial, the consequence is beneficial to the entire society also. The same is true of industry and the market. The bonds of union supporting the community are strong to the measure that producing, buying and selling are beneficial to all concerned even when the individual and local group produces or buys or sells in a way to serve the interests of those so engaged regardless of any good will they may have for the other parties involved. The family helps to hold the community together when children reared to satisfy the affection and pride of the parents become serviceable to the large community by reason of this rearing. The government serves the community if it is so organized that ambitious persons seeking high office for prestige and power must do what serves the community in order to win prestige and exercise power. A government not so organized does not serve the large community even when people in high office seek to do so with sacrificial devotion.

Of course good will, idealism and devotion to the common good always add strength and virtue to any community. But no ruling group, even though its members should love others as themselves, can ever be wise or powerful enough to uphold a world community. To have a community of many diverse peoples, institutions must be so ordered as to channel the consequences of individual behavior in ways that serve the entire community, even when the individual has no desire to help others. The best of people are at times unconcerned, if not hostile, to the good of others.

There is every reason to believe that we have today sufficient experience, skill, and technology to establish institutions fit to channel the consequences of behavior in a way to support a world community. Furthermore, we are striving as never before to establish such institutions. There is one great obstacle that stands in the way, however. Two opposing groups approximately equal in power are each striving to create world community but each wants a different kind of social system, i.e., one promotes communism and the other Western democracy. Each does everything in its power to prevent the other from bringing the world into the kind of community sought by the opposing party. This blocks the way to the formation of any kind of comprehensive social system which might unite the world.

Thus far the communists have been more aggressive in seeking world community. Indeed communism was designed from the very start to bring the whole world under its control, and that has been the ruling purpose of its leaders all the time. While the Western world by way of Christian missionaries and other groups has also sought world community, the powerful agencies of government and industry were not thrown fully into this endeavor until the danger of the world's going communist made the problem of world community a major concern for the organized might of the Western world. However, even since this problem has come to dominate the minds and plans of the West, it has been treated more as a matter of protection rather than aggression. The major question has been how to stop Communism rather than how to create a world community. The political and economic system of the West was not originally planned for world community while the communist system was. The ruling purpose of the political and industrial leaders of the West was to serve their own people rather than to bring the world into a single system, whereas the ruling purpose of the political leaders of communism has always been to form such a world-wide order.

Under these conditions it seems that a world community is inevitable if a World War does not intervene. But what kind of World Community? Will it be communist or will it be that of Western democracy? Actually, however, these questions represent a totally false notion of the likely outcome. We have no reason to think that communism and Western democracy are the only ways in which the world might become a single community. In fact, all the evidence indicates that the world community will not be either that of communism or that of Western democracy.

People who think that the world community must either be controlled by communism or by Western democracy labor under the illusion that change does not occur in the social orders prevailing at any one time in history; and that the ideals of social order in the minds of people do not change. Both communism as it is in fact and in ideal, and Western democracy as it is in fact and ideal, are transitory phenomena in history, as transitory as was the city state. In fact, in an age of accelerated change, communism and Western democracy will pass off the scene much more swiftly than did the ancient empires before the city state arose. It is impossible that these two social systems of our time should continue as long as did the ancient political system of China, because our social order rides the back of a technology that changes its character in a decade more than ancient technologies changed in centuries. What is even more important, the political systems of our time are much more deeply involved in operating the industrial technology than the political systems in the past were involved in the peasant agriculture that sustained them. About the only connection the political systems of the ancient world had with peasant agriculture was to collect the taxes and uphold the system of irrigation. Often they did not even do the second. In China the local landlords with the peasants produced whatever was required to support the social order while the government limited itself very much to the collection of taxes.

Today the political order and the industrial technology are so intimately intertwined that one can predict with considerable assurance that the prevailing political system will assume whatever form it must to keep the industrial technology producing enough wealth to prevail over any alternative system. The people of the world will choose whatever political and industrial system that can create the most power in the form of wealth, political efficiency and loyal devotion of the people. These three combined into one system will prevail over all other kinds of social order either because all people will want to have it for themselves or, if they do not choose it, will not be able to resist the dominance of its control.

This is true and if industrial technology is changing its character with ever increasing acceleration, the conclusion seems to be obvious. The present social systems, both those that go by the name of communism and those that go by the name of Western democracy, will undergo whatever change they must to operate the industrial technology in a way to achieve the synthesis of the three components of social power just mentioned, namely, wealth, political efficiency and loyalty of the people. Therefore, the world community will have a social order different both from Communism and from what now prevails in the West. To say that one or the other in the form it now exists must win over the opponent is to totally misunderstand the major social problem of our time. When it is understood, however, a further question arises: What is the task and responsibility of those committed to the Christian faith when confronting this problem? According to the interpretation of faith here given, that question can be reworded thus: What is the task and responsibility for world community on the part of those who give first priority to the kind of interchange creating communion and wholeness of being?

According to what has already been said, no world community can be based on universal love nor on communion of each with all nor on our belonging to a universal family, excellent as these are to the measure they can be cultivated. Neither does Christian faith demand that we strive above all to make Western democracy prevail over communism. This is not the way in which world community can be achieved. If the road to world community is not by way of our belonging to a universal family and not by way of Western democracy, then what is it? There is a road leading to world community if it is faithfully followed; and none are so well equipped to follow it and lead the way as those who are committed to the kind of interchange just mentioned.

First of all, let us be clear on one point already stated which must be emphasized because controversies now raging have greatly obscured it. One hundred years from now Communism will not exist if the word "Communism" is defined as the kind of government, economy, habits, customs and mentality now existing in Russia and China, or the Utopia pictured by Karl Marx. One hundred years from now Western democracy will not exist if the word means the kind of government, economy, customs, habits and mentality now existing in the Western world. The social order existing in the West one hundred years from now will be even more different from what it is today than it now differs from what it was one hundred years ago, at the time of the Civil War. The difference will be greater because social change is more rapid. Not only is social change rapid, but it cannot be stopped so long as modern technology continues to undergo revolutionary change. Of course, technology may not continue to undergo revolution after revolution. We hope it does not; we hope that in time it will attain stability so that the energies of people may turn to other kinds of social development. But within the near future, with automation and other radical changes gaining ground, there is no prospect that these revolutions will cease. Since the entire social order is woven into modern technology, these revolutions will drag the social order after them.

The conclusion from this is what was previously stated: The road to world community is not by way of Western democracy and not by way of communism. Therefore, they who seek world community intelligently will not seek it by either of these routes. The road to world community is by way of that social order which can most effectively operate modern scientific technology.

Great social changes such as we are now considering do not come by way of the plans and purposes of people *unless* these plans and purposes are shaped to serve underlying social processes. Hence, intelligent action should search out the social developments which move in the direction desired and work with them while opposing counter developments. For this reason we point to the most powerful social process shaping the social order and the course of history today—the development of modern scientific technology.

In accord with this general principle that should guide social action, we should note that democracy cannot be introduced where the underlying social process does not support it; nor can a dictatorship be established unless social conditions favor it.

We can now state the distinctive responsibility for world community which rests upon those who are committed to the divine creativity in Christ. It is to do what no others are able to do. It is to search out and promote those social developments that do not support Western democracy and do not support communism but which operate to transform both. These developments operate to create a society fitted to use the full power of scientific technology in the production of wealth with minimum labor and with maximum devotion to the goals of that social order. Only they can do this who serve Christ first and who recognize that the divine creativity cannot be confined to any social system or its ideals. People not thus committed are bound to serve either Western democracy with its ideals, or communism with its ideals, or some other social system commanding their loyalty. Being thus bound they cannot serve developments that would undermine and transform every system now existing. This bondage is intensified when the systems are opposed in bitter conflict because this conflict makes each side identify all good with its system and all evil with the opposing one.

The chief obstacle to world community is the inability of people to rise above the raging conflict sufficiently to discern the road leading to world community when this road runs counter to the ideals of both the conflicting parties. They who seek above all to promote Western democracy cannot promote developments that would change Western democracy in any radical way. They who seek above all to promote communism cannot promote developments that would change communism in any radical manner. Yet the only social developments leading to world community will change both these social systems.

There is a commitment of faith that saves us from passionate partisanship for an existing order. It is not neutrality (when neutrality means uncommitted), it is a faith as passionately committed as any of those who are engaged in the conflict of one system against the other. But its commitment is not to any social system, or to some transcendent ideal or supernatural order. It is commitment to something actually operative in society, in history and in the life of every person, a commitment to the divine creativity which transforms every social order, every ideal and every organization of personality. In this way commitment to Christ transcends the social conflicts, the social systems, and the ideals that bind and limit and blind so that people cannot see the road to a better world. But this transcendence is not by commitment to something outside of this world. It is commitment to what operates in this world.

The social developments here to be considered that will bring on world community if adequately promoted are not in themselves the divine creativity, although the divine creativity also works to this end. But commitment to the divine creativity liberates individuals from bondage to the conflicting systems and their ideals. Being thus liberated they can recognize the significance of developments that undermine and transform the established systems and commonly accepted ideals. Being committed to what transcends the conflict, they can promote social developments that lead to world community when these run counter to the goals of both the conflicting parties. This is the vocation of those committed to Christ when great conflicts rage between divisions of humanity.

This explains the statement previously made. The only people well equipped to work with the social processes leading to world community are those who are ultimately committed not to Western democracy and not to communism. Neither are they neutral because they are passionately committed to the kind of interchange which creates communion among people. They have the vision and the devotion to promote those social processes which can lead to world community by transforming both opposing systems of social order now in bitter conflict. Such being the case, the primary task and responsibility of those committed to Christ stands clear. It is to search out those social processes of the sort mentioned and work to promote them above all else and do this with all the power of their commitment.

With this understanding of the responsibility resting on those who share faith in Christ, let us examine a little further the social processes which can bring on world community if promoted by devoted endeavor, providing conditions favorable for their development.

As said before, the one over-riding component to be examined in this context is the scientific technology which the United States and Russia are developing and which they are extending to all the rest of the world. This technology is the same in Russia as it is in the United States; and it will continue to be the same because as soon as either discovers and adopts a new method or a new machine to increase the power of the technology, the other does much the same, either by taking over what the other has discovered or by directing research to find out what it is and how to do it.

Developing the same powerful technology both in the Western world and in the communist countries will eventually produce in both countries very much the same kind of economic and political system. That economic and political system will prevail which can most fully exercise the power of this technology to produce wealth and at the same time win the devotion and loyalty of the people. The economic and political leaders of these two divisions of humanity fully recognize this fact and are bending every resource and energy to develop the system which can use this scientifically developed technology most effectively. This results, contrary to the intention of the leaders, in developing in both East and West the same kind of economic and political order. The peoples concerned are striving to keep themselves as different from one another and as opposed to one another as possible. But the consequence of seeking the kind of social order best fitted to operate the power of modern scientific technology is a process of social change producing the same kind of political and economic order wherever this technology is effectively used.

This does not mean that all parts of the world will have the same culture in all respects. Not every form of cultural development is given over to the control of productive technology. At present it is true that the intense rivalry between the two drives both to subordinate all branches of culture to the quest for maximum power in order to prevail over the other. But when the kind of system is established in both parts of the world which is best fitted to make use of the power of industrial technology, so that this problem is practically solved and there is no longer any marked difference in the two systems of power, other forms of culture can develop which are not subordinated to this one function of operating the technology. What these other forms of cultural development might be, when released from the domination of the technology, was explained in previous chapters. When thus released, the unique cultural developments rising out of diverse histories and mentalities of the different peoples can arise.

Let us first look at Russia to see how it is being transformed by this struggle to achieve maximum power through the development of a political and economic system best adapted to actualize the potentialities of scientific industrial technology. The first thing to note is the breakdown of tyranny in Russia, not because the dictators want to relinquish centralized control, but because the extreme dictatorship developed under Stalin is unfit to operate the developing system of power. Initiative, imagination, responsibility and authority had to be distributed more widely to keep the wheels turning. They were becoming clogged with red tape and grinding toward a stop. The necessity for wider distribution of power and authority is quite obvious in a highly industrialized country including a wide expanse of territory and millions of people of diversified culture. It could not be avoided if Russia was not to fall behind in the race for power. This breakdown of tyranny and this wider distribution of power are bound to continue as industrialization goes on, requiring not only more technical training on the part of greater numbers of people but requiring also wider distribution of power, authority and ability to win the loyalty and cooperation of diverse peoples living in remote regions and with very different histories. This is a compulsion under the necessities of power which no dictator can resist and still keep a place of eminence in world affairs.

Another social process which breaks down tyranny in Russia and changes the entire social system, whether or not the governing body so wishes, is the universal extension and intensity of education. It has been said that this education is largely technical and that technicians do not concern themselves with social problems beyond the demands of their own special competence. While it is true that technical training is greatly emphasized in Russia, the social order would break down if people were not also educated to use the arts of organization, administration, persuasion and inspiration. People who read as the Russians are doing, who are having an increasing amount of leisure and discussion, must be persuaded; and the persuasion must appeal to educated minds. Technicians who are nothing but technicians cannot do this. It requires cultural education and this education must be both intensive and extensive.

Another aspect of the social process transforming Russia is the gradual deliverance from the clutch of the Czars. For centuries Russia had been under the control of an absolute monarchy; and before that under the rule of the Tartars. At the time of the revolution in 1917, it would have been impossible to form anything like a democracy. The great mass of the peasantry could neither read nor write and had no experience in managing affairs beyond the simple local community. All governmental officials and persons in control of the social system had training and experience fitted only to operate under a system of centralized control like that of the Czars. Only after a generation of indoctrination with the system and goals of the new regime could the general public take part in the administration of affairs. Now a second generation of this sort has arisen and is taking far more part in shaping the social system of Russia than did the mass of people under the Czars. The Russian people must still cast off the mentality developed under the dictatorship of Stalin, and this they are doing.

Two or three other factors should be mentioned that intensified the communist dictatorship in Russia but which are now being cast off. These are further facets in that total process now transforming the social system of Russia beyond the control of the rulers except as they shape their plans and purposes in adaptation to it.

The immediate consequence of a radical revolution, such as that of 1917 in Russia, is inevitably either a dictatorship or anarchy or both. In Russia it was both. This revolution was not merely a change in government such as occurred in the American revolution. Instead it was a change in the whole social structure. Also when property, power and prestige are violently taken from those who previously possessed them, the dispossessed are bound to struggle by way of counter-revolution to regain their wealth and privilege. Only a military organization of society, hence a dictatorship, can resist the counter-revolution with its hidden spies and saboteurs, its insurrections and its armed attack. All this happened in Russia. But all this is now history. The social system has become stabilized. Habits, customs and expectations of the people have been conformed to the new order. The generation of the dispossessed has either died or passed the age and opportunity when attempt at recovery could make sense. Hence the conditions supporting dictatorship in Russia are no longer applicable.

Another condition which made for dictatorship in Russia was fear of attack from foreign countries. Russia was invaded by foreign armies during the early years after the revolution. It was invaded again by Germany and suffered more than any other country in the second world war. It is now ringed with planes and rockets ready to hurl destruction at a moment's notice. The tension is maintained as every day American planes with missiles start toward Russia in the direction of the north pole and if given the signal would proceed to drop their bombs on the Russian people.

This constant fear of attack has supported the dictatorship in Russia just as such danger tends to do with any people because a centralized, military organization of society is the only way to keep in readiness to meet the sudden onslaught of an enemy. But even this condition is relaxing in Russia for the same reason that it does not drive America into a dictatorship. Today the Russian people believe they have such power of retaliation that an attack is not likely.

Rapid industrialization without accumulated capital is another development that has supported dictatorship in Russia and will do so with any people if they do not get sufficient capital from external sources. Without available capital the resources for rapid industrialization must be squeezed out of the people. Also when industrialization is very rapid, it must be forced because the habits, the skills and the established way of life are not adapted to it. The Russian leaders correctly believed that they could not protect themselves against attack from Germany or other countries if they did not industrialize with breakneck speed. If they had not industrialized to the point they did, they would not have been able to drive back the German army. Neither could they have done it without American and other foreign help; but help from foreign sources cannot save any country if it does not have resources and organization to use this help along with sufficient power of its own.

Russia is still undergoing rapid industrialization, but the demand now is the reverse of what it was in the early days. Today Russia has accumulated capital. Also today the habits, customs, skills and expectations of the people are adapted to the process of rapid industrialization as they were not in the beginning, so that coercion is not needed as it was when this adaptation was lacking. Rather, as previously stated, the reverse of centralized control and coercion are required when a high level of industrialization is attained with accumulated capital under conditions now prevailing in Russia.

This process of decentralization going on in Russia is forced by the requirements of modern scientific technology and the struggle for power. It is transforming the social system, not necessarily according to the plans of the rulers, but under the dictates of the development here sketched: intensive education; historical casting off of the mentality developed under the Czars; the rise of a generation no longer living in the shadow of the revolution under Lenin and coming out from the shadow of Stalin; the ability to resist attack by other means than continuous military organization of society; and a level of industrialization where centralized control can no longer make the wheels turn effectively.

This transformation going on in Russia does not mean that Russia will develop the kind of democracy seen in America and in Europe. But neither shall America and Europe continue to have this kind of social order. Our own social system is rapidly undergoing transformation. Indeed the change is so rapid that in many cases it is not recognized. We retain the old names and apply them to an order which no longer conforms to what these names are supposed to designate. Our society is becoming more centralized as Russia is becoming more decentralized. Thus the two societies are approaching one another from opposite directions and will continue to do so until they become very much alike in respect to that sector of the social system which operates the science and technology of power. This we cannot avoid, no matter how much we denounce one another as though the opposing system represented the extreme of evil in contrast to our own virtue. Forty years of propaganda have produced a mental attitude that will not be easy to overcome. This bitter antagonism calls for the ministry of an ultimate commitment, not to one side or to the other, but to the kind of interchange creating insight whereby one is able to see the common interest and the common good of both sides. This is what commitment to God as revealed in Christ will do in those who are faithful to this commitment.

This shows a further relation of science to the Christian religion when "Christian religion" is understood to be commitment to Christ and not merely commitment to Western culture. When scientific research and its application to technology become the all-dominant power shaping the order of society and the course of history, great conflicts are created because cultures and social systems previously isolated must now live in intimate connection with one another. It is the mission of the Christian faith in such a time to rise above these conflicts, not by way of being aloof and unconcerned, but by being passionately concerned for the kind of interchange creating appreciative understanding and communion among people.

With this understanding of Christian faith in its relation to the problem of world community in mind, let us now turn to an examination of the way American society is being changed by the struggle to control and operate the power of modern technology in competition with Russia.

In the United States the central government is taking over increasing responsibility for education and for the health of the people; for preventing unemployment, economic depression and inflation; for care of the aged, the unemployed and the disabled; for conservation of natural resources and development of new resources such as atomic energy; for regulation of wages, labor disputes, labor unions and employment practices. This list, of course, might be considerably lengthened. Centralization is done not because officials of government want to extend the powers of government and not because the people generally want to magnify its power. It is done because there seems to be no other way to exercise to the full limit the potential power of our scientific technology.

Another change is occurring which is scarcely recognized. Private property is disappearing in the form in which it once existed. Big industries are no longer owned by individuals with full power to dispose of them; they are owned in fragmented form by great numbers of individuals, and these owners have little power over the management of the industries. Even homes and cars and other property used by the individual are not owned by the individual except in small part since they are bought by installment, by mortgages and other devices which prevent the individual from full ownership and right of disposal. Ownership of property, both personal and corporate, is being taken over by insurance companies, mutual funds, banks, credit unions, mortgage companies and the like. Even private income is not fully controlled by the individual since it is heavily and progressively taxed and there is much reason to believe that the proportion of income paid in taxes will increase.

These changes in our social system are here recorded neither with praise nor with blame. They are mentioned to indicate a social process which apparently cannot be stopped because it is required by the scientific technology which produces our wealth, supports our culture and gives us the power to protect ourselves and play our part in the conduct of international affairs.

The social process transforming American and European society is due to the same scientific technology that causes changes in Russia. Both social systems are rapidly becoming different from what they were in the recent past and both are becoming more like one another. The same technology is spreading to all the peoples of the earth. It will have the same transforming power upon all. It will establish the base for a world community in which all people can live together cooperatively. As said before, this does not mean harmony and good will over all. It does mean the possibility of establishing institutions fit to channel the consequences of self-interested action in a way to serve the society generally. It means also that the problems and difficulties arising will not always be those of communism versus Western democracy. Neither will they be those of Western democracy by itself nor communism by itself because these two kinds of society will both be "buried" by the kind of social system shaped to meet the demands of what science discovers insofar as these discoveries can be applied to the conduct of human life.

One of the imperative demands of science which even now breaks through the restrictions imposed by the opposing governments is free, full and open interchange of knowledge, methods and theories among the scientists of different countries. International conferences of scientists gather to read papers and confer with one another. The Russian scientists and those of the West discuss freely what they know and what they seek and what they have done. It is to the interest of every country to promote this kind of interchange because science cannot render its proper service to any country if this exchange of ideas is hindered.

This interchange among scientists works at a different level from the kind identified with Christ. Science deals with abstractions most remote from problems involving the whole personality with all its interests. Commitment of faith in Christ involves the whole personality more fully than any other undertaking. But these two kinds of interchange, extremely different as they are, can help one another if they recognize their common concern for interchange and if commitment to science and commitment to Christ can be purged of irrelevant demands which have caused conflict or indifference between them. The cosmic theories of science do not give us knowledge of God, but neither do the cosmic theories of religion. Neither do the ontological and metaphysical speculations of philosophy which at various times have developed either in support of prevalent scientific theories or religious doctrines. These have caused the conflicts between science and religion or, in other cases, mutual exclusion from any cooperative endeavor. But these are truly irrelevant to the two commitments. This cooperation between commitment to science and commitment to Christ is urgently needed as we undergo world-wide transformation of the order of human existence under the coercion of science and technology driving toward world community in the face of fear, hate and mistrust. Under these conditions science and faith need one another and can work together with great help one to the other if they recognize their common interest and are purged of those ingredients which have alienated them.

If science and faith are to join in common cause, faith must be purged of beliefs which go beyond the evidence. As John Edward Carnell in his defense of orthodoxy states: "To believe beyond the evidence—what is this but to believe what may not be true." Instead of belief in cosmic theory, ontology and metaphysics held over from times before modern science arose, faith should be commitment to what operates to transform people in the way repeatedly mentioned. This involves belief to be sure, but the beliefs about what conditions are most favorable for this transformation to occur can be treated as tools to guide conduct in providing these conditions. These tools, like any others, can be cast off for better ones whenever better ones are available. They do not involve the basic commitment. The basic commitment can scarcely be doubted—namely, that people do have varying degrees of wholeness and communion with one another and that these do change when conditions change. Not only is this obvious to ordinary experience, but the sciences which study the human being recognize that this is so.

When one says that this transformation occurred in the fellowship of Jesus and is there revealed as God in Christ, one has a belief that can be doubted. Many will deny and do deny this affirmation about Christ. Neither do the sciences provide any evidence to support this claim. This reference to Christ is a distinctively Christian religious doctrine arising out of a fellowship of faith. This should be fully acknowledged. But this commitment of faith to creative interchange has other roots also which can be supported by what we know about human personality in social relations. The person of faith can stand on this ground with these roots and join with the sciences.

Let us now consider another danger which presents itself when we consider the problem of world community. Thus far we have been chiefly concerned with the difficulty arising out of the conflict between the two parts of the world having greatest power. Even if this conflict should be reduced and even if the necessities of operating the same technology bring about an overall social system much the same in both countries, still a major problem would remain. It can be expressed in a question such as this: What kind of a world community would this be? It might be a mechanized system suppressing individuality, imagination and initiative, reducing us all to functional members of a system without capacity or opportunity to interchange after the manner identified with Christ.

No world-wide system can operate without a bureaucracy. Indeed no complex and far reaching national system can do without one. The word "bureaucracy" has taken on an evil connotation as though it were a nuisance to be cast off. No complex social system can dispense with an organization of many persons assigned to routine and specialized kinds of work necessary to keep the system in operation. But a social system operating in this way always carries a danger. The danger is never so great as when it operates smoothly without violent disruptions, demands no reorganization and brings comfort and ease to everyone. The danger in such a system is that it will destroy in us the one thing for which we are supremely fitted, the one thing which makes us uniquely different from all the other animals, giving to the human species a destiny different from every other animal. It is our capacity to expand the range, variety and vividness of appreciative consciousness in the form of love, aesthetic appreciation, comprehensive knowledge, moral aspiration and religious devotion.

If the global society now coming into being should bring peace and

comfort, economic abundance and entertainment, it still might bring down
upon humanity a fate almost as bad as annihilating war. It might take away
the opportunity to develop and exercise imaginative vision and have the
vivid consciousness of joy and suffering. If this reduction of life to routine
performance and biological satisfactions continued long enough, it might
bring on a weariness and disgust that would reduce the zest for living to the
point where the human race would lack sufficient interest to meet the
demands of continued existence. This problem we shall treat in the next
chapter. Preliminary to that we shall here examine what two other books have
to say about the problem of world community. One of these is *The Structure
of Nations and Empires* by Reinhold Niebuhr. The other is *Evolution and
Culture* by Elman R. Service and Marshall D. Sahlins.

Niebuhr rightly sees that the problem of world community is not new,
although it has assumed a radically new form in our time. In some form or
other it has been a matter of central concern since civilization began. The
ancient Asiatic empires sought world dominion. Since at that time people did
not know the dimensions of the world, they often claimed to have achieved
world community. They extended empire as far as their instruments of
control could reach with the methods of transportation and communication,
of conquest and economic production and distribution, then available. Rome
was the last of these.

After Rome three competing centers of power strove to achieve world
community. One was Islamic; another was Greek Orthodox beginning with
Constantine; and the third was directed by the Roman Catholic church.
These three checked one another. Also their methods of conquest, of social
control and knowledge of the world were limited so that, even though they
aspired to world dominion, they could not attain it.

At the close of the Middle Ages new techniques arose—military, political, economic—together with new knowledge and methods of travel and
discovery. These developed to the point where they could no longer be
controlled by the three empires of the Middle Ages, two Christian and one
Islamic. Out of these new vitalities with their newly developed techniques
arose the nation states of modern times. While these were not empires and
were not organized in a way to extend their borders to world dimensions, the
drive toward expanding dominion did not cease. They developed colonial
empires. First Spain led the way, then France, then England.

Niebuhr sees the evil in these colonial empires but he is always eager to
defend the virtue of the people who have the kind of Christian faith akin to
his own. He tries to show that England especially did much good, along with
the evil, by expanding its control toward world dimensions. Three motives,
he says, led these countries, especially England, to establish colonial empires. One motive was missionary, which included as a major force the
missionary endeavor to bring civilization, better morals, economic benefits
and in general a superior way of life to people who, they were convinced,

were much inferior to themselves. The second motive was economic gain for the homeland. The third was "the power and glory" of empire. The great evil resulting from this, Neibuhr rightly sees, was the arrogance of the empire builders, the humiliation of the people they ruled, with consequent hate and rebellion rising in the colonies. This along with other developments combined with two world wars has led to the liberation of most of the colonies.

This brings the story of world community down to the present. What distinguishes our time from any other is a great number of independent national states with the idea of national sovereignty dominating the minds of people so completely that all people who have not attained national statehood are striving passionately to achieve it. This is the one moment in human history when independent national states cover the earth in great part. Is this moment in human history merely transitory, swiftly passing over into some kind of world organization? Or will independent national states with full sovereignty continue indefinitely? Niebuhr thinks they will continue indefinitely, each upholding its sovereignty with modification by means of blocks of internationally organized states. But it seems more likely that an earth encircling technology will bring all societies under its control and the demands of this technology will bring down the independence of national states. However, all this is a matter of degree. Certainly local regions may well have some measure of independence, self-sufficiency and uniqueness of culture due to a language, a tradition and a history peculiar to that region. Also this change from the present condition of world society, distinguished by independent nations, over to a world-wide organization dominated by a unifying and all dominant technology, will not be sudden. No one knows how long it will take for the change to occur. Thus, since the subordination of the sovereign state to the world community is a matter of degree and not absolute, since the time required for this change is not definite, any difference with Niebuhr on this point may be merely a difference in wording and emphasis, although that is not certain.

Niebuhr is chiefly concerned, as is the present writer, with the conflict and competition now occurring between the two great centers of power, Russian and American, and the bearing of this conflict upon the problem of world community. Niebuhr's argument, however, seeks to discount the prospects of world community.

Russia deliberately and professedly and with passionate organization of every resource seeks to create a world community in the form of communism, in which national states will "wither away." This withering away of the state, according to communism, does not mean the disappearance of all social organization and administration. It only means the abolition of that particular kind of organization which the communists define as the state, namely, an organization set up and operated exclusively to enable one class in society to dominate and exploit the other classes. Niebuhr, in his discussion of the utopia at which communism aims, does not make plain this distinction between the state as an agency of domination and exploitation, which will wither away according to the doctrines of communism, and the kind of social organization and administration that will continue in the utopia.

In opposition to Russian communism, the United States and its allies strive to preserve the independence of nations, upholding the sovereignty of each and preserving the status quo as much as possible by the device of "collective security." This "collective security" means the method of international organizations such as the Marshall Plan, NATO, SEATO and others, including the United Nations which the United States uses whenever it can to control international relations.

Niebuhr seeks to show that both the drive of Russian communism to unify the world by means of a utopian ideology, and the effort of the United States to defend the independence and sovereignty of nations by means of collective security and democratic idealism will fail. The Russian endeavor will fail because the utopian ideology is a fraud which becomes more apparent as time lengthens after the 1917 revolution and more force is required to perpetuate the illusion of success. In time the fraud cannot be concealed and the force used in the attempt to conceal it will become self-defeating.

Also, Niebuhr writes: "The pattern of autonomous nationality is so universal that it will finally prove a hazard to the communist imperialism, even though the latter hides its violations of autonomy by ruling subject nations through subservient communist parties."[1]

In the meantime, as Niebuhr rightly sees, the United States is failing in its efforts to stop the spread of communism, and, unless the U.S. changes its methods, it will continue to fail. The United States must accept responsibility for the exercise of its dominant power and must not pretend to operate within the limitations of the United Nations and other international organizations. The hard reality is that weaker nations are controlled and dominated by the stronger and to pretend otherwise is a source of weakness as well as hypocrisy. But we must learn to express our power "in relation to smaller nations by accepting the sovereignty of the nation as the fixed norm of international morality."[2] He cites our treatment of Mexico as a model when we substituted "contracts between owners and producers for the previous right of foreign ownership" in developing the oil resources of that country. We must protect the sovereignty of the several nations while extending our power through all the many forms of international organizations. "The variations in the pattern of international community vary endlessly. But the fixed pattern in all these variations is a combination of dominion and community above the level of the nations and below the level of the community of mankind. It is safe to predict that no future history will annul this

[1] *The Structure of Nations and Empires* by Reinhold Niebuhr, p. 198.
[2] *Ibid.*, p. 198.

pattern though it may produce hitherto unknown variations in the pattern."[3]
Later Niebuhr states, "Perhaps we are fated, for some centuries at least, to
live in a situation in which global community appears to be a necessity
because of the interdependence of nations, but an impossibility because
there are not enough organic forces of cohesion in the global community."[4]

Niebuhr reaches the conclusion that a world community is impossible
and that we should cease the futile and self-defeating efforts to achieve it. We
can have, and we should strive to increase, the various forms of international
organization below the level of world community; but communism presents
an insuperable barrier to any community of mankind: "Russia had already
proved, and was about to prove more unmistakably, that it was informed by a
fanatic creed, which made mutual trust between capitalist and communist
nations impossible, however much we might nerve ourselves to trust them.
For the organic and given facts of the international situation are more
powerful than a quasi-constitutional system. In a tragic age we have come
upon one of the constant factors in the international situation which men
have tried desperately to obscure in their desire for peace. Constitutional
authority alone cannot create community, either on the national or international level."[5]

Niebuhr is chiefly concerned with the communist attempt to bring all
peoples under the control of a single system of world order. He compares it
to all the past attempts at world dominion. All these attempts of Asiatic
empires and those of the Middle Ages are alike in one respect—they are all
guilty of the sin which is the central theme of all of Niebuhr's writings. It is
the sin of falsely identifying the actual social system and moral practice with
some transcendent order, either religious or secular, thereby winning an
unjustified prestige, a misdirected devotion and often a blind fanaticism of
effort. The ancient empire either identified the ruler with God or with God's
chosen and anointed representative on earth. With Stoicism the Roman
Empire identified itself with a cosmic order. Islam claimed to be the bearer
of God's almighty will. The Greek Orthodox beginning with Constantine
made its rulers semi-divine and holy. The Roman Catholic church identified
itself with the City of God, Augustine himself having opened the way for this
presumptive error (although, according to Niebuhr, Augustine added
qualifications which were later ignored).

So communism today identifies itself with a law of history operating to
achieve utopia. This ideology of communism is its driving power, according
to Niebuhr, generating fanaticism with all its cruelties together with incapacity for self-criticism; "Man inevitably forgets his creaturely finiteness and
pretends to a transcendent and universally valid perspective upon common

[3]*Ibid.*, p. 200.
[4]*Ibid.*, p. 266.
[5]*Ibid.*, p. 265.

problems which is beyond the capacity of mortal man."[6] The vision of a perfect and universal community is the very substance of religion, according to Niebuhr, provided that one truth is not forgotten, which Niebuhr reiterates again and again: "only at the end of history and not within history" can the universal and perfect community be attained. Niebuhr goes on to state: "The negative relevance of such a vision is of course obvious. It is a source of criticism for all the kingdoms of the world."[7]

The communists are guilty of seeking this perfect and universal community in history and not beyond history. From this flows all the evil of communism when equipped with the power provided by Lenin's genius in organizing a disciplined and fanatical party to carry out the orders of the dictator. But this "utopian creed" is a fraud, says Niebuhr, and its fraudulent character will in time become obvious to all.

If the important components of the problem of world community are what Niebuhr seems to think they are, his conclusions might be correct. But the bias of his theological thinking leads him to ignore the most powerful agencies working for world community. This bias leads him to misinterpret the religious resources available in dealing with this problem. The only religious resource, according to Niebuhr, is the transcendent vision; and this vision, according to his own teaching, is the chief source of evil in the world because people seek to actualize it in history when it cannot be had in history but only beyond history. According to Niebuhr there is no actual, operative divine creativity in history which we can accept as God's revelation in Christ to which we can commit ourselves. There is only the transcendent vision, the chief source of corruption in social developments when it is sought as a goal instead of using it exclusively as a standard of criticism.

Contrary to what Niebuhr says, the revolution now going on in the world, and the spread of what looks like Communism, is not driven by the ideology of communism nor by the "fanaticism of its Utopian creed." Communism is not sustained by the vision of a "perfect and universal community to be attained in history and not beyond history." What is spreading around the world with irresistible power is not the utopian dream but something else which has actual power, namely, rapid industrialization and agriculture made more productive by scientific research.

Walter Lippman, as well as many others, has made this point. Lippman writes in his column: "There is no mystery as to why the Soviet Union and even China have the inside track (in the social revolution now occurring around the world.) They do not stand for democracy, which is impossible in most of these countries, or for free and private enterprise, which is also impossible. They stand for dictatorships with technicians. The handful of educated leaders in the backward countries, and also in countries not so

[6]*Ibid.*, p. 136.
[7]*Ibid.*, pp. 91–92.

backward, can imagine themselves following the Soviet pattern. But they cannot imagine themselves following the political pattern of Eisenhower and Nixon and Kennedy and Johnson, of General Motors and U. S. Steel."[8]

The drive toward rapid industrialization and intensified agriculture, together with the scientific research which makes these possible, did not originate in Russia or in communism. It originated in the Western world. Its world-wide spread today is the influence of the West transforming all societies, even when this transformation goes under the label of communism. To see this perspective on the world revolution, in opposition to Niebuhr's view of what is happening, we turn to the second of the two books above mentioned: *Evolution and Culture* by Elman R. Service and Marshall D. Sahlins. (References here are to salient points adapted in *The New Republic*.) This work would not be so convincing if the views presented were not supported by many others. The following statement by Service and Sahlins is the clearest, briefest and most cogent on the issue of dispute with Niebuhr.

Communism is neither the cause of what is happening in the world today nor the cause of the West's deteriorating position. The prior industrial evolution of the West is the cause and Communism is one of its earliest results. As Barbara Ward, a political economist specializing in underdeveloped areas, put it, "The Western powers themselves launched every one of the world's contemporary revolutions. they carried them across the ocean and around the world. They set in motion the vast forces of contemporary change and in doing so never doubted that what they did was of profound concern to the entire human race. Yet today, wealthy, complacent, unimaginative, they appear indifferent to the stirring protean world of change and revolution in which three quarters of the human race are struggling for the forms of a new life.[9]

When the social revolution appears under the guise of communist ideology, this appearance is due to the external wrappings put around the process of change. But these wrappings of communist ideology have very little to do with the driving force of the movement. When this is said, however, the question arises: Then why does this rapid industrialization, especially in Russia and China, take the form of dictatorship and cruel coercion, when it brought democracy to us in the West? Is this not a perversion introduced into it by the ideology of communism?

Analysis of what is actually happening shows that the ideology of communism is not the cause of the tyranny, disruption and cruelty of the process. According to the authors we are now summarizing, as well as many others, the dictatorship and tyranny are caused by four conditions working together.

[8] *Saturday Evening Post*, September 9, 1960.
[9] *Evolution and Culture* by Elman R. Service and Marshall D. Sahlins, *The New Republic*, May 16, 1960, p. 12.

(1) These new areas cannot industrialize with small beginnings, creating capital as they go along as did the West when the industrial revolution began with us. These newly developing lands take over the most advanced technology now in use. This requires a huge investment of capital—far greater than was required to initiate the small beginnings of industrialization in Europe and America. When this capital cannot be obtained in any other way, it must be extracted from the peasantry. This requires tyranny and totalitarian control by government. This is a practical necessity under the conditions existing. When this is done, the Utopian vision of communism may be useful but it is by no means the activating force of the revolution nor the supreme agent of control.

(2) The new areas such as Russia and China (and perhaps in the future India, Indonesia, Africa and South America) carry on the rapid industrialization by dictatorial methods because of the opposition and, often, the actual invasion and constant threat of attack from outside powers. This leads to a semi-military organization in self defense, and military organization is always dictatorial. This is the external cause of the totalitarian regimes as (1) above was an internal cause, according to Service and Sahlins.

(3) The idea and hope of industrialization with its wealth has come to these new areas by way of the picture in their minds of what the West has already accomplished. Thus they begin with this consummated goal in mind and strive to leap to it as rapidly as possible. This makes their procedure far more disruptive and revolutionary than industrialization was in the West. For England and Europe and America there was no such example in actual existence of the wealth and power to be attained. Hence we were not driven to try to make "great leaps" over intervening stages to reach the goal. These disruptive leaps shatter the way of life of the people. The society then requires more police action, and more centralized control than is needed when industrialization proceeds unplanned and groping its way, one stage automatically leading to the next as it did in England, Europe and America.

(4) In the West medical science and hygienic regulations, rapidly increasing the population, *followed after* the increase in production by industrialization. In the new areas this order is reversed. Medical science and hygiene increase the population before industrialization and intensified agricultural production can provide the needed food and other supplies. Furthermore, this has happened in areas that are already over-populated. This is another condition leading to increased dictatorship and centralized control entirely independent of the communist ideology or any "Utopian creed."

Thus we see that communism in the form of "an ideology we abhor," to use Niebuhr's expression, is not the cause of the disruption, turmoil, dictatorship and totalitarian developments around the world. The communist ideology does certainly lend itself to these developments, and in many cases is used, notably in Russia and China. But communism, when that term means an ideology and the fanaticism of an Utopian vision, is not the cause.

If communism with its ideology had never come into existence, very much the same rapid industrialization with its dislocations and tyrannies would be going on much the same as it is now. This is so because the source and cause of it all are the development of modern technology in the West and its rapid spread to other lands. Other peoples want it not because communism demands it, but partly for the wealth it provides and perhaps even more for the power and prestige it brings. It opens the way for these peoples to rise from the humiliation imposed on them by those who first acquired this wealth and power. This is the teaching of Service and Sahlins in the book mentioned.

With this understanding of what is happening in the world, we cannot agree with Niebuhr when he says that the driving force now working to create a universal community is the ideology of communism with its Utopian fanaticism. Niebuhr's second error is closely related to this one. He identifies the attainment of world community with the attainment of a perfect community. Of course no community will be perfect. The virtue of this prospective community is a question entirely different from the possibility of attaining it. Niebuhr confuses its attainment with the actualizing of a vision of transcendent perfection. The achievement of a "universal and perfect community in history" is not the question under consideration. The problem is to achieve a community sufficiently regulative of all peoples so as to assure the continued existence of human beings on this planet and the continuance of a high level of civilization. This is not at all the same thing that Niebuhr is rejecting, although he does not seem to recognize that this very different problem is actually the one imperatively demanded by the predicament of human society in our time.

There is no certainty that we shall escape a third World War with its dire consequences. Even if a third World War does not occur, we have no certainty that we shall achieve a universal community sufficiently strong to deliver us from the "balance of terror" that keeps us always on the brink of annihilation. This condition may continue indefinitely. But we are not discussing certainties nor even probabilities. Rather we are trying to discover what is the most effective way to work for a world community, even though we might fail. The possibility of failure is always with us, no matter what we do. That possibility is involved in every worthy enterprise. But that is not the question. The question is this: What is actually going on in the world which *might* bring about a world community provided that we do all in our power to promote it?

With respect to the power of technology in shaping the social order, Niebuhr himself sees that the national states now so widely prevalent arose to meet the demands of a newly developing technology. They were brought into being by the kind of industry and commerce that created a middle class beneath the feudal aristocracy. The rising power and wealth of this class created by the new technology enabled them to win the cooperation of the king on the one hand and the working class on the other. In this way they could resist the feudal class and establish parliaments. All this Niebuhr relates. But he fails to see that the very characteristics of this process which created the nation states can, under present conditions, break down the exclusiveness of the nation states and transform them into a world society. This feature of the social process which created the nation states, but is now driving on toward a world community, can here be sketched in only a few sentences.

The new industry with the middle class in control of it created the nation states because the technology of that time was tied down to the localities and geographical conditions favorable to the rise of industry equipped with the technology of that day. For example, industry arose in those localities where coal and iron were readily accessible and where rivers and harbors permitted transport by boats. Of course, many other factors entered into the formation of the nation states. The mentality of the people, the traditions, language, dynasties, wars, diplomacy, even marriages, courtesans and love-making had their parts to play. But amid all this, as Niebuhr notes, the rising power of industry carrying the middle class with it was one necessary component without which the nation states would not have developed as they did.

Now precisely the one factor in the rising power of industry which was most potent in creating the nation states has now reversed itself and is creating a world community. This one factor was the tying down of industry to those localities where the raw materials and needed transportation could be had. Industry today equipped with modern technology is not tied down in that way. With the power of electricity transported like lightning across continents, with electronics and synthetic chemistry soon to be followed by organic chemistry, with fission and fusion and automation and with modern methods of communication and transportation, the nation state becomes a barrier to the development of the power of industry. Hence the class that operates industry today, very different from the middle class of earlier times, cannot be contained within the limits of any national state. States are becoming internationally organized under the compulsion of industrial and economic necessity. Furthermore, the demands of industry equipped with modern technology cannot even be kept within the limits of regional organizations. Despite the utmost efforts of national governments to prevent economic interchange between the communist countries and the Western democracies, this interchange is breaking through the barrier with ever increasing volume.

What is here said about the social process driving toward world community should not be interpreted to mean that a world system is inevitable. Many processes are working against it. A world war might prevent it from ever being realized. The point we are trying to make is this: Moral idealism, devoted endeavor and Christian commitment cannot achieve a world community unless they recognize the underlying social process that will help to attain this end if we work with it. What is meant by working with the social process driving toward world community is partly described in the following quotation:

> It must be apparent by now that I am suggesting a policy that will aid as much and as rapidly as possible, rather than continue to impede, the industrialization of the rest of the world. And I mean *the rest of the world*, not merely small portions of it selected for their political compliance or strategic location. But some of the backward areas will probably move beyond us. Is this not a paradox? Would not aiding them in this be something like digging our own grave?
>
> It is not digging our own grave to abolish the causes of strife, despotism, and militarism, but the only way to save ourselves and the world at the same time, for we and the world are in this crisis indivisible. It would be a policy for *us;* at the same time it is a policy for the non-industrialized nations. To cease our opposition and our unworkable containment policy would certainly lessen world tensions. Then the next great need is capital for the new industrialization . . .[10]

After this correction of the picture which Niebuhr gives us of what is happening in the world relative to the attainment of a world community, we turn again to his interpretation of the moral and religious resources available in seeking to alleviate the evils of our existence. The only moral and religious resource recognized by Niebuhr is the vision of transcendent perfection which becomes a source of moral corruption as soon as we try to achieve it in history.

For Niebuhr Christ is nothing more than "an expression of the validity" of "the vision of a perfect individual or collective virtue" and "also the expression of the final answer of divine mercy for the perplexities and frustrations" people encounter in their struggle to achieve social justice within the conditions of our actual existence.[11] He adds that "the truth expressed in these religious symbols is created not by a particular faith but by the human situation. It is validated therefore not by a dogma but by historical experience."[12] Just what is meant by saying that this vision of perfection and divine mercy "is validated . . . by historical experience" is not clear. It certainly does not mean that the envisioned *perfection* is ever attained in history because Niebuhr is never weary of denouncing the belief that perfection can ever be reached in history. Also it is not clear what is meant by saying that *divine mercy* "is validated . . . by historical experience." The only point that seems to stand out clearly in this statement is that

---

[10] *"The Future of America" by Elman R. Service. The New Republic,* May 16, 1960, p. 12. Italics in the original.

[11] Niebuhr, op. cit., pp. 223-24.

[12] *Ibid.,* p. 224.

the religious symbols and the dogma involving Christ are not necessary to validate the vision of perfection because it is "validated . . . by historical experience."

The whole of religion for Niebuhr seems to be contained in this vision of transcendent perfection. When this vision is properly treated by resisting the temptation to identify oneself and one's works with it, the moral and religious value of it appears. It enables one to take a stand above and beyond what is actually occurring in one's self, in one's society and the cause one serves, and in history as a whole. This makes possible an objective, relatively unbiased judgment of good and evil and thus saves from the blindness of fanaticism which sees all evil in the opponent and all virtue in oneself and in the party with which one has identified oneself. This is Niebuhr's gospel.

This objectivity of moral judgment is indeed the most difficult achievement in human life, and the greatest virtue. Nothing is more precious and nothing more noble. But does this vision of transcendent perfection enable us to attain these noble virtues? We are convinced that Niebuhr is mistaken on this point and this is our criticism of him although we honor him most highly for the magnificent criticism he has made of the evils in society and in the practice of religion itself.

In opposition to Niebuhr it is here claimed that Christ does not merely serve to validate a vision of transcendent perfection and give expression to divine mercy, especially since, according to Niebuhr, these seem to be validated by historical experience in any case. What Christ provides is an actual operative presence working in human life to transform one as one cannot transform oneself to deliver that person from the corruption of evil and toward the greater good when required conditions are present. As Niebuhr truly says with profound insight, people "seek collective compensation for their individual insignificance" by pretending to be identified with "a meaning and system of ends which transcends these historically contingent and precarious political configurations." The problem is how to be saved from this corruption.

For Niebuhr there is nothing actually going on in history or in human life anywhere to which one can commit oneself in religious faith. Neither can one commit absolutely to the vision of transcendent perfection, and this for two reasons. For one, as Niebuhr repeatedly asserts, absolute commitment to the eternal leads to irresponsible disregard of the actualities of human life where the greater evil is to be fought and the lesser evil promoted. Second, every person's vision of perfection is limited and corrupted by imagination. All the bias and prejudice entering into human life, so well depicted by Niebuhr, infects our vision of the eternal perfection. Hence this vision, even when they make it, as Niebuhr recommends, the norm for judging the good and evil in actual existence, still is corrupted by the bias of the culture, and all the distortions of judgment arising out of the complexities of life and the complexities of human personality. Every vision of transcendent perfection entertained by the human mind has in it the limitations and corruption of that mind. This is inevitable. Hence the alleged way of salvation offered by Niebuhr cannot be *the way* of salvation.

The best that Niebuhr's vision of transcendent "perfection" can do for humans is to stimulate negative criticism. One can always point out what seems to be evil by the standard of one's own corrupted vision. One cannot point out anything that is worthy of our complete religious commitment of faith. Not even the vision is worthy of this for reasons just indicated.

Niebuhr is right in what he says about the limitations of economic and political action and the inevitable self-defeat when any political or economic or ecclesiastical organization or established institution of any kind claims to embody the will of God or human destiny or the predetermined goal of history. In all this his criticism is invaluable. But he is blind to the underlying work of Christ in human life where the divine presence is truly revealed and where the highest possibilities of people and history are truly to be found. Niebuhr can find the divine presence nowhere in history. While he claims to find it beyond history, this is an illusion when based upon the validity of his vision of the eternal because his vision is the work of his own human mind and that mind in every person, according to Niebuhr's own teaching, is corrupted by the actualities of existence. The vision itself is corrupted. Consequently, he cannot even find the divine presence in what he calls the eternal or the vision of transcendent perfection, although he claims that this vision is the way of salvation and the only way.

Niebuhr is not acquainted with the revelation of God in Christ. The revelation has never come to him. He is a noble and dedicated idealist, looking to nothing save what the human imagination can construct in the form of an ideal order.

CHAPTER VII
CHRIST CREATING COMMUNITY

The most obvious links holding people together in community are the political and economic connections. Although these connections are most obvious, they are not the strongest. The economic and political, merged into one order, constitute the top level of community, which is superimposed upon the deeper, more spontaneous and prior bonds between individuals and groups. This political level is made up of legislation, judicial decisions, executive decrees, administrative devices and systems, directing agencies and many other contrivances by which human society is constructed more or less according to human plan and purpose. This level of community commands attention and hence comes first to mind when the problem of community is considered. It is conspicuous while the other levels are more or less hidden, because the economic and political agencies are always being constructed or reconstructed. Also they are enforced by specified and conspicuous penalties so that people keep this level of cohesion in mind to avoid the penalities for deviation. For the same reason the economic order is a focus of attention. It is always being revised, criticized and reordered. Also it is enforced by sanctions such as loss of income.

While the economic and political order is necessary to hold a complex community together, it becomes highly unstable and generates discontent rising to rebellion when not sustained by prior bonds of cohesion. This brings us to the second level of community, that of economic and political need.

The economic need, normally arising prior to any economic order, is that condition of society in which one group or division needs the products of other groups or divisions, while the others reciprocally need the products of the first. When a group has no sense of economic need for trade with other groups, an economic system imposed upon it, requiring it to engage in trade with other groups, creates dislocations, discontent and resistance. The colonial powers of Europe imposed an economic system of trade upon peoples who had no sense of need for this trade. This, with other features of colonialism, led to discontent and finally to rebellion, so that the European nations have been compelled to relinquish their colonies. Of course an economic system once imposed can in time create economic need, because trade leads to division of labor and interdependence. But this topsy turvy procedure is likely to generate resistance, hatred and fear which continue long after the economic system is truly needed.

What is said about the economic order applies also to the political. The political need is prior to, and should underlie and sustain the political order. A political need arises when conflicts within the society disturb the peace and the security in such a way that the established political system cannot control or pacify them. In such case a further development of the political bond is needed. When a political order is superimposed prior to need, it arouses resistance.

It is plain that the development of modern technology is creating the need in all the regions and divisions of human life for a world-wide economic order and a world-wide political order, superseding or overlying the economies and governments now restricted to national states. Hence an economic and political order encircling the earth would be sustained by a prior economic and political need. Such a world order stands in contrast to the ancient empires and in contrast to the more recent colonial empires, because these were extended over peoples who did not feel the need for the imposed system.

This brings us to the third level of cohesion, a level more deeply laid in human existence and more tenacious than either of the two levels we have considered thus far. When the demands of this third level conflict with the economic and political demands, social disruption and dislocation break out and the economic and political interests are often sacrificed for these deeper demands of cohesion. At this moment a very conspicuous example of the sacrifice of economic and political interests to satisfy these more deeply laid bonds can be noted. It is the trouble between blacks and whites both in the United States and in South Africa. It has also broken out in other parts of Africa as well as many other places. The ethnic bond of white with white against the black bond is disrupting both the economic and the political order in these regions.

This third level of cohesion, however, is not limited to the ethnic bond. Rather it is a very complex web of intricately interwoven bonds of cohesion. These all might be brought together under the heading of a sense of likeness or kinship. Sometimes this sense of likeness takes the form of ethnic likeness. But in other cases the sense of likeness may be dominated by likeness of language or likeness of dialect; or likeness of customs, manners and habits; or likeness of ideals; or likeness of a social class; or likeness in poverty or wealth; or likeness of culture, tradition and history; or likeness in having shared in a common experience which has become momentous and symbolic of what is best in human life. Not least in these bonds of cohesion at this third level is likeness in religious belief and practice.

It should be noted that these bonds of community derived from sense of kinship and shared interests are restrictive and exclusive. They bind together those who have the likeness which happens to be the dominant interest among the people at that time and place; but they exclude all who do not have this likeness. Often these bonds do more than exclude; they often generate hate, fear, suspicion and violent conflict between communities each of which is united by a kind of likeness excluding the other. Most conspicuous today is the kind of likeness called communism, uniting one community under the ideology which goes by that name while the opposing community is united under the ideology of capitalism or free enterprise. Of course communism and capitalism are not merely ideologies; they are also political and economic organizations. But we are now looking at the ideological bond, which represents the third level of community in contrast to the political and economic. This third level is sometimes called the organic community.

An ideological community is, perhaps, not a good example of the organic bond since it is often constructed as a political device for controlling the people and inducing the action desired by the political leaders. Yet an ideology can be a shared interest binding people together to serve a common cause apart from any economic or political mechanism. People inspired by a revolutionary ideology may be opposed to every economic and political system in existence.

There is a fourth level of community underlying all the other bonds of cohesion. It is so deeply implanted in human existence that it is created in the very same creativity which creates the human level of existence. As soon as the human infant begins to acquire a human mind by way of understanding words and sentences, this level of community is being created. As soon as the infant can understand that kind of meaning which is capable of being expanded indefinitely in range and variety of reference, the infant has become a member of the universal human community. This is a community inextricably wrought into the structure of human existence. No one can use language without membership in this community. No one can have the mentality capable of using human language without sharing in this community.

All languages, no matter how alien to one another, have logical and grammatical structure. This is not only the structure of language; it is also the structure of the human mind, because language and mind create one another. This reciprocal creation is done by the kind of interchange creating communion between human beings. This includes more than the rational structure of mind; the structure of linguistic and other human symbols convey all those sentiments and all that sense of better and worse which human beings are able to communicate. Thus, while individuals and cultures differ greatly in what they judge to be better and worse—and languages are very different—there is a basic structure of the value sense common to all human beings by reason of language.

In addition to a basic structure common to all, languages have many meanings in common along with all the diversities of meaning, because they can be translated into one another with some approximation. Also the use of language creates a subjectivity and self-consciousness common to all users of language. This does not mean that the content of the subjectivity is the same for any two individuals and least of all for individuals in different cultures. What it does mean is that every individual who uses a language thereby develops a self-consciousness and a self-concern, different from any animal which does not use the human kind of language.

This interchange creating this basic level of community which is wrought inextricably into human existence is the same interchange revealed in Christ. It actually creates the human level of existence by creating the language-user, with the mentality and organization of personality which go along with use of human language. Also by thus creating the human mind in the infant, it creates an individual who can share meanings with all other human beings when required conditions are present; and the use of language makes possible a scope and depth of shared meaning not otherwise possible. Thus the creativity in this kind of interchange exemplifies the parenthood of God and the family unity of all humanity, not merely as ideals or dogmas but as demonstrable actualities.

Community created at this level is not restrictive and exclusive as are the other kinds built on this level. This human community created by God in Christ is unlimited because it can expand and deepen beyond any known limit when conditions are favorable. It can break through or penetrate the barriers set up by exclusive communities. When children born into diverse and exclusive communities have been tenderly reared so that fears and hatreds have not been built into the organization of personality, the white child readily forms community with the black child; the child of communist parents shares meanings with the child born into the family of a capitalist. The child of parents speaking a foreign language forms community with one whose parents speak the native tongue; the child of the rich forms community with the child of the poor; the child of one geographical region, culture and tradition forms community with the child of another heritage; the child of parents holding ideals or religious beliefs diametrically opposed to the ideals and beliefs of the parents of another child forms community with the other child, and no opposing ideals intervene.

The point is that children, before the exclusive communities have taken hold of them, live in the universal community which has been created in them. They are guided by it in seeking association with other children, provided that adults have not implanted fear and prejudice in them. Children fight and quarrel but their fighting and quarrelling arise out of their community with one another; it does not break their community with one another.

This fourth level of community created by the interchange creating the use of language and other human symbols is the basic level of community. Upon it all other levels of community are reared. Apart from it no kind of community distinctively human can arise. Helen Keller, born deaf and blind, testifies of the wonder and joy of entering into the human community when she first learned the meaning of human symbols. Only then did the great world of human culture and human community open to her. Only then did that kind of interchange begin which made her a member of the community including those long dead as well as those living and yet to live, including also many individuals whose personal identity was unknown but who shared with her the meanings carried by human symbols.

Profound and supremely important as it is, this basic universal community which is not merely an ideal but an actuality sustaining us day by day in all we do is largely ignored. It is hidden because human attention is focused largely upon political and economic problems or else upon the exclusive communities previously mentioned as the third level of community. But when the infant begins to respond to the meaning of human symbols, this basic, universal community is being created. In time this will be overlaid by the exclusive community of family, culture, ethnic group and intimate fellowships. Yet the community of the symbol-using animal with all other symbol-using animals is being created in the child by the interchange whereby one becomes able to understand the meaning of humanly used symbols. These symbols carry a kind of meaning which cannot be carried by the signs used by other animals. It is a kind of meaning which can be expanded indefinitely to encompass more and more; and it is a kind of meaning which can be communicated without limit to other human beings when required conditions are provided. For these reasons we have at the human level of existence a universal community inextricably involved in the existence of every human being. It is rightly called the family unity of humanity.

It is not correct to say that culture is the frame within which meanings are shared. At a superficial level that is true, but at a deeper level it is more correct to say that communication creates the culture in the first place. It is the communication of these meanings that extends the culture to include more people. Also, by this communication from one generation to the next, those long dead have community with those now living and those yet to live. Thus history is created.

Certainly this expanding community of shared meanings is obstructed and often turned back by the exclusive and restrictive communities. But these barriers are not absolute while the universal community *is* absolute in the sense that it is built into the human self so that there can be no human existence without it. This universal community built into the structure of human existence is not beyond history; it is in history and actually creates history. Without it there could be no human history.

The exclusive communities are not necessarily and essentially obstructive to universal community. They are reared on the basis of this universal community and they can be contributors to the universal community. To some measure they always are. Every family by rearing children provides conditions under which the child not only acquires the meanings peculiar to the prevailing culture but also becomes a language-using individual and thereby becomes a member of the universal community.

Intimate, exclusive communities will always have their proper place, no matter how inclusive and profound the world community may become. Rather it should be said that the universal community cannot become most inclusive of many meanings unless the exclusive communities contribute their new creations of meaning to the larger fellowship. The intimate and exclusive group is just as indispensable to the human level of existence as is the world community. Both are needed and each can contribute to the other.

The world community would be reduced to barren forms if it did not permit a great diversity of more intimate communities. Even separate and distinct "nations" are needed when nation means a people having a history of its own, a culture, a language, and insights and appreciations peculiar to it. No doubt these exclusive communities will always fall into conflicts. But they also contribute meanings to one another and to the world community. The problem is, and will always be, to increase the contributions of each to the others and diminish the hatred and fear. This will be accomplished to the measure that people commit themselves to the kind of interchange which is the revelation of God in Christ. All manner of structures and procedures must be reared to keep communication between exclusive communities open and free; but people will not do this effectively unless they give priority above all else in their lives to the kind of interchange which creates wholeness and communion between individuals and groups at the level underlying exclusive communities.

Communication between communities is most rewarding when their endowments are unique and their resources are different from one another; but this requires that ultimate commitment be given not to the intimate community with its unique endowments, precious as this may always be, but to the interchange of God in Christ which is the interchange creating world community.

Local governments will always be needed. World government is needed but it can never take the place of concentric circles of control reaching down to the family or local fellowship and reaching out to the regulation of affairs of common concern to all the peoples of the world.

We are not painting the picture of Utopia. We are not suggesting perfection in any of the respects above mentioned. Indeed our major concern is not with ideals or prospects of the future at all. It is with actualities operative here and now in our lives every day. It is with these that we must work rather than with ideals and future prospects. These actualities point out the direction and manner of change for which we work. To these actualities we look to point the way rather than to ideals. It is with these actualities that we shall try to break down the obstruction of limited communities when they set up barriers to the kind of interchange creating world community. Yet we are not predicting that these obstructions will be overcome. We are not even saying that they will become less than they are now. They might become worse. Nobody knows enough about the future to make such predictions, whether one is a pessimist or optimist. What we do know is the present actuality of God in Christ. To this we are committed, win or lose. In this commitment we find the best that life can give, regardless of what the future may bring. We do not live in the future; we live in the present. In the present we already have a basic, universal community created and sustained by God in Christ. In this and with this and for this we live.

Predicting what can be attained, and what cannot be, throughout the indefinite future of history, far exceeds the competence of the human mind. If we fail when we work for, and in, and with the interchange that creates wholeness in communion, it still is better to fail thus than to succeed in anything else. But we are not predicting failure. We are only saying that it is better to live for this and die for this than for anything else.

The statement that the way to world community is through commitment to God revealed in Christ must not be confused with the notion that world community can ever be attained by inducing the peoples of the world to accept this formulation of religious belief. This is impossible for many reasons. This formulation of religious belief is peculiar to one special religious tradition. It carries with it the unique endowments and resources of this one tradition and community of belief. Nothing has been more divisive than the formulations of religious belief cherished by a people whose minds and organization of personality have been shaped from infancy by one special tradition. Such beliefs are held with a tenacity and passion that make this kind of community exclusive.

God revealed in Christ is the way the Christian community, when it keeps close to the ancient tradition, refers to what calls for the final commitment of faith and leads to world community. Every intimate fellowship, whether religious or not, has symbols that are profoundly meaningful in the fellowship but without significance for others. This is right and good but it has a danger in that the words will command passionate devotion in disregard of any kind of being which empirical inquiry can demonstrate to be designated by the words. Even this clinging to the words, over against any rational demonstration of descriptive truth they convey, has its virtue for the reason we have repeatedly stated. The concrete wholeness of being expressed by symbols in an intimate fellowship is always more than what they demonstrably and descriptively designate. But if the symbols are not to perpetuate illusions and mislead the commitment of faith, there must be in addition to their symbolic power some descriptive truth.

Here is where science (or empirical inquiry of some kind) should join with language of religious faith. Some demonstrable and descriptive truth should be found in what the symbols of faith represent. When this is done, it is possible to shift from the use of the symbols of faith to the use of language that conveys descriptive and demonstrable truth concerning what calls for commitment and what leads to world community. Throughout this writing, this has been our practice. We have shifted constantly from the symbols of faith, such as revelation of God in Christ, to descriptive language such as interchange creating wholeness of being in the individual and profound communion among individuals.

The way to world community, with deliverance from the hate, fear, tyranny, cruelty and destruction hanging over us, cannot be found if we insist on the symbols of faith peculiar to any one religious tradition such as the Christian one. These symbols we need and must have. But if we refuse to translate them into descriptive statements demonstrably true, we shall obstruct the work of the very Christ to which we are committed. Perhaps nothing has divided the world into exclusive groups so difficult to reconcile as religious fellowships insisting that their peculiar religious symbols be accepted by all other people.

A third alternative which may seem to be open but actually is not sometimes goes by the name of rationalism. It repudiates symbols of faith which carry the depths of individuality and communion far beyond the reach of rational, descriptive statements. These symbols belonging to an intimate fellowship cannot be repudiated if we are to have love and devotion, religious faith and profound experience of beauty. But we must have bridges with which to pass from one fellowship of faith to another, from one intimate communion to others. These bridges must be built by reason and by descriptive statements scientifically demonstrable. In respect to the profoundly true symbol "God revealed in Christ," the descriptively true statement corresponding is "interchange creating wholeness in the individual and deep communion between individuals." If this is not the best statement correctly describing what is demonstrably true in the referent of the symbol "Christ," then some other statement of it should be found. Our present insistence is not that this statement of ours be accepted; our insistence is that, for the sake of the cause of Christ and world community, some statement correctly descriptive and demonstrably true be found.

The claim here being defended can be summarily stated thus: Affirmations, whether religious or otherwise, can most readily spread to all peoples across the barrier of diverse cultures and traditional faiths when they are confirmed by empirical or scientific evidence and thus assume the form of knowledge. If this is true, then religious beliefs not thus confirmed will strive in vain to win the world to Christ and cannot lead the way to world community.

Another source of misunderstanding in this discussion should be removed. We have said repeatedly that world community is already with us at that basic level where the human mind is created by the use of language. We have also said repeatedly that our salvation depends upon attaining a world community we do not now have. These statements may seem to be contradictory but are not. World community created at the basic level where the human mind is created in the new-born infant is with us always and includes all humanity. It unites all the peoples now living with one another. It unites all the peoples now living with all that have lived and all that will live. It is the family unity of humanity created in us by God when God means the kind of interchange creating the human level of existence.

If we have this world community already, one may ask why we seek world community. The answer should not be difficult. We have this world community already, but we must give this community priority over the exclusive communities. We should do this not by abolishing these intimate, exclusive communities but by subordinating them to the service of universal community created in all peoples. The common practice today, and generally throughout history, has been the reverse. It has been to subordinate the world community we have in God to the service of our special tradition and exclusive community. This is what we do when we insist that all people should accept the formulation of faith expressed in the words "God revealed in Christ." However, when we are willing to translate these words into statements demonstrably descriptive of what does in truth create world community among all people, we are not repudiating the unique Christian fellowship with its endowments and resources different from every other. Rather what we are doing in such case is to subordinate our own intimate fellowship with all its precious values to the service of that community in God which all people share, rightly called family unity of humanity.

But commitment cannot be made to the generalization of family unity. If it is to be effective, it must be made to the interchange between you and any person with whom you deal, provided it is the kind of interchange that creates communion with another not as the member of a special group but as an individual important in one's own right. This is the only kind of interchange and communion that can be extended to all people regardless of their membership in special groups. This is what creates the universal community. Generalizations and ideals about human bonds and love and good will have their place; but Christ is not in any of them. Christ can be found only in the actual concrete interchange between you and the other person when it creates wholeness in each individual and depth of communion between you.

Certainly this kind of interchange is never pure and free of mixture with other kinds. Therefore it does not create perfect and complete wholeness nor the whole depth of communion. But it is present to some degree, more or less submerged, and more or less dominant, more or less mixed with other kinds of interchange and more or less clear of them. Christ is found in this actuality and not in any ideal or any transcendence when "transcendence" means what is not actual and present here and now. This actuality is the living Christ; this actuality is the power of God unto salvation. This actuality is what we need to distinguish and clearly discern and serve above all.

Non-theistic humanists as well as many others identify religion with devotion to the "highest ideals." The expression "highest ideals" must be put in quotation marks because highest ideals for the communist are not the same as for the Nazis; and neither of these are identical with ideals prevailing in Western democracy. Furthermore, all of these ideals differ from the highest ideals of the Hindu and the Buddhist. Trying to unify the world by devotion to the same ideals presents the same difficulty we found standing in the way of religious belief. Ideals, as ordinarily professed, are said to represent what ought to be. What ought to be can never be derived, so it is said, from what actually exists. But empirical and scientific evidence is always about what actually exists, together with predictable possibilities to be actualized by specified forms of action guided by probabilities derived from this evidence. Since *ought* can never be derived from *is*, according to the cliche, moral ideals cannot be confirmed by empirical or scientific evidence. So here we are in the same predicament with ideals that we were with religious belief in seeking a way to basic community for all the world.

It has been said that we can find the same ideals in the teachings of the supreme representatives of all the great faiths of the world. In verbal form this may be true. The statement of the ideal in the teaching of one great historic representative of moral idealism and religious aspiration may be translated into the languages of the other teachers most highly honored in the great traditions of the world. But the level at which these ideals seem to be the same is a level of abstraction so remote from the actual way in which human life is conducted that for all practical purposes the similarity is lost.

There is another and much more important objection to ideals as guides to any significant change in the order of human existence. The actuality of human existence and the actuality of what creates and sustains human existence is always immeasurably more powerful than any ideal and any devotion to ideals. On this point the practical, hard-headed person is correct over against the idealist. The order of human existence cannot be changed by ideals. The only way that ideals can be effective in changing the order of human life is to guide human conduct in service of some actuality already present and operative in creating and sustaining human existence. This is precisely the difference between moral idealism and religious commitment of faith. Commitment of religious faith, when rightly directed, is commitment to an actuality operative in creating and sustaining human existence. It reverses the commitment of moral idealism when the latter is not religious. Moral idealism seeks to transform the ideal to serve an actuality already in existence. What this actuality is for Christian faith we have repeatedly stated within the limits of our competence.

In this respect religious faith, when joined with scientific inquiry after the manner above described, is realistic and practical as opposed to the dreaming of the non-theistic humanist and the moral idealist. This does not imply the repudiation of moral ideals. It does mean that moral ideals shall be held subordinate to, and in service of, a divine actuality rather than striving to subordinate actuality to the ideal.

Let us examine still another proposal concerning what might create world community or at least move in that direction. It is claimed by some religious leaders that we can break down the barriers of opposition and exclusion among diverse religious communions if we recognize that all religion is our ultimate concern and ultimate concern is always directed to ultimate reality—otherwise called Being. Being underlies and is common to all distinguishable kinds of being but cannot be exclusively identified with any distinguishable kind of being because it includes them all and extends infinitely beyond all kinds of being accessible to human cognition. Being in this sense is common to all humans, to all ages and cultures. Every individual, together with all society and all human history, derives existence from infinite Being. All are equally and ultimately dependent upon it. So, it is claimed, when we recognize that the ultimate concern of all is for Being, we have the basis of world community.

This sounds plausible, but when examined it is found to lead nowhere. Being, in the sense of what underlies every distinguishable kind of being while infinitely transcending them all, is not itself distinguishable. It has no distinguishable character. It points in no one direction more than another; it guides toward no outcome more than to any other. It is equally receptive to every form and kind of existence. The concentration camps of Hitler, the bloody tortures and cruelties of history, every horror that can be imagined as well as every horror that ever was perpetrated in existence, are all equally sustained in being, whether they are forms of existence or possibilities imagined or possibilities not imagined. Being is all-inclusive and infinite. Everything possible and actual is included in it.

Plainly ultimate reality in this sense can provide no basis for world community nor for anything else since all are equally participant in Being. The only way that Being in this sense can seem to have character and direction and support for life in one form rather than another is by ontological speculation. So we have all the different ontologies and metaphysical systems of human history, not only those of the Christian West but all others as well. These fantastic constructions in all their diversity and opposition cannot be shown to be false except in the sense that evidence is lacking sufficient to persuade those who prefer a different construction of Being. Neither can they be shown to be true because they are about the unknowable. To say that ultimate Being is unknowable is true in the sense that a tautology is true. Ultimate Being cannot be identified with any distinguishable kind of being. What is not a distinguishable kind of being is unknowable because to be knowable is to be distinguishable from other being. So we have our speculative ontologies, creatures of the human imagination with all the bias and prejudice of the culture and the age in which they are reared. On this point Karl Barth is entirely correct: the Christian faith must not be subordinated to a speculative philosophy.

Yet this subordination of religious faith to speculative philosophy is almost inevitable, given the propensity of the human mind, unless an empirically demonstrable actuality can be shown to be designated by the symbols of faith. The symbols of faith must point to something, or else they are vacuous. As said before, we must be able to translate them into language which correctly describes a distinguishable kind of being to which we commit ourselves. If this is not done by means of science (or some form of empirical inquiry) it will be done by means of fantastic constructions allegedly describing the unknowable. Here again we see the need to join commitment of faith with science.

We know God by revelation when the revelation exposes to empirical inquiry an actuality operating to create, sustain, save from self-destruction and transform toward the best. When metaphysical speculation is substituted for empirical inquiry concerning what has been exposed by revelation, we have begun to wander through trackless realms leading nowhere.

On the other hand, if metaphysics does not mean speculation, seeking to endow the unknowable with a definable character, but is analysis of actual concrete experience to distinguish within it the basic, distinguishable forms of which it is composed, it can be very helpful to religious inquiry. It can contribute to our understanding of what has been exposed to inquiry by revelation when revelation means a fellowship so lived as to render conspicuous and accessible to empirical inquiry one component universally and necessarily present in all human experience. The kind of interchange here identified with the revelation of God in Christ is such a component.

Different cultures have brought to dominance different components of universal human experience. When a fellowship and a tradition bring to dominance a distinguishable component of all human experience and when this component is the one that creates the human level of existence, sustains it in being, saves it from its self-destructive propensities when required conditions are met, and transforms it toward the best it can ever attain, then in that fellowship the revelation of God appears. This revelation of God must first of all be lived before it can be intellectually understood. At first it cannot be intellectually understood by those who live it because they do not yet have the concepts for putting it into intellectual form. But in time this knowledge is required and inquiry should be directed to this end, so that revelation in life may become also revelation in thought.

Teilhard de Chardin, who is both an eminent scientist and a devout Christian, has a magnificent statement to this effect in his book *The Phenomenon of Man*.

> We are given to boasting of our age being an age of science. And if we are thinking merely of the dawn compared to the darkness that went before,

up to a point we are justified. Something enormous has been born in the universe with our discoveries and our methods of research. Something has been started which, I am convinced, will now never stop. Yet though we may exalt research and derive enormous benefit from it, with what pettiness of spirit, poverty of means and general haphazardness do we pursue truth in the world today! Have we ever given serious thought to the predicament we are in?

Like art—indeed we might almost say like thought itself—science was born with every sign of superfluity and fantasy. It was born of the exuberance of an internal activity that had outstripped the material needs of life; it was born of the curiosity of dreamers and idlers. Gradually it became important; its effectiveness gave it the freedom of the city. Living in a world which it can justly be said to have revolutionized, it has acquired a social status; sometimes it is worshipped. Yet we still leave it to grow as best it can, hardly tending it, like those wild plants whose fruits are plucked by primitive peoples in their forests. Everything is subordinated to the increase of industrial production, and to armaments . . .

The truth is that, as children of a transition period, we are neither fully conscious of, nor in full control of, the new powers that have been unleashed. Clinging to outworn habit, we still see in science only a new means to providing more easily the same old things. We put Pegasus between the traces . . . But the moment will come . . . when man will be forced . . . to admit that science is not an accessory occupation for him but an essential activity, a natural derivative of the overspill of energy constantly liberated by mechanization.[1]

Chardin lists some of the tasks that science has to perform in service of God and man. I have inserted numbers to indicate the several distinct undertakings which fall to science in this service:

(1) The future of knowledge . . . As a first approximation it is outlined on our horizon as the establishment of an overall and completely coherent perspective of the universe . . . the world can fulfill itself only insofar as it expresses itself in a systematic and reflective perception . . . intellectual discovery and synthesis are no longer merely speculation but creation . . . some physical consummation of things is bound up with the explicit perception we make of them . . . they are (at least partially) right who situate the crown of evolution in a supreme act of collective vision obtained by a pan-human effort of investigation and construction . . .

(2) the march of humanity, as a prolongation of that of all other animate forms, develops indubitably in the direction of a conquest of matter put to the service of mind. Increased power for increased action. But finally, and above all, increased action for increased being.

[1] *The Phenomenon of Man* by Teilhard de Chardin, pp. 278–9.

(3) . . . our ambition . . . is no longer to find gold but life; and in view of all that has happened in the last fifty years, who would dare to say that this is a mere mirage? With out knowledge of hormones we appear to be on the eve of having a hand in the development of our bodies and even of our brains. With the discovery of genes it appears that we shall soon be able to control the mechanism of organic heredity. And with the synthesis of albuminoids imminent, we may well one day be capable of producing what the earth left to itself, seems no longer able to produce; a new wave of organisms, an artificially provoked neo-life.

(4) The dream which human research obscurely fosters is fundamentally that of mastering, beyond all atomic or molecular affinities, the ultimate energy of which all other energies are merely servants; and thus, by grasping the very mainspring of evolution, seizing the tiller of the world.

(5) I salute those who have the courage to admit that their hopes extend that far; they are at the pinnacle of mankind; and I would say to them that there is less difference than people think between research and adoration. However far knowledge pushes its discovery of the "essential fire" and however capable it becomes some day of remodeling and perfecting the human element, it will always find itself in the end facing the same problem—how to give to each and every element its final value by grouping them in the unity of an organized whole.[2]

If civilization continues, this is the kind of power which people will possess by way of science. Humans may quite likely "sieze the tiller of evolution" and direct its course. They may get control of that deepest level of energy which is the source of all energy and thus change extensively the physical universe and the course of its development. They may create new forms of life and determine the kind of living forms which inhabit the earth, shaping them to human purpose. All this power people may have; but there is an ultimate power which is mightier than all this and this ultimate power we can never control. One can never make oneself love what one does not love and has no desire or impulse to love. One can never make oneself value supremely what has no appeal and is rated of no importance. One can never make oneself adore what one has no impulse to adore; nor make oneself want or seek what one most profoundly and sincerely does not want. There must be some hidden and minimum level of wanting and seeking before any conscious cultivation of it is possible. In sum, people cannot create their own sense of values.

No matter how vast our power may be, our sense of values will determine how this power is used. Therefore, what creates our sense of values is mightier than all the power we may ever exercise because it determines how this power shall be used, whether to develop the constructive potentialities of human existence or the self-defeating and self-destructive propensities.

[2] *The Phenomenon of Man* by Teilhard de Chardin, pp. 245–250.

Thus, no matter how great human power may become, the ultimate power can never be ours because the ultimate power is what creates in us our sense of what is good and what is evil, what is important and what is trivial, what should command the last devotion and the final obedience.

The basic problem of human existence is to find and commit ourselves to what creates progressively, as we live our lives, that sense of values which can be expanded indefinitely without self-destructive consequences. This is the religious problem. To be intelligent in the conduct of the Christian religion we need to understand this problem of human existence as thoroughly as it is possible to understand it. To this end we should draw upon those fields of research which help us to understand it. *Young Man Luther: A Study in Psychoanalysis and History,* by Erik H. Erikson, exemplifies how research can help solve this problem by applying a combination of psychiatric, sociological and historical knowledge. This and other works of Erikson illustrate how science can serve the Christian religion. Throughout the present writing I have defended by argument the claim that science can render a service to the Christian religion far beyond anything yet done, provided that certain barriers are removed which heretofore have hindered this service. But argument is not enough. I wish to present an actual instance of this service rendered by recent developments of science in the field of psychology of personality combined with sociological and historical knowledge. At the risk of being unduly repetitious, I must again ward off the criticism of those who will insist that the fields of inquiry just mentioned are not fields of science. I do not want to argue over the word "science." Whether or not this word is used, I mean to refer to research which draws upon every available resource in our culture to test, criticize and correct any proposed statement. That is the sense in which I have used the word "science" throughout this writing.

That combination of knowledge derived from psychiatry, history and sociology, when applied to the study of the problems of human personality, can contribute greatly to the understanding of these problems; and this is the type of understanding the Christian religion must have to discharge its responsibility.

This responsibility of the Christian religion is not merely that of the clergy. It is the responsibility of the Christian individual in the home, in the school, on the playground, in the various branches of business, industry and the professions, in theology and philosophy. The Christian religion is a term that applies to the conduct of life in all these areas. The basic, persistent crises through which every individual must pass from infancy to death, must be understood as thoroughly as possible if the Christian man and woman are to be effective in what their Christian faith requires of them.

The work of Erikson represents the kind of knowledge and the kind of research sorely needed by those who seek to conduct human life in the way of Christ. There is nothing final or authoritative in what Erikson says. No

knowledge entering the human mind from any source is exempt from criticism because the human mind is always subject to error. But knowledge to
be had from the human services, and illustrated by the work of Erikson, is
the most reliable knowledge we have concerning the crucial problems of
human existence. To ignore it is to be irresponsible and unfaithful to the
Christian commitment.

The central problem of human existence, according to Erikson and many
others working in the same field, is the "problem of ego identity" or "identity
formation." This problem, as analyzed and treated by Erikson and others, is
very complex; but in substance it comes to much the same as achieving
wholeness of being, the term used throughout the present writing. Although
this problem of identity formation is discussed by Erikson in *Childhood and
Society* as well as *Young Man Luther*, the clearest and most systematic
treatment of it is in his article "The Problem of Ego Identity." (*Journal of the
American Psychoanalytic Association*, vol. 4, 1956, pp. 56–121).

Crudely stated, the problem of ego identity can be expressed in such
questions as the following: What kind of a being am I and what am I good for?
What can I do and what can I become that will be worthwhile? What can I do
and whom can I love that will not arouse in me a hatred of the work I do and
the person I love? How can I live and how can I develop in such a way that
one part of me is not disgusted or opposed toward some other part of me?

Of course individuals do not consciously formulate this problem in the
words suggested. In most cases they do not consciously formulate it in any
words. Generally they do not understand what it is that troubles them. It is a
problem lived but not intellectually understood. Indeed Erikson and those
who work with him do not use the word "problem" to refer to this difficulty.
They call it a series of crises. It generally becomes most acute in late
adolescence; but it is a life-long problem, beginning in the first year of
infancy and continuing to the day of death.

The problem is to find a way to live so that the following demands will
not conflict to the point of frustration: Biological demands of the instinctual
drives, the institutional demands, the demands of those persons intimately
involved in one's life, the opportunities for some occupation, the distinctive
talents and interests of the individual, the goals of life set forth in the
prevailing culture. This is only a partial life of the enormously complex and
sensitive combination of demands entering into the life of the individual
which must somehow be made to work together. One of the many ways in
which Erikson states this problem appears in his description of the way
George Bernard Shaw struggled with it. After describing some of the crises
through which Shaw passed, Erikson quotes G.B.S. and then adds a comment:

The end of the crisis of younger years, Shaw sums up in these words: "I
had the intellectual habit; and my natural combination of critical faculty

with literary resources needed only clear comprehension of life in the light of an intelligible theory; in short a religion, to set it in triumphant operation." Here the old Cynic has circumscribed in one sentence what the identity formation of any human being must add up to. To translate this into terms more conducive to discussion in egopsychological and psychosocial terms: Man, to take his place in society, must acquire a "conflict-free" habitual use of a dominant *faculty*, to be elaborated in an *occupation;* a limitless *resource*, a feedback, as it were, from the immediate *exercise* of his occupation, from the *companionship* it provides, and from its *tradition;* and finally, an intelligible *theory* of the processes of life which the old atheist, eager to shock to the last, calls a religion. The Fabian Socialism to which he, in fact, turned is rather an *ideology* . . .³

Note that in this quotation Erikson does not agree that the "intelligible theory of the processes of life" is a form of religion, although it is one necessary part of that total combination required to achieve ago identity. It could be called an ideology, a philosophy, or a guiding set of principles, derived from the prevailing culture but interpreted and modified by the individual in such a way as to fit into that unified way of life which an identity formation requires.

It is plain that this wholeness of being, or ego identity, cannot be achieved merely by conforming to all the diverse demands entering into one's life from parents and family, from friends and chosen occupation, from the institutions and prevailing ideology of the time, from one's own biological organism and unique individuality. One must somehow reinterpret and reorder them to fit them to oneself and oneself to them. One must repudiate and fight some of these demands with all one's power, because they would disrupt wholeness and create "identity diffusion" if one accepted them as legitimate. The problem is to know what to accept and what to reject, what to modify and how to modify and what interpretation to give to all these demands as they arise in the form of biological drives and social interests. Sometimes the society in which one lives makes the problem much less difficult than it is in other social contexts. Also the native endowment of some individuals renders the problem more difficult than for others. Perhaps most important is the relation of the individual in infancy to the mother and father. This relation will be helpful or harmful in achieving ego identity, not primarily by what the parents consciously and deliberately do, although that is certainly important. Most important in determining success or failure in identity formation is the organization of personality in the parents. That in turn depends on the kind of parents they had when they were infants. This does not mean however, that success and failure for the individual is hopelessly predetermined from infancy by the parents. There are eight major

³"The Problem of Ego Identity" by Erik H. Erikson. *Journal of the American Psychoanalytic Association*, vol. 4, 1956, pp. 56–121. Italics are his.

turning points, or crises, in the life of every individual, according to Erikson. While the crisis of infancy, if unsuccessfully encountered, will make the crises arising at later periods more difficult, there is always the possibility, with proper help and favorable conditions, that these later crises will rectify some of the harm done by the earlier ones.

It is worthwhile here to list the eight crises of individual development as set forth by Erikson and briefly explain each one. It will then be possible to suggest the responsibility of the Christian religion for providing favorable conditions and guidance in meeting each of these crises. By "Christian religion" we mean, as previously indicated, not only the church; we mean the responsibility of every man and woman in the home, the school, in forms of entertainment, in industry and business, in government and politics, in scientific research and art, in the professions and avocations, and in every other area where men and women committed to Christ are active in shaping conditions and the course of events.

Each of the eight crises is described as having two alternatives, one representing the successful outcome of that crisis, the other the unsuccessful. "Successful" means contributory to identity formation or, to use our own expression, wholeness of being in commitment to what sustains that wholeness and its development. It should be remembered that each of these crises represents a problem not only for the individual but also for society and for history and for all the institutions and vocations. Basically every one of these crises involves religion; and for the Christian that means the Christian religion. The way the Christian religion is interpreted and practiced by the participant individuals will determine the success or failure of the individual undergoing the crisis, insofar as the person lives among Christian people. But in a complicated society such as ours, dominated by science and technology and exercising enormous power over the conditions of human existence, the interpretation and practice of the Christian religion will not ordinarily be helpful in dealing with these crises if the individuals concerned are not guided by an understanding of the crisis and what is needed to make the outcome successful. Here is where research (science) must come to the service of our faith.

The first of these crises, arising in early infancy, is called *Trust versus Mistrust*. The trust developed in this crisis, if trust is developed, is called basic trust. That means it is a trust not dependent on knowledge or skill or any achievement or any striving but underlies all these so that all these are dependent on it. That is to say, one will be able to acquire knowledge dependent on the measure of one's trust in the source of knowledge. One will be able to develop skill or achieve a goal or undertake difficult striving to the measure that one can trust oneself to what will sustain and guide in seeking knowledge, skill, etc. This basic trust is not a trust based upon any understanding of what sustains when one trusts oneself to it. It is prior to all understanding. In later life the individual may seek to understand what sustains when one trusts oneself to it. But always this basic trust must be lived first of all. Only after it is lived can one get some understanding of it. Even then, this knowledge about what sustains one who trusts will be imperfect, partial, and superficial relative to the wholeness and depth of that to which the individual trusts in the wholeness of being.

While this basic trust developed in infancy depends on the trust-worthiness of the mother, her faithfulness, responsiveness and consistency in meeting the needs of the infant, the infant has no intellectual understanding whatsoever of the mother. The trust developed in the infant is a trustfulness that is lived without any recognition of what sustains the trust. In a sense the infant is right, and the sophisticated adult is wrong, when the latter says that the mother is the one who provides the basis of this trust. It is not basically the mother when "mother" means the consciously formulated plans and purposes, ideals and intentions of the mother. As said before, what sustains the trust of the infant is the deep laid organization of personality in the mother, reaching far beyond her conscious purposes and good intentions. This deep laid organization of personality in the mother is, in turn, created in her by the kind of interchange that occurred between her, when an infant, and her mother. Therefore, what sustains the trust of the infant is God in Christ when this expression refers to that kind of interchange continuing through history which creates mutual trust and profound concern between individuals when required conditions are present. This does not mean, again to repeat, that this kind of interchange came into the world for the first time in the fellowship of Jesus. What occurred in the fellowship of Jesus was the revelation that this kind of interchange is God, meaning that it calls for the most complete self-giving of trust and commitment, to live and die in it, and by the sustaining power of it.

All that has just been said about basic trust developing in the infant applies in reverse to the basic mistrust that develops. Always there is some mistrust. The crisis creates more or less mistrust in the infant, depending on the kind of interchange occurring between infant and mother and other intimate associates.

This problem of trust versus mistrust continues to the end of life but is initiated in the first year of infancy. While this initiation of the crisis is not finally determinative, it will always be one factor in all later struggles to attain basic trust. The religious name for basic trust as developed in later life is faith. Basically faith is not a matter of belief or conscious purpose or striving of any kind. It underlies all of these. Certainly belief and conscious purpose and striving have a part to play. Even more important are the conditions that happen to prevail, or are provided by devoted and intelligent people. But faith does not have its genuine religious character unless it possesses the individual more than one possesses it, so that one does not have to think about it or cultivate conviction in the truth of some belief, or strive after it. One thing, however, that the person of faith needs to do is to occasionally take time out for meditative, worshipful periods when lesser matters can fade away and the deep unconscious level of faith can rise again to the borders of consciousness to restore that sense of peace and power which is not dependent on any intellectual understanding of the issues of life but possesses the individual at levels beyond the reach of understanding. The beginning of this kind of basic trust is in the first year of infancy. The beginning of its opposite is also at that time. Since the outcome can be either a predominance of basic trust or a predominance of basic mistrust, this period is called a crisis.

The second crisis occurs in early childhood and is called by Erikson *Autonomy versus Shame, Doubt.* The infant must develop some independence of its mother. It must stand on its own feet and learn to walk without anyone holding it. It must learn to control its bowel movements. It must develop consciousness of itself as being observed, approved, blamed, shamed, questioned, requiring self-justification. The problem here is to stand over against the mother and father and other associates, as one who is approved or disapproved, praised or blamed, accepted or rejected, recognized for what one truly is or accepted only on condition that one strive to be something other than what one is.

Here again we see a problem that persists throughout life; and here again we find the ultimate resource is God revealed in Christ. This is so because the sense of autonomy, independence, self-confidence and self-worth will develop to the measure that the interchange between the small child and its parents is the kind creating recognition and appreciation for one another of the genuine individuality of each. Shame and doubt of one's own worth develops in childhood when one must pretend to be something other than what one is, or else try to hide oneself and sink into oblivion. When this continues in one's further development, it brings on the self-destructive and socially destructive propensities of the human being.

The third crisis develops at the time called by Erikson the play age, before school age is reached. It is the crisis of *Initiative versus Guilt.* The child develops initiative in the form of play. When one does this, one will cause trouble at times and will be destructive, sometimes by intention, sometimes unintentionally. Here again is a problem that never ceases throughout life. Whoever exercises initiative will cause disturbance and dislocation. Any extensive change will inevitably involve destruction as well as construction. In the play of children, as well as in the far reaching projects of adult initiative, the destruction resulting may far outweigh any benefit. Thus the child and the adult become involved in guilt.

Here the crisis centers in the question: What shall I do about my guilt? Shall I inhibit initiative to avoid guilt? Shall I deny my guilt. Shall I try to compensate for it by good works? Shall I become burdened with the sense of guilt to the point where I make myself and my associates miserable? Shall I project my guilt on some other person or group and punish them as though they were the guilty ones and not myself? There are many different ways in which people deal with the problem of guilt. The right way, according to the standard used by Erikson, is the way that will best promote identity formation, to use his expression. To use our own expression, guilt is treated in the right way when it promotes wholeness of being in commitment of faith.

This way of treating guilt requires, first, that one acknowledge oneself for what one truly is with whatsoever guilt and virtue are present. Only when one does this can one meet the second requirement, to commit oneself as one truly is, guilt and all, to the divine creativity of interchange able to weave this guilty self into the fabric of life to create a goodness not otherwise possible. Thus does the self, guilt and all, become something precious.

As a child, one will not be able to acknowledge one's guilt in such a way as to commit one's guilty self to the interchange between oneself and one's parents if this interchange is not of a kind revealed in Christ. If this is to happen, the parents must recognize their share in the guilt along with that of the child, while never ceasing to accept the child as one who is precious. In this way one can learn to commit oneself with full acknowledgement of one's guilt, to that kind of interchange which can create out of such honesty and completeness of self-giving a range and depth of appreciative awareness which is the glory of human existence. In this attainment the guilt, confessed and repeated, has a part to play.

At school age comes the fourth crisis, called *Industry and Inferiority.* Here the child must undertake tasks more serious than play. The child must be able to master, in some measure, what is required in school, both in learning and in the competitive life of the students with one another. Will one come through it with a sense of inferiority which cripples and incapacitates one for any worthy work, or will one find a place and a part in the school and in the work of the world where one's achievement wins recognition?

The next crisis occurs in adolescence, extending from the middle teens to the late twenties. For some this period may be longer or shorter. This crisis is called *Identity versus Identity Diffusion.* This is a consummation of all the previous crisis. The relative success, or the relative failure, of the previous struggles with the issues of life bear their fruit at this time. None of them, nor all of them together, will determine with finality the outcome of this crisis in adolescence. But the struggle to achieve identity at this time will be more or less difficult depending on the outcome of the previously encountered crises. We shall not attempt to go into the complexities of this crisis of identity beyond what we have already explained concerning it. It is the central theme of Erikson's work and any attempt to discuss its ramifications would lead too far afield.

The next crisis is that of *Intimacy versus Isolation.* This intimacy is not only with a member of the other sex, although this is included, but it also refers to the ability of the individual to enter into relations of reciprocal appreciative understanding of individuality with others. The outcome of this crisis determines how freely and fully and at what depth the individual can communicate reciprocally with others? Over what range of diversity and over what barriers of estrangement and hostility can this sharing and this reciprocal understanding of individuality take place between the individual and other? These are the questions to be answered by this crisis.

The seventh crisis is *Generativity versus Self-absorption*. Generativity refers to productivity. It includes what the individual produces in a chosen field of work that bears the stamp of the individual's own unique individuality. It refers also to children and parenthood and the ability to rear children who can pass successfully through the crises here listed. Also it refers to what one is able to do in shaping social and cultural conditions that will be helpful in enabling the next generation, and not alone one's own children, to encounter these crises successfully. It refers to the development of a personality and way of life that will enable the rising generation to find a person who increases their basic trust, their autonomy, their initiative, their industry, their ego identity, their intimacy with others and their own generativity.

The last crisis, reached in late maturity, Erikson calls *Integrity versus Disgust, Despair*. By this he means that a person comes at last to appraise the life one has lived, the kind of personality one has become, and the effect one has had on other lives. Will self-appraisal of oneself and one's life bring a sense of disgust or despair? Or will one be able not only to say, but profoundly to feel, that after all it was good to have lived. Can one say and feel this with full and free acknowledgement of what one has become and of what one has done? If so, this is what Erikson calls integrity. One has met this test if one can say in all sincerity and without self-deception that one would undertake again the kind of life one tried to live and the development one followed. This is the final test of a lifetime of struggle, meeting crisis after crisis, and finally becoming the kind of person which all this has produced.

On this point Erikson makes a comment about the great persons of history who have done most to reconstruct the order of human life and have introduced new and better ways of enabling individuals to undergo the crises of personal development. He says that these great persons who have been transformers and innovators have often ended their lives in disgust or despair. This has come upon them for two reasons. First, they are more honest with themselves in judging the actual outcome of their life's work, searching more deeply and judging more severely. Second, their innovations rightly broke through the old constraints and limitations that produced hypocrisy and in that sense their work was good. But this liberation is almost always used by many for their own destructive ends. Hence the more immediate outcome of these innovations may be a series of disasters. Their lives, their teachings, and the new order is misunderstood and misinterpreted and made to serve ends the opposite of what was intended. Erikson makes this plain in his study of Martin Luther in his book *Young Man Luther*. Such being the case, Erikson suggests that these great persons should die very soon after their constructive work was done. Jesus died young, says Erikson, and we cannot imagine him as an old man. He suggests that Jesus could not be so high and holy had he not died young. Lincoln died at the right time. Socrates lived to be an old man. We do not know if he experienced disgust or despair; but perhaps he died before the misinterpretations of his life's work and the consequent disasters became manifest.

This suggestion made by Erikson that the great persons of history who have done most to open the way for human salvation should die before the misinterpretation and misuse of their innovations brought on great evils is quite peripheral. It is only an aside, thrown out by him in the discussion. There may be a way of achieving integrity even amid the disasters resulting from misuse of innovations that would be beneficial if rightly used and understood. But this suggestion helps to understand and more vividly appreciate this last crisis through which the life of every person must pass. Will it be integrity in the sense of acceptance and approval on the whole or will it be disgust or despair?

Any one or more of these eight crises may be hidden and unacknowledged by the individual. People for the most part have no understanding and no conscious awareness of these crises, even when they suffer the consequences of failing to meet them successfully or even when they derive the benefit of going through them successfully.

These problems of personality, making for well-being or ill-being, are like the problems of health for the biological organism. Only the medical expert and diagnostician has much understanding of the crises through which the organism passes, resulting in sickness or health. But regardless of this unawareness and lack of understanding, the organism undergoes the crises of digestion, the crises of resisting infectious disease, the crises of maintaining the right body heat when the temperature changes radically, and all the other crises which the biological organism must meet in maintaining its vitality and health. The health of the organism has been greatly improved where research has made people aware of these crises of biological vitality and has provided scientific knowledge concerning how to meet them and maintain good health.

All this applies in like manner to the human personality and the crises of its development. As biological health will be better or worse depending on research to provide the conditions required for healthful living, so the development of the human personality can be made better or worse depending on research to show the conditions required for its salvation *from* basic mistrust, shame and doubt of self, unmanageable guilt, self-defeating inferiority, identity diffusion (which is disintegration of personality), isolation (which is inability to enter into intimate relations with others), self-absorption and final despair. This is the problem of salvation *from*. The problem of salvation *to* is the reverse of this list.

While biological health and the salvation of human personality have in

common this need for knowledge gained by research, there is one major
difference of first importance that must never be forgotten. This major
difference makes the salvation of personality a religious problem while the
problem of health, taken by itself alone, is not religious. For biological health
one does not need to commit one's total being to anything. One only needs to
commit one's biological organism to the regiment and treatment required for
health. But when it comes to salvation of the individual personality in the
wholeness of its being, the total being of the individual must give itself in
faith to what creates, sustains, saves and transforms toward the best that
human life can ever attain. For this reason the basic problems of personality,
called crises by Erikson, are religious problems, even though he does not
present them in the context of religion. They cannot be solved, and the crises
cannot be passed successfully, unless one at some level of maturity commits
oneself in faith to what creates basic trust, free and unashamed autonomy,
initiative with guilt confessed and forgiven, industry free of the distortions
and inhibitions of inferiority, identity which can bring all the resources of the
individual into action, ability to engage in deep and multiform intimacy,
generativity and, last of all, integrity in the final survey and judgment on life.

So we reach the conclusion: these crises through which every individual
must pass with fateful consequence are, every one, religious problems.
Consequently the Christian religion, just as every other religion, has responsibility for every one of them. This Christian responsibility for each of these
basic problems of human existence is sevenfold: Cognitive, educational,
evangelical, institutional, cultural, historical and philosophical-theological.

These imperative responsibilities of the Christian religion for the conduct of human life cannot be adequately met in our time without organized
research as thorough, persistent, penetrating, and critical as it can be made.
If some insist that this kind of research is not science, considering its subject
matter, let them use another label. We are using the name of science in this
context—with apologies if those are demanded.

The first of these imperative responsibilities of the Christian religion for
the salvation of the individual, involving also society and history, is here
called cognitive. By this term is meant responsibility for getting the best
possible intellectual understanding of what calls for commitment of faith by
reason of its creative, sustaining, saving and transforming efficacy. Again to
repeat, this does not mean that intellectual understanding by itself is sufficient for any person's salvation nor will it by itself induce the commitment of
faith. But they who seek to provide conditions most favorable for the transforming power of Christ do require this intellectual understanding so that
their efforts will not be misdirected.

Any intellectual understanding we may ever have of the saving power of
God revealed in Christ will be partial and superficial. This is true of all
knowledge that the human mind can ever possess of any concrete actuality.
Every actuality is always more than our true statements about it. Especially

is this true of anything so complex, deep laid and intimately involved in human existence as Christ, when Christ means what carries us most successfully through the major crises of human life to the end of our salvation. Not only is our knowledge very limited, but it is also partial in the sense that it is always adapted to some one approach. When we approach the same actuality with other interests and in a different cultural, historical context, we need a different knowledge of the actuality. This does not mean that the first form of partial knowledge was false, any more than knowledge of a mountain viewed from one valley is false, even though knowledge of that same mountain when viewed from the other side gives us a very different perspective.

This change in our approach and perspective, with consequent need to revise our knowledge, applies to every vitally important actuality with which we deal in order to live. It applies to our knowledge of the earth and sky, our knowledge of our own organisms and of society, our knowledge of history and of love and friendship. So also it applies to our knowledge of the saving power of Christ. Knowledge fitted for one approach, due to one context of culture, society and history, will not be fitted to guide the commitment of faith in another context. The old forms of knowledge become obsolete because the approach to the actuality in question is different from what it was when those forms of knowledge may have served well enough. The knowledge fit to guide the traveler to the top of the mountain from one valley is not the knowledge required when one starts from the other side of the mountain.

Here, then, is the first responsibility of the Christian religion for showing the way of salvation. It is the cognitive responsibility because every new social, historical situation gives to people living at that time a perspective on all reality which is different from what it was in other social, historical contexts. Within this new perspective, our knowledge must take on a different form, exposing a different aspect to earth and sky and love and death and all else. Today the social-historical condition has changed so radically and swiftly during the last few decades that our intellectual understanding of Christ, held over from other times, is not fitted to guide the commitment of faith, at least for many people. It is a Christian responsibility to develop a form of knowledge that is fitting.

The second responsibility of the Christian religion applies to education. In going to school the student should be equipped by the teaching received, by study and by association with other students in school to undergo successfully the crises of personal development. This in turn means a commitment of faith of such sort that the student is guided and sustained through these crises. Education must assume this responsibility not for the sake of any particular kind of religion but to save our civilization from self-destruction as well as save the individual from a like fate.

This responsibility of every Christian man and woman for the conduct of education does not mean that the church should control and direct education. To repeat, the Christian religion and its responsibility is not limited to the church. It is life as lived by Christian men and women in relation to every institution of our society. Hence the responsibility of the Christian religion for education has nothing to do with the relation of church and state.

Research is required to find what kind of education is best fitted to enable the student to develop a sustaining faith fit to carry one through the crises of personal development and at the same time enable one to become participant in guiding society through the crises of its transformation. The church might engage in this kind of research just as any other institution might do. But this should not be done to bring education under control of the church. For the most part this research should be done by Christian men and women (and others) in connection with the educational institutions themselves.

The third responsibility of Christian men and women is evangelical. By this is meant conduct best fitted to induce people to make the commitment of faith. This is not merely a matter of public preaching, although preaching has its part to play. It is not merely a matter of formal worship and going to church and having meetings specially designed to induce this commitment. Nor is it merely a matter of speaking to people about Christ. Something else is far more effective in evangelism. It can be called evangelical conduct— living in profound readiness to respond with appreciative understanding to the unique individuality of the other person. In short, evangelical conduct is living day by day (and not alone in church) under the dominant control of that kind of interchange which is Christ present in our midst.

Living in this way is not merely a matter of knowledge. But some conditions are more favorable than other conditions can be for the development of this way of life and for this responsiveness. To discover and provide these conditions for effective evangelism is a problem for research. In this way the evangelical responsibility of the Christian religion calls for scientific research as much as the other responsibilities.

Still another Christian responsibility calls for examination in respect to its relation to science. It is here called institutional responsibility. This means the responsibility of Christian men and women to modify the major institutions so that the demands of these institutions upon the individual will not hinder but will help the individual undergo the crises of personal development. If Christian men and women are to do this effectively, if their efforts to modify institutions are to do more good than harm, they should be guided by knowledge relevant to this problem. Research such as that of Erikson illustrates what is needed, not because Erikson is an infallible guide but because he is working upon problems that bear upon this Christian responsibility.

A further responsibility, here called cultural, means the responsibility of Christian men and women to develop what Erikson calls an "ideology" that will be helpful in guiding the developing personality through the crises of existence. Erikson recognizes that the word "ideology" has taken on evil connotations. What he means is a perspective on human history, human society, the human personality and interpersonal relations and the world generally. Instead of calling this perspective an "ideology" we might call it the truth. Certainly what we should seek is the truth. But, as said before, our knowledge is always very incomplete and partial and the best we can hope to achieve is knowledge relevant to our situaion in the context of the society and period of history in which we live. If "truth" is understood to be knowledge developed in this way and for this purpose, there is justification for Erikson's use of the word "ideology." Ideology is truth when "truth" means knowledge confirmed by evidence but at the same time shaped to guide conduct in dealing with the major problems of the culture and historical situation where we are. Any such guiding perspective adequate to our time will include an interpretation of the significance of science and its integration into the comprehensive view of the way life should be lived.

The need of organized and directed research to achieve such "truth" or "knowledge" or "ideology" is obvious. Here again science must be made to serve faith, if the Christian religion is to measure up to its imperative responsibility in shaping the cultural perspective.

We listed two additional responsibilities called historical and philosophical-theological. But these are not different from what has just been described as the cultural or ideological responsibility. The only reason for mentioning them is to make more specific certain essential parts of this work of developing an ideology for the conduct of human living in our time. The historical responsibility is to find that interpretation and understanding of history which is a necessary part of any adequate ideology. The philosophical responsibility is to analyze human experience in such a way as to expose those basic forms or categories of human experience which also form a part of any guiding cultural perspective. All of this sevenfold responsibility of the Christian religion calls for research and in that sense requires the service of science.

The worth of any community is determined by the way it fosters the development of participant individuality in the persons who belong to it. Hence the problem of community properly includes a study of the crises of growth through which every individual passes in the development from infancy to old age. These periods are called crises because they are forks in the road of personal development. One fork leads to greater wholeness in Christ. In the technical jargon of psychology this is called "identity formation." In the scientific study of the problem, no reference is made to Christ and quite properly because the study is not carried to this level. The nearest that Erikson comes to it is in his reference to "limitless resources" mentioned in one of our quotations.

The other fork in the road leads to breakdown of wholeness and alienation from Christ. In the technical study this is called identity diffusion.

While alienation from Christ is not mentioned, and again for good reason, the psychological study makes it plain that the individual who goes down this fork in the road of personal development is alienated from what creates ego identity. There is no division and no opposition between the psychological interpretation of the problem and the theological understanding of it provided that the Christian religion assumes what is here called its cognitive responsibility as described above.

To symbolize the inseparable connection of the problem of community with the problem of developing individuality, we have put the two together in this one chapter. The responsibility of the Christian for both of these problems demands that one make use of scientific research. Otherwise one cannot serve Christ faithfully and effectively. Adherents of other faiths have a similar responsibility; but the Christian who shifts responsibility over to them is unfaithful.

CHAPTER VIII
SCIENCE, CHRIST AND EXISTENTIALISM

Existentialism represents a great reversal from the direction in which Western thought has been developing during the past centuries. Existentialism is a turning away from the objective world as known to natural science and from the goals sought by scientific technology of prediction and control. This is the negative side of existentialism. On the positive side it is a turning to the consciousness of the individual to discover what may be found there. It stands for subjectivism in opposition to the objectivism of scientific knowledge and scientific technology.

Edmund Husserl with his phenomenology was not an existentialist but he was one influence leading to present day existentialism. For Husserl the shift of inquiry from the objective world to the inspection and analysis of the structures of consciousness was intended to establish the foundations of scientific knowledge. Husserl is mentioned here to illustrate the difference between studying the structures of consciousness in order to understand the cognitive powers of the human mind and studying consciousness in a very different way which is the way of the existentialists.

The existentialists study consciousness of the individual because it is for them the all important reality. They seek to rescue consciousnes in its depth and wholeness from being ignored and submerged beneath the structures of the objective world as known to science and from the rational systems constructed by reason. The existentialists do not deny the truth and the importance of scientific knowledge and rational order. They only insist that consciousness is vastly more than these. They also insist that one in the actual depth and wholeness of one's being is this total depth and wholeness of consciousness which is ignored and devalued when the structures of reason and objective scientific knowledge are given priority over all else.

This consciousness in its wholeness, which the existentialists want to rescue from the outcast regions and put at the center of human concern is the actual individual person. To ignore this wholeness and depth is to ignore our humanity and deceive ourselves into thinking that we are identical with the rational order constructed by science and systematic philosophy. This is "bad faith," "lack of authenticity"; it is repudiation of responsibility for the total being of self and others; it is refusal to face up to reality and acknowledge the self for what it is.

What we actually experience is vastly more than the scientifically confirmed generalizations about the world around us; it is vastly more than the purposes sought by means of scientific technology. Above all it is more than what people are taught to think and feel and seek under the control of those techniques by which the crowd is managed by dictators, advertisers, popular slogans and the mass effect of conformity to customs and fads.

The existentialists strive to rescue the total content and capacity of human consciousness from subordination to the techniques of prediction and control, and the massive impact of social convention whether these are imposed directly upon the individual or whether they are imposed indirectly. They are imposed indirectly when people become so fascinated with the narrow specializations of scientific inquiry and technology, or so bound to social convention, that they exclude from consideration all the variety and fullness of consciousness which arises when the individual honestly recognizes in oneself all one's motives, desires, fears and hopes. But the full import of existentialism does not become apparent until we go beyond this. The deeper meaning of existentialism is found in the teaching that the actual individual is one's total consciousness. This is one's total being, one's actual existing self. Furthermore, this actual existing self is, in their teaching, ultimate being.

This teaching of existentialism about the actual existing self as ultimate being stands in opposition both to materialism and to idealism, both to naturalism and to supernaturalism. It denies materialism because it denies that the conscious mind of the individual can be explained in terms of organized matter. It denies idealism because it denies that there is a cosmic mind or any other kind of mind upon which individual minds depend or from which they are derived. It denies naturalism when this means that scientific knowledge of the world around us can give us knowledge applicable to an understanding of the individual self. It denies supernaturalism because it denies that we can know any kind of being greater than we by which we are created, sustained, saved from evil or moved toward a greater good than we can achieve by our own freedom and purpose.

Some existentialists believe in a supernatural being or other being with power to create and save humans from their evil ways. But they deny that such a being can be known by way of intellectual inquiry. Kierkegaard accepted the traditional Christian beliefs but he denied that they can be sustained by the kind of evidence on which knowledge must rest. So also Jaspers believes there is a cosmic being, called the "Encompassing," but this being can never be distinguished from other beings by any characteristics accessible to human inquiry. Others such as Gabriel Marcel, Martin Buber, Reinhold Neibuhr, and Paul Tillich affirm a supreme being of some sort but deny that this faith can be established as a form of knowledge. The individuals just mentioned are religious existentialists or, if they repudiate this characterization, they are greatly indebted to existentialism.

Existentialism is not new. Many a great mind in the past denied the priority of the objective world and turned to consciousness itself to find ultimate being and all the important goods and evils of life. In some form and to some degree this way of dealing with the problems of life is very ancient. But existentialism is new in the sense of having a character more or less distinctive of our time and in having a wide influence not only in philosophy and religion but also in art and literature, in psychology and psychotherapy, and in the field of popular discussion and popular reading. Its impact is wide and powerful both on those who reject it and on those who accept it and on those who are critical but "see something in it."

This raises the question: why has existentialism become so powerfully influential in our time in many intellectual circles? The answer to that question appears when we note what existentialism is fighting for and fighting against. The overwhelming domination of scientific knowledge, technological control and rational order has been building up for centuries until now it has created in the minds of many a vague but deep and disturbing anxiety. Existentialism comes forth with a message that seems to explain and justify this anxiety. Scientific knowledge, technological control and rational order are of course indispensable. Human beings must have them. They are precious and our existence depends upon them. But when they submerge and exclude from consideration the total being of the individual, they can become monstrous evils. They are not evil in themselves. They are a great and necessary good. But when they subordinate, dwarf and impoverish the wholeness of one's being, their tyranny must be cast off. Existentialism has arisen to cast off this tyranny. Great thinkers, especially those concerned with the fine arts and religious faith are pre-eminently concerned with that wholeness of being which is ignored when interest is directed exclusively upon the structures of reason and science.

For the sake of science on the one hand and for the sake of the Christian faith on the other, it is our responsibility to listen to the existentialists and learn what we can from them. They have something to say which is worthy of very serious consideration. In order to appropriate whatever truth they have to offer, we shall ask again, more searchingly than before, "what are the existentialists trying to accomplish?"

By asking this question we are seeking to comprehend the vision of such writers as Pascal, Kierkegaard, Nietzsche, Dostoevsky, Tolstoy, Heidegger, Jaspers, Sartre, Buber, Marcel, Camus, Beauvoir, to mention a few of the individuals generally classed under the heading of existentialism. Some of these writers have denied that they are existentialists because they seek ends very different from others who bear the name. No doubt they differ greatly among themselves and in some respects their aims are contradictory. Some of them strive passionately to eliminate all belief in God while others just as passionately defend this belief. Some of them find God as a living person with whom they commune, while others insist that the ultimate concern is with pure being and not with any distinguishable kind of being.

Some of them are chiefly concerned with what they call nothing or nothingness. Nothingness is the absence of seeking which we experience in some encounters. If I eagerly seek a friend with high expectation of meeting in some location, and if my life is wrapped up in that meeting, I have the experience of nothingness if I fail to meet and cannot find my friend. When someone dies with whom my life is intertwined, the experience of nothingness comes over me. If I seek life and find death awaiting me, I encounter nothingness. So likewise many experiences are of this sort. They are blanks, leading on to nothing whatsoever.

These encounters we ordinarily try to forget and keep out of consciousness because they are very disturbing. They are the source of deep laid anxiety from which we cannot escape because they are inevitably involved in our finitude. Our reach in always exceeding our grasp and when it does we encounter nothingness. Death as the limitation of all our strivings is the most obvious example of our finitude because we try to reach on beyond death. "Going to heaven" may be a compensation, but almost everyone strives to continue earthly existence. Some of the existentialists have much to say about this encounter with nothingness in the anticipation of death. They emphasize this not because they want to be morbid but because we ordinarily refuse to acknowledge this experience honestly and openly and assume responsibility for meeting death in whatsoever way may be the best and right way. What that best and right way may be is the open question. The existentialists insist that every person must answer that question responsibly with full awareness of what is involved, without evasion, self-deception or any dishonest device. When death is not met in such a way as to make it contributory to the purpose for which I live, it is my encounter with nothingness. It is also on that account called my experience of finitude.

So likewise failure in an enterprise on which I have staked my all is a dead end. It is empty of meaning, hence a case of nothingness if it contributes nothing to any striving or any purpose in my life. It is another manifestation of my finitude. Or again, rejection by one I love, to whom I have given my utmost devotion, is such a dead end if I can discern no meaning and no purpose for living thereafter. Examples of this sort might be multiplied but these may serve to suggest a line of inquiry pursued by the existentialists.

With these examples before us we come back to our initial question: "What are the existentialists trying to do?" Certainly they differ among themselves. At some levels and in some forms they are diametrically opposed to one another. But insofar as they can all be classed together as existentialists they have something in common; and it is this common goal of endeavor, given the name of existentialism, which we here seek to understand and articulate as quickly as possible.

Put very briefly, what the existentialists are trying to do is to make the individual more fully conscious of all that is involved in existence, particularly what is ordinarily concealed, denied or unacknowledged. People try to divert their minds from the kind of encounters described in previous paragraphs. They try to overcome their limitations, otherwise called their finitude, by thinking and acting as though these limitations did not exist for them. People find it very difficult to give attention to what has no meaning, precisely because it has no meaning for them. Nevertheless we have seen that what has no meaning is truly involved in our experience. It is there inevitably and plays a large part in our lives. We conceal it and cover it over with limited purposes insecurely pursued, and these keep us going. But these purposes are not sufficiently comprehensive to draw into their service the total being of the existing individual. They cannot in this limited form give meaning to my death by making it contribute to what I seek above all else. Neither can they endow my failure with meaning by making it contributory to the total striving of my life. So likewise with many other encounters with nothingness inevitably involved in the existence of the human being. All these dead ends might be transformed into open roads leading on to the ultimate purpose of my life if I had the right kind of purpose. But what kind of purpose might that be? That is the basic problem of human existence. It is the problem with which the existentialists struggle.

The existentialists try to uncover what is unacknowledged, concealed and denied, and thereby enable the individual to understand the basic and comprehensive problem of personal existence. We cannot ask the question rising out of the imperative demands of human existence until we understand what those demands may be. We cannot understand these demands so long as we conceal them and will not acknowledge them.

The existentialists do not deny that people have many purposes for which they live, and many meanings concern them in their daily lives. But when we get beneath the surface and do not conceal what is actually happening, we find that the individual ordinarily does not have any purpose fit to gather one up and thus enable one to overcome the nothingness involved in personal existence by endowing it with meaning through making it contributory to the overruling purpose of existence. Also such a purpose, if it is to overcome the emptiness of life, must gather all society and all history into its service along with the wholeness and uniqueness of each individual. It must give meaning to death and failure, to suffering and uncertainty so that those also become contributory to the activating purpose of life. The absence of such a purpose in the ordinary life of a person is what the existentialists are exposing.

After the existentialists have done their work of exposure, removing the illusions which conceal this condition, three alternatives are open. Search for a purpose of the sort just mentioned, which can endow with meaning what is now meaningless by making it contributory to this purpose; give up in despair; deny and conceal what the existentialists have exposed and thus revert to the ways of self-deception.

This condition of human existence exposed by the existentialists calls for further examination. Many things in the world have meaning in the sense of utility. I can use them to serve some purpose or other. But the question asked by the existentialists is not about these utilities. The question they ask is this: "Does my own existence have a purpose to serve?" Does it have a purpose beyond merely serving itself and serving the existence of other selves like myself? Or is human existence a dead end in itself with nothing to seek except to survive, be comfortable and try to be happy with nothing to do except to be happy? When people have power and wealth to satisfy every biological need and achieve every biological pleasure, they resort to extravagant follies and desperate ventures to keep this question out of mind.

At the peak of human power, with science and technology getting control of the ultimate sources of cosmic energy by way of nuclear fission and fusion, with the possibility of economic abundance for all, suppose we succeed in abolishing war and attain peace and harmony. What then? Is this a dead end? Is this the goal of all our striving? Or can it be that this total existence I call myself, with its suffering and its death, its failure, sin and guilt, its ignominy and defeat, just as it is without pretense to be anything else, can it be offered up and given over as a very precious contribution to a creative and transforming power working to bring forth a glory beyond human power?

Can it be that my death and my failure, my sin and my guilt, my ignominy and my defeat, add to the value of this gift of my total self when it is offered up in complete self-giving to this saving and divine being? Does complete honesty and openness concerning the true state of my total being, called confession and repentance, add to the value of this gift of myself?

The question about human existence emerging after the existentialists have done their work might be worded thus: What possible purpose for human existence can I find and adopt as my own which will give high meaning and precious value not only to my success but also to my failure; not only to my pleasure but also to my suffering; not only to predictable outcomes but also to uncertainties and unpredictable outcomes; not only to honor and popular favor but also to ignominy and rejection by those I love; not only to the days of my life but also to my death; not only to my virtue but also to my sin and guilt; all this provided that required conditions are met. What purpose can I adopt for my life which will enable me to say: The weak things of the earth and the things that are despised did God choose, yea, and the things are not, (even the nothings) that he might bring to naught the things that are?

This is the question calling imperatively for an answer out of the depths of human existence when this depth is given a voice by the existentialists. It is a question which cannot come to consciousness until after the concealments and cliches, the distractions and subterfuges have been wiped away. Also the contradictions and uncertainties resulting from a study of the different theologies and philosophies must be recognized before this question can be asked with all the passion generated by the struggle to escape despair. Meanwhile they who are blinded by the social conventions of concealment or by the speculative theologies and philosophies, live comfortably and complacently.

This question exposed by the existentialists is not the one most commonly asked about human life throughout the history of Western culture. The question that has ordinarily been asked by Western people has taken one or other of two forms. Both of these should be distinguished from the question rising out of the study of the existentialists. One of these Western style questions asks, "What purpose can I adopt for my whole life and for all humans which will satisfy more fully than any other possible purpose all my desires and felt needs along with like satisfaction for all others?"

This is one form of the question about human life most commonly asked by Western peoples. The second form is different. It requires a revolutionary change in the conduct of human life, but still is not the same as the question we are asking after disillusionment. It runs like this: "What possible purpose can I adopt for my whole life and for all humans which will satisfy more fully than any other all the desires and felt needs of human existence *provided that all these desires and felt needs are transformed to meet the demands of this purpose?*"

The first of these two ways of asking the question is put by the epicurean. The second is put by the stoic. According to the first question, my desires and felt needs are the standard to which the purpose must conform. According to the second question, some alleged cosmic purpose is the standard to which my desires and felt needs must conform. We are here using the word "purpose" to take the place of the word "ideal," which is more commonly used. But in this context the two words are equivalent. An ideal is irrelevant to the problem here under consideration unless it becomes a ruling purpose, absorbing the whole of one's life so far as that is possible.

While the two questions point in opposite directions so far as concerns the kind of purpose or ideal sought, they are alike in one respect. They both seek to bring all desires and felt needs under the control of a ruling purpose and in this way give some measure of satisfaction to them all. But if it should be the case that not all desires and felt needs can be brought under the control of any possible ideal or ruling purpose, if the individual in the totality of personal existence is at cross purposes and if the forms of finitude exposed by the existentialists are wrought inextricably into human existence, then these dead ends will be left standing. They will be without meaning, without contribution of any kind to the purpose of my life. They will remain the dark areas about which nothing can be done except to conceal them, deny them, divert attention from them. In this way, perhaps, one can make oneself think that one has found the road to happiness or fulfillment or satisfaction or whatever term will best serve to hide what one does not want to acknowledge.

Over against the two kinds of questions we have just mentioned is a third kind of question arising out of the study of the existentialists. The existentialists themselves do not necessarily ask this third kind of question although some of them seem to suggest it. (But just now we are not looking to the existentialists to solve this problem of human existence. Rather we are looking to them to remove the concealments obscuring the actual conditions of human existence so that the problem in its true character can be discerned.) The third way of putting the question about human existence might be worded thus: "What can I serve of such sort that I can say, 'Not my will but thine be done' and thereby commit myself to a creativity which needs such a one as I, namely, one who struggles against the limitations of personal finitude." Only such a one can be creatively transformed to larger dimensions of appreciative consciousness. Only such a one can be the creature and creator of history by both one's life and death, one's death being as great a contribution as one's life, because one's death opens the way for millions of others through a sequence of generations to contribute their lives to the creativity running through history as described in previous chapters.

Only the people who struggle against the limitations of their finitude can be vividly aware of a creativity reaching beyond their own lives to which they can commit themselves with such completeness that all the possibilities of this divine creativity become their own possibilities. My forms of finitude, when I struggle against them, yield the experiences described by the existentialists as nothingness, meaninglessness, guilt, sin, failure, death and the like. But it is precisely these forms of finitude and my struggle against them which enables me to identify myself with a divine creativity which can realize values immeasurably beyond my powers and even beyond the specific forms of my imagination although I can know that this creativity under required conditions is able to realize them.

Thus when I say, "Not my will but thine be done" what I am saying is this: "I commit myself to be transformed creatively in communion with others and through a sequence of many generations to the attainment of ends which I cannot foresee nor imagine but which I know are of greater value than what I can foresee and imagine." My very limitations make me fit and able to participate in this divine creativity and take to myself in communion with others all the values it will ever create. In this way does my struggle, yielding the experience of nothingness, endow me with transcendent value. This transcendent value is the value of the divine creativity to which I commit myself when I say, "Not my will but thine be done." These words were uttered in Gethsemane by Jesus on the night before he was crucified, knowing that he would be crucified the next day. It is in such an hour, if ever, that a person discovers the transfiguring power and ultimate blessedness of this commitment. It is the hour when a person seems to be engulfed in the great night of nothingness. As previously explained, it is the last despair beyond which is found the buoyancy of life.

In this way a person can offer one's failure and sin, one's uncertainty and blindness, one's defeat and rejection, one's absurdity and death, one's total self just as one is, in communion with others to be transformed in whatsoever way the divine creativity can expand the range and vividness of appreciative consciousness. Nothing is fit to undergo the kind of creative transformation expanding the range of appreciative consciousness except one who struggles against the limitations of personal existence in all the several ways mentioned in the previous sentence.

All this will make no sense at all to many persons because they have not found the way of salvation. For them only the second and third alternatives are open: Either give up in despair or divert the mind from the problem of human existence which is now being exposed by the existentialists. In this way one can conceal the dead ends by many devices commonly practiced.

Let us return now to the two ways of asking the question about human existence which have been most common in Western culture. They are the questions, with relevant answers, asked by the Epicurean and the Stoic. Why have Western people not, generally speaking, asked the question in the third way? The third way, of course, is to ask about a divine creativity which can given value to one's limitations, finitude, dead ends, frustrations, sin, guilt and death. To understand why Western people, as a rule, have not asked the third question, we shall examine a little further this Western culture of ours. This examination may help us to understand the special significance of existentialism for our culture at this moment of its history. It may show how the exposure of our condition by the existentialists is related both to science and to Christ.

The supreme achievement of Western culture has been its science and technology with consequent power to produce economic abundance and to organize great numbers of people for collective action. In this way people of the West have been able to exercise power immeasurably greater than was ever had in any other time by any other people, although other peoples of the world are now acquiring this power first created by the West. The social and historical conditions making it possible for Western people to create this power are also the social and historical conditions preventing us from asking the third question, although a minority in the West have asked it and found the answer.

The Greeks taught that reason is supreme. This started the development that has finally resulted in modern science and technology and methods of social organization, giving to Western people a mastery over subhuman nature and over the social process never had by humankind until now. The claim that reason is supreme means, first of all, that the totality of all being, so far as it is worthy of serious consideration, is an order as perfect and precise as a mathematical structure. It means, secondly, that this order of being can be comprehended perfectly and completely by the intellect, provided, of course, that the intellect attains that level of competence and comprehension. No human intellect can know this order of being perfectly and completely, but there is no known limit beyond which human inquiry might not go in approaching comprehension of all-inclusive being, since all being has the structure knowable to reason. Of course, the Greek tragedians had a strong sense of the irrational in human existence, but the dominant influence reaching us from the Greeks has come to us from Plato and Aristotle, the Greek mathematicians and scientists of Hellenism, the stoics and, later, the Roman jurists and administrators.

Not only did we get from the Greeks the notion that being is identical with the kind of order to be known by logical thinking; this order was also prescriptive for human conduct. Furthermore, it was taught that a human is a rational animal. This means that what distinguishes humans from every other animal is the intellect that can know the logical order of being—and the moral ideal that can bring human conduct into conformity with this logical order.

Thus was given to Western culture, at the beginning of its historical development, a vision which has continued more or less dominant up to our time. It was a vision of human destiny in kinship with the order of being, which was commonly represented as God, the supernatural Person, who created the rational order of being for the intellect and prescribed the moral ideal for human conduct.

This brief sketch is very much over-simplified in that many deviations from this line of development could be found in the history of Western culture. But just now we are tracing that strand in our historical development that became inordinately dominant in the eighteenth century and that, so far as it was dominant, prevented Western people from asking the third question, leading them rather to ask the question about human existence in either the first or the second forms above mentioned.

This does not mean that Westerners have been throughout their history Epicureans and Stoics. Rather when they asked, "What purpose can bring the largest measure of satisfaction to all my desires and felt needs?" they answered with Paley and many others, "God wills the happiness of all creatures. *Therefore seek happiness for yourself and for all people because that is God's will.*" If, on the other hand, they asked the second question, they received an answer provided by John Calvin and others like him: "*Seek out that purpose for your life which conforms to the will of God and bring all your desires and felt needs into conformity to it, not for your happiness but for the glory of God.*"

This vision of reality, this picture of humanity and human destiny, has given to Western culture its conquering power in science and technology, in government and industry, in commerce and war. It is one of the great visions and supreme achievements of human history. All the rest of the world is now reaching out eagerly to take over and adopt to their own use this power created by Western people. Other cultures have given great gifts to human kind; this is the gift given by the West and it is no mean thing.

But now at the peak of our power, in the hour of our triumph, Western people are beginning to look within. We are beginning to search our own subjective state of existence, our own consciousness; and this searching is call existentialism. It is a reversal of the whole course of history. Heretofore, Western people, when dominated by the vision derived from the Greeks, did not look inward; we looked outward upon the world and devoted all our searching, all our discipline and all our energy to getting the knowledge and the methods for prediction and control in order to master subhuman nature and organize society for action.

Of course many individuals in Western culture searched their souls and not a few spent their lives and all their powers trying to understand the total subjectivity called the Self. All this diversity in the way individuals live, and what they primarily seek, can be found in every culture and not least in the West. But we are now speaking of one ruling propensity. Otherwise stated, we are speaking of that one great thing which Western culture has produced and given to the world beyond any other: science, technology and the power of prediction and control. All the world is now eagerly receiving from the West, not its religion which is Christianity, but its science, its technology, and its methods of social organization.

But no great thing is ever achieved in human life without sacrifice of other things. The achievement of Western culture is no exception. In achieving scientific knowledge and scientific power of control, something has been lost; and this something lost is what the existentialists are seeking to recover.

When our power is narrowly limited, what we ignore or do not know about the constitutive demands of the human beings may not lead to serious consequences except for certain unfortunate individuals. But when power becomes gigantic and reaches out to control and direct the whole movement of human life and the course of history, these blind spots concerning what is necessary to the total being of the human self can lead to irremediable disaster. This is what is new about the present situation.

The reference to irremediable disaster is not primarily to nuclear war and the danger of annihilation. People have always been concerned about survival. There is nothing new about that, although the survival of the human race and not alone of a people or a culture is now in question and that, of course, is new. But the problem raised by the existentialists is not the problem of biological survival. The blind spots which the existentialists are trying to correct in the exercise of gigantic and massive power pertain to what is necessary to protect and develop what is profoundly and distinctively human in the total subjectivity of the individual. This is what is in danger of being lost when all power and all concern are given to mastery of the external world and the massive movements of society without regard to the hidden needs of the individual person. This is what we must come to understand, cry the existentialists, and this must be our central concern, in the day of triumphant mastery and dominant control over nature and society and the mind of the individual. We have the power to reduce the individual human being to a brainwashed puppet; and regardless of our intention, this is what our exercise of power will do if we disregard what is necessary to save the depth and wholeness of being of each unique individual person.

The protest, whether it comes in the voice of Kierkegaard or Nietzsche, Heidegger or Jaspers, Sartre or Marcel, Camus or Buber, runs something like this: The all comprehensive system of rational control guiding our exercise of power misinterprets or distorts or suppresses much that is necessary to the total being of the human being. Certainly the existentialists disagree on what is necessary to the total being of the human self and what should be done about it. In some cases, as with Nietzsche, they may denounce humanity itself. But all this disagreement, and all this diversity in the use of language, should not blind us to the common intent of them all, however mistaken their theories may be.

The scientific organization of life, say the existentialists, is an artificial strait jacket which distorts and corrupts the individual self because the human being cannot be fitted whole into such a system. When one seems to fit, and above all when one forces oneself to fit, a large part of one's total self is excluded. Hence, if one persists in trying to live in conformity to the system, one is divided: one part operates according to the system, the rest rebels against it, whether or not one recognizes this split in one's own existence. For the sake of one's own integrity, to save oneself from division into a rational part subject to prediction and control and the non-rational part not thus subjected, one must repudiate the demands of the system and deny its right to rule one's thoughts, actions, sentiments and passions. One must acknowledge oneself for what one truly is and recover the wholeness of personal being. The whole person must come alive, not merely that fragmentary part of the individual that can be controlled by the instruments of power.

Great evils have resulted from the acquisition of power achieved through science, technology and social organization. On the other hand, to reject or condemn science, technology and massive social organization because of the evils resulting from their misuse is folly. This power is one of the most valuable acquisitions ever attained in human history. The problem is to learn how to use it. What shall we seek to achieve or serve by its use?

Two answers have been made to this question and both are wrong. They are the two answers we examined above when the question was asked about human existence. What is our existence good for? What shall we seek or serve supremely? Previously we labeled these two answers as epicurean and stoic, because we were then searching for the sources of our historical development. But these terms, while they communicate well when applied to the two alternative ways of using power in our modern world, are likely to be confusing because the life we live today is very different from what it was when these two terms were current. Today the two alternative ways of using the power of science, technology and social organization are given the names of democracy and communism.

In democracy power is used to satisfy the desires and needs of each individual so far as that is possible. It takes the form of producing goods and services for profit. Profit is made by intensive study of what the public wants, or can be persuaded to want, and then goods and services are produced to satisfy these wants. Critics of the way this is done are numerous. One critic, George Gerbner, of the Institute of Communications Research at the University of Illinois, in an article in *Saturday Review* (June 18, 1960), describes the perverse nature of the way this system works today. Because his points are so cogent, I will quote at length from his argument:

> Television alone, only ten years old as a mass medium, now demands one-fifth of the average person's life. Comic books, twenty years old, can sell one billion copies a year at a cost of $100 million—four times the budget of all public libraries, and more than the cost of the entire book supply for both primary and secondary schools. Movies, developed within a lifetime, reach 50 million people who still go to theatres each week. The same number stay home and watch movies on TV each night—a total of 400 million a week.

> . . . The strategy of private-enterprise mass production is geared to careful assessment, cultivation, and exploitation of marketable desires. A detachment of intelligence specialists probes public fancy; reconnaissance brings in the sales charts, cost-per-thousand figures, consumption statistics; corporate headquarters issues a series of battle orders; an army of popularity engineers prepares compelling messages designed to make the public want what it will get. Then vivid images of life roll out of the "dream factories," produced to exacting specifications to sell the public what it wants. These are the images and messages through which millions see and judge and live and dream in the broader human context. And the conditions of sale are implicit in the content and quality of the dream. What are these implications? How do these conditions of sale affect the individual's image of himself? How is that image changing?

> . . . But existence by itself is not consciousness of existence. Between human existence and our consciousness of existence stand the symbolic representation and imaginative re-creation of existence that we call culture. Culture is itself a historical process and product. It reflects the general productive structure of society, the role and position of communications institutions, the dominant points of view their role and position impart to these institutions, and certain overriding myths, themes and images . . . food for our thoughts and even for our doubts has become a mass-produced commodity.

> . . . Educators especially wonder about the consequences inherent in the commercial compulsion to present life in salable packages. They

observe that in a market geared to immediate self-gratification, other rewards and appeals cannot successfully compete . . . And there is suspicion that the appeal to juvenile fantasy, role experimentation, curiosity, and even anxiety and revolt, may be based more on the private necessity of developing habits of consumer acceptance than on the public requirements of developing critical judgment and of defining essentials of a useful life in society.

. . . The charge of the critic is, in brief, that for all its attractions and private satisfactions, our mass culture does not link the individual to that real world of existence in which he can become an autonomous person, in which he can base his direction on an awareness of the existing structure of his relations to others, in which he can find the representations and points of view necessary to judge and change reality in the light of human values.

. . . We are unable to mobilize much cultural support for aims which do not yield an immediate payoff for somebody producing some commodity for some market. Public agencies are effectively excluded from the mass-cultural field. This leaves the field clear for the privately controlled consumer-oriented media to play the roguish, indulgent uncle.

This extensive quotation shows how the power of science, technology and social organization is used to serve the needs and interests of the individual. It is one of the two alternative ways in which this power is now being used and is called the way of democracy. Its ruling purpose in the use of power is to satisfy the conscious wants of all the people, so far as that is possible. The best method thus far devised for doing that is the market. What can be sold is what the people want. Of course the people who have wants different from those of the mass market, and those who have not the money to buy what the market offers, cannot be served. That is the limitation in this method of serving the wants of the people; but is there any other method that can do it better? Every method has its limitations and its evil consequences. All we can do is to choose the method that most fully achieves the purpose and results with less evil than any other alternative, when good and evil are judged by the end sought—in this case the satisfaction of the desires and needs of all the people so far as these can be sufficiently uniform to be served by any method whatsoever.

This is one way in which the modern world answers the question: "How shall we use our power?" We have already seen how the existentialists condemn this way of using power. It splits the individual into two parts, one part conforming to the system of service while the other part is suppressed or breaks out in revolt because it cannot be served by such a rational order.

The second way in which the massive power of the modern world is used is represented by communism. In principle this is the reverse of the democratic way. Instead of using power to serve whatever interests the people happen to have, it is used to transform the interests of the people to serve the purpose adopted by those who exercise the power. These two seem to be diametrically opposed and in theory they are; but in practice they have a good deal in common. We have seen that when the market is the method for finding out what the interests of the people may be, to the end of producing what they want, a massive conformity to the demands of the market results. The producers certainly are compelled to produce what can be sold for a profit on the market. The market registers what the people will buy and this is what they want. This looks like freedom of choice for the people and service rendered to the people by the instruments of power and so it is within limits. It is certainly not the same as communism. On the other hand, the market, with its vast equipment of advertising and salesmanship, with its scientific research devoted to discovering what the people will buy in massive quantity when proper methods are used to shape and mold their wants, exercises a subtle tyranny of its own over both the producers and the consumers. It does not develop the full potential powers of the individual; neither does it create a community in which each assumes responsibility for all the others while receiving from others those suggestions and insights which expand the range and depth of values accessible to appreciative consciousness, and the limitations of the alternative way of using power, communism, are so widely proclaimed and so continuously denounced that there is little need to repeat them here.

This brings us to the third way of using our science, technology and methods of social organization. It differs radically both from the prevalent form of democracy and from communism. In this third way power is not used to mold and direct the interests of the people to serve some purpose conceived in the imagination as the purpose of history or the purpose of human existence. Neither is it used to serve the interests which the people happen to have at any one time. In distinction from both of these, it is used to provide the conditions most favorable for that kind of interchange which we have discussed throughout this writing as the living Christ in our midst. This cannot be identified with any foreseen outcome of history nor with any foreseen outcome in the development of the individual because it transforms the imagination and appreciative consciousness in such a way as to widen and render more comprehensive, diverse and profound what the imagination can apprehend and consciousness evaluate.

To be sure, what has just been stated can be called a foreseen outcome. But outcome in this sense is very different from an outcome which our present, limited imagination can specify in terms of a definite system of values and structure of human existence. It is an outcome which transcends our present limited imagination and present capacity for evaluating what is good and what is evil. Verbally these two are both outcomes, namely, what our present imagination and appreciative consciousness can anticipate in definite form and content, and what our present imagination and consciousness cannot foresee except to know that it will be more comprehensive and discriminating of good and evil than any vision within reach of our present powers. These two should not be confused because they are opposed to one another. The one is confined to the reach of the vision we now have; the other is directed to transforming this vision so that it will comprehend more of the possibilities of good and evil, distinguish the good from the evil more correctly, and be able to achieve the good and avoid the evil more effectively.

This is not a prediction of inevitable progress. Indeed it is rather a denial that progress is possible when progress means to attain the specific goals which we now can imagine to be most desirable. Also it is a denial that progress is possible when progress means what can be produced directly by the exercise of our power in the form of science, technology and social organization. When these are thought to be the means by which the greater good is achieved and when this power is used to reconstruct the world, the order of society and the minds of people, the outcome, as we have stated, is not good but increasingly evil *unless all this is done to serve the creativity of Christ*. But when it is done to serve Christ in the sense of providing conditions most favorable for the kind of interchange previously described, then it is Christ and not science, technology and social organization which brings forth the greater good although the latter operate indirectly to this end by serving Christ first.

Also we previously made plain that when power is used in this way and people commit themselves to Christ by applying their science, technology and methods of social organization to this service, the finitude of humans in all its forms, combined with the individual's struggle against personal finitude, takes on positive value because this is what makes one fit for the transforming power of Christ. All the perversities, rebellions, frustrations and dark realities explored by the existentialists and the analysists take on positive value, not because perversity and rebellion in themselves are good, but because these are manifestations of the structure of human existence whereby one is shown to be made not for one's present state of existence but for creative transformation.

But this creative and transforming power cannot operate to save us from our self-destructive perversions and rebellions against our finitude unless the resources of our culture are used and enjoyed not as ends in themselves, and not as means for serving this creative transformation. This does not mean that ends and means must be separated. The resources of our culture can be, and should be, enjoyed for their own sake provided that they are also and at the same time used as means to provide conditions most favorable for that kind of interchange between individuals and groups which creates appreciative understanding of one another and generates insights in each whereby the appreciative consciousness becomes more comprehensive and profound.

Western culture in our time has produced four magnificent creations.

We have thus far considered only three of them, namely, science, technology and methods used to organize society for collective action. The fourth is modern art. It must be considered in this context because a recent development in art is an expression of the same development called existentialism. But before we do so, we repeat that these four creations of Western culture will bring on either the degradation or the destruction of people if they are not put to the service of Christ. So far they have not, in general, been so applied. So long as they are not, we live in great danger and in mounting evil. The Christian religion has concentrated on bringing the individual to Christ but this is not sufficient. It must bring the science, the technology, the methods of social organization and the art to this service if we are to be saved from the misuse of this power. This is the hour of our greatest triumph when judged by the magnitude of our power. It is the hour of our greatest danger when judged by the way we use our power.

By art we mean not only painting but also music, fiction, poetry, dance, sculpture and architecture. Recent art as seen in the short story and the novel, in painting and in poetry, to speak of these especially, is often shocking. It exposes the degradation, the perversion and the horror in the subjective existence of the individual. In this sense it is existentialist. But before examining the significance of this development in art, let us look at the function of art in general.

To understand the service of art in the conduct of human living, we need to make a distinction at the level of metaphysics. It is the distinction between objects selected and shaped to guide practical action and logical inference and, in contrast to these, the total process of existence out of which these objects have formed and from which they have been selected for the purposes mentioned. This ongoing process we experience intimately but, in general, obscurely and dimly. As animals struggling to survive and striving to achieve goals of many kinds, our attention is focused on objects which we want to get or avoid, control or cast off. As rational animals our attention is focused on those structures narrowly and precisely defined which are fit to guide the operations of logical thinking. But these objects of practical endeavor and these structures of logical order are only a very small part of that total process of existence from which they are derived and out of which they are developed to serve our practical and theoretical interests.

Underlying these objects and these structures is the total process of existence surging on, sometimes destructively, sometimes sustainingly. But this total process is not an object and it has no defined structure except those narrowly selected portions of it which the culture of the day has found useful for practice and for logical inquiry. Yet this total process is being experienced all the time, obscure and confused and peripheral as that experience may be. This dim, obscure experience of the process of living provides the material out of which all new objects and all further development of logical structure must arise. This process so dimly experienced, because attention ordinarily is diverted from it, is the matrix, the mother, so to speak, out of which all new creation must come forth.

This process of existence which cannot be identified with any knowable object because it is not an object, nor with any logical structure because it has no definable structure, is ordinarily represented by non-cognitive symbols and myths which have no definite referent and by sentiments and moods not attached to anything. Under some conditions the individual may experience this process vividly, not as an object or structure but in the way called mystical. This mystical experience may be an experience of bliss or of dread, yielding a sense of transcendent glory or of horror or disgust.

One may ask why this same process is experienced under some conditions with bliss and under others with dread or deep anxiety. It is experienced in one way or the other depending on whether the process threatens to destroy the objects of practical endeavor and the structures of reason or whether it seems to sustain them and surround them with an aura of beneficence and blessedness, so that the common objects of daily life "trail clouds of glory" to use Wordsworth's expression. This destructive or sustaining relation between objects and structures versus the total process of experience depends, in turn, on whether the practice and theory of the prevailing culture have developed a high degree of independence and separation from this process or have kept in close connection with it. If the former, the process, when and if it reaches consciousness, seems destructive and hence is experienced in the way described by Jean-Paul Sartre in his essays and drama, by Faulkner, Camus, Becket and many others. It is experienced with disgust or horror or dread. This does not mean, however, that the process of existence is necessarily destructive. It is destructive of those objects and structures which depart from that relation to it wherein they are sustained and further developed by it. It operates to sustain when the forms of thought and perception maintain that relation to it in which they can be sustained and further developed.

This distinction between the unformed process of existence and the objects and structures of practice and thought shows the function of art in contrast to science and technology. The function of art is to bring to consciousness more or less vividly the process of existence underlying the practical and theoretical constructions. The artist may do this by presenting rather well-defined objects but the objects do not serve the distinctive function of art if they are presented merely as reproductions of objects and structures relevant to practice and theory. The distinctive function of art is to present the object (if an object is presented) in such a way that one becomes more or less aware of a total process of living in which the object is merged. By reason of this merging with the total process, the artistic object is able to trail clouds of glory or clouds of horror or some other kind of cloud which is more than the bare object defined for the utilities of practice or the structures of logical inference. Works of art are dripping with the process of existence and this process is always more than any object by itself can ever be.

Now we are prepared to deal with why the most recent developments of art in story and novel, poetry and painting, suggest horror or disgust or corruption, anxiety, despair, frustration and futility. This of course is not a prescription to which all present day artists must conform. The work of many is not of this sort. But Camus, Faulkner, Gide, Becket, and Sartre are examples of a great many literary artists that do this. In painting we have Picasso with his *Guernica* and many who follow him. Also we have the non-objective painting which presents, or tries to present, the most intimate and direct experience of the unformed process of existence.

Present day art presents our experience of the process of existence in this way because the objects and structures developed by modern science, technology and massive organization of society have become separated and alienated from the process of existence so that this process cannot be sustaining relative to them but threatens them with destruction. Or, if it does not threaten, at least it cannot endow them with the aura which surrounds, sustains and encompasses the objects and structures that are intimately and lovingly experienced. This is not a statement that applies universally and without qualification to everything. But it is perhaps more widely true than has been the case throughout most of human history. Our power has become so great that our objects designed to guide practice and our structures designed to guide rational inference have broken free of the process in which and by which we exist. When our power is very limited, we cannot separate our objects and theories very far from this process. But when our power becomes as great as it is today, this separation and alienation from the sustaining process of life is likely to occur unless the power is deliberately used to prevent this opposition between the structures of efficiency and precision on the one hand, and the total sustaining process of living in which our being is submerged at levels beyond the reach of these constructions.

This opposition between the scientifically designed constructions and the sustaining process is disruptive of the human personality. A part of the total being of the human person lives in the unformed process and part is shaped by the scientific constructions. When these diverge or conflict, the individual is inwardly disrupted.

What is needed to correct this disruption both within the individual personality and between persons and groups? What is needed is that kind of community in which individuals assume responsibility for one another, have appreciative understanding of one another, generate in one another insights which widen and deepen the appreciative consciousness of each. This kind of community is created, we have seen, by Christ when Christ means what transforms the lives of people in the kind of fellowship Jesus had with his disciples.

What is needed is not the rejection of science, technology, massive social organization and art but the application of these to promote this kind of fellowship.

So far we have spoken only of one strand of history creating our Western culture, the one derived from Greece. Another is derived from the faith of the Hebrews. This strand also is relevant to the problem of our time as revealed in existentialism, so we must examine it very briefly.

The ancient Hebrew was bound to God not by any theology or philosophy, not by reason in any form, but by membership in the community. The community of Israel belonged to God and could not separate itself from the divine presence. Neither could the individual member of that community. The faith of the Hebrew was not a belief when belief means an affirmation which might not be accepted as true. The Jew could not deny that one was a member of the community of Israel; therefore, one could not deny the presence of God because the two were inseparable.

We do not have this relation to God and under present conditions cannot because we do not have this kind of community. But if ever we develop the kind of community repeatedly described in this writing, God in the form of Christ will be with us intimately and inseparably involved in our lives. It will not be the same as it was for the ancient Hebrew. It will be God revealed in Christ. But when Christ is understood to be the creator and sustainer of the kind of community described, then Christ can no more be doubted than one's membership in that kind of community, because the two are inseparable. Furthermore, in that kind of community the objects constructed for efficient practice and the theories constructed for reliable thinking will not be divorced from the sustaining process of existence because this process will be that very kind of interchange between persons by which the individual personality is created and sustained and the range of appreciative consciousness is widened.

We are not predicting that this kind of community will ever be attained. We are not even predicting that it will be approached beyond what we have now. To some degree it is present with us even now because without it human existence could not continue nor could the newborn infant acquire a culture, a human mind and the capacity to respond to other persons with any appreciative understanding. So long as human beings continue to exist, Christ in some form and in some measure is with us. Such being the case, we do not need to wait for a better and deeper community to find Christ. Also it may be impossible to improve the human community by any kind of change in the direction of providing better conditions for the work of Christ in our midst. But if we are to do anything at all in any situation, in any interpersonal or social relation, we must know what kind of change would in truth be a change in the direction of what is better. The purpose of this writing is to make plain the kind of change for which to work if we strive to make any improvement at all. The first and most important thing to know is not that we shall be successful. The first and most important thing is to know what kind of change would be an improvement if we should be successful. That is the purpose of all that is here stated—not a prediction of what will happen in the future but a pointing to the direction toward which to strive. One who will not act until one can be sure of avoiding failure can have no part in this undertaking. But there is a commitment that can move the world into the ways of hope.

APPENDIX

CHAPTER IX
WHAT IS SALVATION?

To answer the question posed by our final chapter, four subordinate questions must be answered: What is the saving agency and how does it work? What are we saved from? What are we saved to? What must we do to be saved?

Salvation can be viewed in terms of what happens after death. But all the great religions, including Christianity, have insisted that what happens after death depends on what we accept as our ruling commitment before death. This further requires an understanding of what such a ruling commitment must do for a person in order to gain salvation. We strongly believe that such a ruling commitment must do at least two things if it is to provide salvation.

One of these is to bring anxiety under control so that people will not do reckless and irresponsible things to drive anxiety out of consciousness but will use it to criticize, correct and drive toward constructive action. Bringing anxiety under control can be called the "forgiveness of sin" or "awareness of the infinite love of God" directed to me no matter what kind of person I am. These are only two examples. Different forms of Christianity and different forms of religion throughout the world have brought anxiety under control in different ways, but all have sought to do this and have done it more or less successfully.

The reason this is imperative is not only that it brings peace and saves us from endurable anxiety. Anxiety not controlled in such a way as to make it critical and corrective of the evils of life, impelling toward better conduct, becomes a source of fanaticism with all the consequent evils. The rewards are full of the wars and tortures and suppressions and perverted personalities resulting from this barbarism.

Religious commitment becomes fanatic, with all the evils resulting from fanaticism, when one dare not criticize and correct the beliefs on which commitment depends. When any such criticism or marked change in the sustaining belief brings on undue anxiety, the individual becomes a fanatic and a dogmatist unable to recognize the evils, error and illusion in the beliefs sustaining commitment. The wars and persecutions motivated by religious fanaticism may have involved other interests such as political, economic, racial, and cultural, but the point is that fanatic religious commitment did not correct these other interests but served to implement them.

This brings us to the second part of the question about salvation. What form of religious commitment combines these two parts, one bringing anxiety under control without fanaticism, the other opening the way to the creative transformation of human existence and the cosmos in which we live? To answer this question let us examine human existence to expose, if we can, what might be called its basic problem, or at least one of its basic problems.

Human existence is a great complexity of goal-seeking activities more far reaching, more complex, more tangled and conflicting than can be found in any other form of life. The biological organism is itself a great complex system of goal-seeking activities. These are not goal-seeking in the sense of consciously seeking goals, but they are goal seeking in the sense that the total system called the living organism is kept alive by these activities working in mutual support of one another and changing constantly in such a way as to maintain that system called the living organism. Biologists sometimes call this homeostasis.[1]

Added to the goal seeking activities of the organism are those at the psychological and cultural levels. These also are in great part below the level of consciousness except when brought to consciousness by some problem that can only be solved by conscious thinking, or some action that can be performed only by bringing some part of the total system into consciousness.[2]

If the systems of mutually sustaining and self-regulating activities at the biological level are disrupted, the individual dies; if at the psychological level, the individual becomes neurotic or psychotic; if at the social level, society becomes more or less chaotic and self-destructive. Extreme breakdown of and self-regulating system at any of these levels makes human life impossible. It should be emphasized, however, that these so-called levels are not independent of one another. They are all bound together into a coherent, mutually sustaining the self-regulating system, extending from the atoms and molecules to the cells and the organism and on to the pyschological and institutional systems, including the family, the political, the industrial and economic, the educational and the religious. The religious, when it fulfills its proper function, is commitment to what orders and directs the totality of these activities so that they sustain and promote one another rather than break down into inhibitions and frustrations. The totality includes wide reaches of the environment and cosmos that have been integrated into the system which sustains human existence.

The point of all this is to say that this progressive creation of an ever more comprehensive and complex system of mutually sustaining and self-regulative activities, finally reaching the level of human existence, and continuing to sustain and create human life, is not the work of humans and could

---

[1] See the Work of Alfred Emerson.

[2] See *Experiencing and the Creation of Meaning* by Eugene T. Gendlin, (Glencoe: The Free Press, 1962).

not be. It operated for millions of years before we came into existence and it has continued to operate in human existence without our having any knowledge of it until recent years. Even after we understand it, human purpose cannot create or sustain these homeostatic systems but can only cooperate with them.[3]

Here we see the other side of the meaning of salvation. The side first considered was salvation from uncontrolled anxiety that is destructive of human life and all its values. The second side is to increase the values of human existence. Every goal-seeking activity is a value. The good of life is increased to the measure that goal-seeking activities are brought into relations of mutual support across wide ranges of conflict and diversity.

There is a form of creative evolution which progressively creates these systems of mutually sustaining and self-regulating goal-seeking activities. We cannot by our own powers alone create and expand these homeostatic systems, but we can acquire the knowledge, the technology and the religious commitment enabling us to cooperate with the creativity that does this. We can cooperate by providing some of the conditions which must be present for its more effective operation.

A further feature should be noted concerning religious commitment to creative evolution. The beliefs which sustain and guide this commitment are based on scientific knowledge which is constantly subject to correction. There is no attempt in science to defend any affirmation against contrary evidence. Rather the opposite attitude prevails. Scientific inquiry is chiefly engaged to search out error and falsify whatever is accepted as true. Therefore, religious commitment based on scientific knowledge will not be driven to affirm beliefs with fanatic dogmatism in order to sustain the commitment. Fanaticism arises from fear that the beliefs keeping anxiety out of consciousness may not be true. In science this is reversed. Anxiety drives the scientist to try to falsify the affirmation with every test available. Thus, religious commitment based on what science can discover about the most coherent, comprehensive and expanding system of mutually sustaining activities is not subject to fanaticism. It saves from uncontrolled anxiety, and it puts us into the keeping of what sustains and creates the greatest good that human life and the cosmos can embody. This is so because good is precisely the most comprehensive, coherent and expanding system of mutually sustaining goal-seeking activities.

At this point a serious misunderstanding may arise. What has just been said does not mean that our religious commitment should be given to science. That would be an absurdity. Our religious commitment should be given to the creativity which expands indefinitely the range of mutually

---

[3]We use the expression "homeostatic" in this more comprehensive sense following the practice of the biologist Alfred Emerson. In his usage, processes outside the organism are called homeostatic when they both regulate, and are regulated by, activities in the organism.

sustaining activities. All science can do is to give us knowledge about it so that our commitment can be more intelligent and also give us the technology so that our commitment can be more powerfully effective. As said before, our religion should take science into its commitment along with all the other institutions and ruling interests of human life, of which science is only one small part.

Not science, not politics and government, not industry, not accumulation of economic abundance, not art, not awe and wonder, not the family, not education, not love between persons and peoples—none of these can command the ruling commitment of our lives if we are to be saved from self-destruction in the day of our magnified power. These all are sub-systems within that total system which is human existence together with whatever ranges of the cosmos are or can be integrated into our existence. The ruling commitment of our lives cannot even be given to this total system in its present form which is full of destructive conflicts, especially at the human level. These conflicts will destroy the whole system if not corrected. Therefore, our ruling commitment must not be given to the total system in its present form. It must be given to the creativity operating to transform destructive conflicts into creative conflicts and to bring diversities into that kind of interaction which transforms them into mutually sustaining parts of a more comprehensive system while retaining their diversity. This and nothing else can save us from the destructive use of magnified power.

A further qualification should be made to avoid misunderstanding. We are not saying that the ruling commitment of our lives should be given to evolution in all its forms. Only that one form issuing in human existence should command our commitment because it is the only form of evolution that expands indefinitely the range of mutually sustaining activities. Evolution has many forms. In some forms it has created plant life as it now exists and this form of evolution began long before others. Furthermore, plant life is fit to survive under conditions where human life cannot. The same is true of insects and other forms of evolution. Therefore, mere fitness to survive is no guide to the ruling commitment of our lives, important as survival certainly is.

This distinction between evolution of sub-systems, and evolution of a more comprehensive system that can integrate subsystems into itself is here called creative evolution. This evolution of the most comprehensive system brings wider ranges of goal-seeking activities into relations of mutual support across more conflict and diversity than any other form of evolution. Also, this form of evolution, issuing in human existence, is the only form that creates a valuing consciousness that expands indefinitely in range of what can be valued. If this most creative form of evolution operates on other planets, so much the better. But our responsibility is here on earth and we know nothing about the creativity on other planets. When we do know, if ever, or if representatives of this higher creativity (if it is higher) should visit this earth, we shall have to solve that problem when it comes, if it ever does.

All we can say at present is that we should try to solve that problem in the way we solve our major human problems, by the creative interaction that integrates diverse systems into more comprehensive systems, after due modification of each. If that should be impossible with the visitors from another planet, that fact in itself would indicate that they do not represent a higher creativity because this capacity for expansion by integrating diverse systems is the mark of higher creativity. This is so because creative interaction integrating systems of goal-seeking activities into more inclusive systems is the standard for judging what is better and worse, or superior and inferior. Ways of life doing this less well than other ways are inferior because they cannot carry so great a content of value. The better way of life also requires that the participants symbolize the more inclusive system of mutually sustaining activities. Only in this way can the valuing consciousness expand indefinitely.

Here we have the demonstrated fact, apart from all prejudice in favor of humankind that the creative form of evolution operating in human existence creates values far beyond any other form. It does so for the two reasons cited: (1) only in this form of evolution is the way opened for an ever more comprehensive system of mutually sustaining activities; and (2) only in this form of evolution is there a valuing consciousness capable of indefinite expansion because only here are organisms capable of symbols that can represent these expanding systems.

It is a tautology to say that what expands the range of the valuing consciousness expands the range of experienced value in vividness, diversity and coherence. Therefore, it is only in that form of creative evolution operating in human existence that the cosmos can contain an ever greater content of value, so far as life on this earth is concerned. It should be further added that only in this form of evolution can all the other forms of life be brought into the widest range of mutual support across the widest range of diversity and conflict. It is true that humans have been at times the most destructive animals in existence. But if our ruling commitment is given to the creative form of evolution operating preeminently in personal existence, and if we commit our resources of inquiry and power of control to this creativity, we will bring wider ranges of life into mutual support than can be attained in any other way.

If ever the "lion is to lie with the lamb" and if ever a new cosmos is to be created with far-ranging activities mutually sustaining one another, and if ever the stars in their courses are to join with human action to expand the valuing consciousness indefinitely, commitment to creative evolution is the only way it can be done.

After saying all this it is imperative that we recognize how precariously valuing consciousness is maintained, due to its self-destructive propensity. This self-destructive propensity arises from two characteristics inherent in human consciousness. One of these we have already examined. A valuing consciousness capable of indefinite expansion is an anxious consciousness and cannot be otherwise. If this anxiety is not controlled in a way to fulfill its proper function, it drives the valuing consciousness into self-destructiveness.

The second characteristic of the valuing consciousness making it self-destructive is an undirected drift of human existence, occurring when human life is not brought under the saving control of the right kind of religious commitment. This drift is accelerated and becomes more dangerous when equipped with powerful scientific technology.

Under the influence of this drift, four different ways of life become increasingly dominant over people who prefer one or another. These four have always been present in human life, but heretofore the power of technology and economic abundance was not sufficient to enable people to devote themselves so exclusively to their chosen ways. In the future, if the saving power of religious commitment does not control us, these four ways will become increasingly obsessive, enslaving those who follow them. A fifth way is exceptional. It is the way of salvation, to be explained when we get to it.

One of these four ways which some people have always preferred is the way of sensuous enjoyment. Of course, sensuous enjoyment has its rightful place in life except when it becomes obsessive, enslaving the person devoted to it. This enslavement to sensuous pleasure is often accepted to keep anxiety out of consciousness. While this way of life has always been a lure, not many could give themselves fully to it because they did not have the necessary wealth, freedom and other favoring conditions. As the power of technology and economic abundance increases, more and more people may choose this way to attain sensuous bliss never before possible.

Competent scientists seem to agree that by the year 2000 the way of sensuous ecstasy for many would be quite possible. Economic abundance and other material and social conditions would provide for it. In addition, technology would then be available to stimulate the brain in ways to yield the experience of sensuous ecstasy in a great variety of forms, and with a continuous stream of blissful consciousness. If past history shows anything about the way of life that some will choose, this way will be chosen unless a ruling commitment otherwise shapes and directs the way of life. Those who choose this way will sink to the level of human vegetables, devoted to the bliss of the senses, assuming responsibility for nothing else.

Others who do not choose sensual pleasure may prefer power. This has always been the case throughout human history and there is every reason to think it will continue. Here again the scientific technology now developing will give these persons a magnitude of power never before possible. It will be not only power of coercion but also power of persuasion—power to keep

people under control with blissful sensuous pleasures and also by con-
ditioning their minds in other ways. It will be not only power by inducing
fear but also by presenting the power seekers as heroes of courage and
generosity—by informing people of what is happening and will happen, and
by selecting the information in a way to make the people submissive to the
dictates of power. The multiform ways in which a ruling minority can control
the minds and impulses of the great majority are increasing rapidly.

"By ruling minority" is meant some million individuals, but they will be
a minority opposed to the many millions subject to their control. The
complexity and power of society will require millions to control it, but they
will be much fewer than the total population, many of these made helplessly
submissive with sensuous enjoyment and by the other ways of life to be
described.

There is still a third way that some will follow because some have always
gone this way throughout human history. People driven by the feeling of
inferiority yet unable to exercise the power of social control will often seek to
exercise power irresponsibly to give themselves a feeling of power. When
equipped with scientific technology, these people become increasingly dangerous. Reckless driving of the automobile is an example. But there are many
other ways this is done. An outstanding example is Lee Harvey Oswald's
assassination of President Kennedy. Perhaps Jack Ruby who killed Oswald
was also an example. The history of Oswald's life shows that he was always
seeking power but unable to attain it in any notable way. He had no known
motive for killing a president except that it could give him the sense of power
in shaping the course of history.

As technology magnifies the instruments of power, these individuals,
and also gangs of individuals, seeking to overcome a feeling of inferiority,
become increasingly dangerous unless they are saved by religious commitment to the creativity of evolution. By identifying themselves with this
greatest of all creative power, and serving it above all else, their sense of
inferiority can be overcome in a way that is constructive instead of destructive.

Unless we are all saved in this way, the presence of these dangerous
individuals and groups scattered through society will require the ruling
minority to increase their power, putting policemen and spies pervasively
among the people to guard against the danger. This is already being done.
Protection against reckless driving is an example. Increasing numbers of
policemen are placed to watch the traffic, and often placed where dirvers will
not know of their presence. This is necessary to check the increasing slaugh-
ter on the highways. But reckless driving is only one example, perhaps a
minor example, of the way the increasing power of modern technology can
be misused by people who feel the necessity to overcome the feeling of
inferiority. This indicates that we shall have a police state and a totalitarian
government if we do not find the way of salvation in the form of a ruling

commitment to what widens and deepens the mutual support of all goal-seeking activities. A common example of the way the government plants hidden agents among the people to control what they say and do is the case of the Central Intelligence Agency putting their agents in youth groups without the knowledge of their presence by the rest of the group.

A fourth way of life which some have always chosen and will continue to choose is narrow specialization. There is nothing wrong in this way of life any more than seeking sensuous enjoyment and exercising power provided the chosen way of life does not become obsessive to the point of excluding all important interests of human existence save this one. The danger lies in having a technology and other conditions making it possible for people to devote themselves to some narrowly specialized interest that excludes all else. Of course this is a matter of degree. Perhaps no one will ever do one thing and one thing only. But everything depends on having a ruling commitment that regulates and interrelates these diverse ways so that they can be not only mutually sustaining but also of common concern to all involved. Only in this way can these diverse ways be saved from self-destruction when technology becomes sufficiently powerful.

The specialized interest that becomes obsessive may be a form of scientific research; it may be a form of art; it may be chess or golf or tennis or some other sport; it may be wandering over the planet in quest of new sights and sounds. When these interests become obsessive, all power of centralized control is handed over to the ruling minority who exercise power for the sake of power and little else. This kind of power becomes self-destructive because it is not regulated, informed, and controlled by the many other activities subject to it. The ruling minority, exercising power for power's sake, cannot regulate a vast system of activities all equipped with gigantic power of technology unless representatives of these activities participate in the control and all are concerned to regulate the activities in a way to make them mutually sustaining and of value for all. This is impossible without the kind of religious commitment we have described. Without this, conflicts will arise in the system, no matter how the power group may try to control it in their own interests. These conflicts will make the system self-destructive, and when implemented with sufficient power, may destroy the total system of life built up by creative evolution.

This brings us to the fifth way of life. It also has been chosen to various degrees throughout human history and for some has been a ruling commitment. But when we speak of different people being committed to these five different ways of life, we do not mean that they necessarily did so with understanding of what they were doing and with deliberate intent. For the most part they were guided by myths and non-cognitive symbols, by images and impulses, without understanding what they were doing. But now with the power of modern technology we must understand what these different ways of life are and where they lead.

This fifth way of life is commitment to creative evolution. It is the way of salvation. It is the way opposing systems are brought into a more comprehensive system. This does not mean that conflict or diversity disappears. Diversity must be retained, if not magnified, and conflict also, but in such form as to open the way to creative evolution.

This kind of interaction bringing diverse systems into a more comprehensive system does not occur merely at the level of human consciousness. To be effective it must reach into the subconscious and even beyond the subconscious into the biological. The entire organism is involved, and also the environment, the material world and the society of associated individuals and peoples. Therefore, this commitment is given to the entire system of creative evolution as embodied in human existence. This system is like a vast hidden iceberg with only the top tip in reach of human consciousness and control. Our commitment must be given to the entire system, reaching down to atoms and molecules and reaching out into whatever ranges of the cosmos are integrated into this system.

By no means is the total cosmos a part of the system of mutually sustaining activities integrated by creative evolution operating on this planet. The explosions of billions of stars, and the vast spaces in between, have no goal-seeking activities to be integrated. The forces in the stars and in the spaces in between would destroy completely the goal-seeking activities by which we live. Our knowledge of this cosmos and our valuing of it are created and sustained by the creative evolution on earth. But the material forces themselves, except as harnessed to the creative evolution embodied in human existence, are no part of the system of activities which sustain and expand our knowing and valuing consciousness. Creative evolution is progressive on earth but not throughout the cosmos.

Yet human existence is the conscious, valuing tip of a very complex and extensive system of activities, ordered and directed by creative evolution. We cannot create or control the total system, but with the rising power of our technology we can increasingly help to expand it or break it. If we break it, the knowing and valuing consciousness of humanity will disappear. With its going, the cosmos as known and valued by this consciousness will disappear. In this way our salvation involves the cosmos as known and valued. The creative transformation of our knowing and valuing consciousness, by expanding its range, is also the creative transformation of the universe as *known and valued by this consciousness.*

Salvation in the most profound sense of the word depends on this fifth way of life which is distinguished by the ruling commitment to choose in every time of major decision that alternative which best serves to promote the power of creative evolution operating in our lives to expand the range of the valuing consciousness of individuals in ways that are mutually sustaining. This power that creates us and creates the cosmos in the form in which we can know it and value it, which saves us when we put ourselves into its power by serving it above all, which transforms human existence toward greater content of value as we cannot transform ourselves, can be given the name of God or given the name of Love. But neither of these words give us any adequate understanding of it. When and if they confuse or block our commitment of faith, they should not be used.

It should be added that this kind of religious commitment is the only kind that can bring all the sciences into its service. This is essential for any faith fit to deal with the problem of salvation in our time because science has become the instrument of supreme power under human control.

One further comment should be made relative to the understanding of salvation. Salvation is not merely an idea or concept. It is a transforming event. Therefore, the event cannot be identified solely with the Christian idea or any other idea. We can know an event only by way of some abstract characteristic or characteristics essentially involved in it. Never can we know the total concrete fullness of any event. Most especially is this true of an event so vastly complex as the event of salvation. Furthermore, the same event can be known by way of different characteristics essential to it; and it is not known any more truly by way of one set of characteristics than by others, provided that the alternative ways of knowing apprehend features essential to the event.

The Christian idea of salvation does not make sense to the modern mind. Therefore, we must get some other idea that does make sense. The whole history of human thought shows that as culture and human minds change through thousands of years, events must be known by way of different identifying characteristics—or different models. This is just as true of the event of salvation as of any other. Failure to recognize this fact and on that account refusal to change the concept of salvation to meet human need may cause us to miss the way of salvation. Therefore, they who obstinately insist on holding the same concept of salvation when it no longer informs the human mind betray the faith and are traitors to seekers after salvation.

Some will insist that the form of evolution operating through millions of years in such a way as to expand the range of mutually sustaining activities, finally issuing in human existence and continuing there in the form of creative interchange, is not guided by any purpose or teleology. But to raise that issue is to miss the all-important point concerning salvation. The all-important point is: (1) that there is a form of evolution that has expanded the range of mutually sustaining activities and that it continues to operate in human life with the added equipment of creative interchange with symbolized meanings; and (2) that commitment to this form of creativity is the way of our salvation. If some insist that this form of evolution must be guided by a ruling purpose, let them. If others insist that a scientific understanding of this evolution shows that it cannot be guided by a ruling purpose, let them.

If people must disagree in their metaphysical and cosmological interpretations of this creativity, so they must. But this disagreement becomes suicidal when it blinds them to the way of salvation. I am not saying that the truth about this form of evolution is unimportant. But the point at issue can be shown with an analogy. Suppose a deadly contagion were spreading and threatening to kill the entire human race. Suppose scientific research discovered a way to stop the contagion and save humankind but the vast majority of people, not having the required specialized scientific training, could not understand the remedy or interpret it. Should we refuse to apply the cure until everybody had a correct understanding of it? The question shows the absurdity of such procedure.

It is not necessary that everyone understand what saves the biological organism from sickness and death. If some medical experts understand and apply the remedy, the remedy should be applied whether or not people have a completely formal understanding of it. In many cases, the medical experts do not themselves understand fully how the remedy operates. They only know that it cures the ill. So it is relative to the salvation not only of the biological organism but also of all the values of human existence. If there be a way of salvation, we must follow it, no matter how incomplete may be our understanding of it. Our understanding will always be incomplete, and probably there will always be different ways of interpreting such complex events as biological health. To even greater measure will there be incomplete understanding and different interpretations of events far more complex, such as the creation and saving of all the values which make human life worth living. These include much more than biological health.

Different interpretations of what saves, whether it be the life of the organism or the values of human existence, can be tolerated so long as they do not misdirect or obstruct the course of action required to meet the demands of the agency that saves. This applies whether the agency be the homeostasis of the organism or the expanding system of mutually sustaining activities throughout the whole of human existence.

This brings us to a major point of dispute in theology, in religious belief and in religious practice. A widely prevalent form of religious belief and religious practice must be disputed and cast off if we are to be saved, not merely because it is in error, but because it misdirects in many cases, and in other cases prevents, the course of action required of us if we are to be saved.